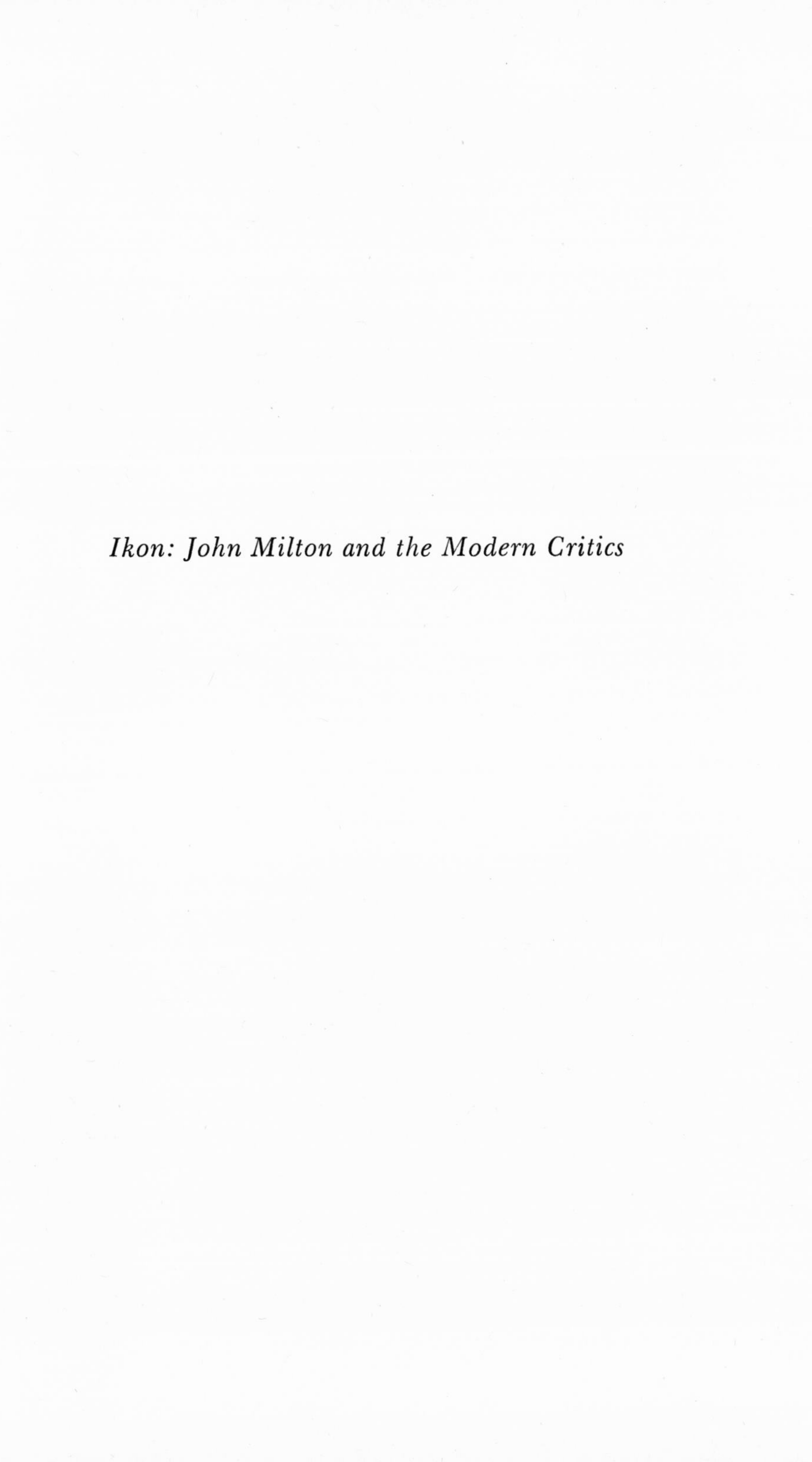

Ikon: John Milton and the Modern Critics

Ikon: John Milton and the Modern Critics

Robert Martin Adams

DEPARTMENT OF ENGLISH

CORNELL UNIVERSITY

CORNELL UNIVERSITY PRESS

Ithaca, New York

Cornell University Press

London: Geoffrey Cumberlege

Oxford University Press

First published 1955

PRINTED IN THE UNITED STATES OF AMERICA BY THE

VAIL-BALLOU PRESS, INC., BINGHAMTON, NEW YORK

FOR *Harrison Ross Steeves*

WE freely acknowledge Him to be the Inventor of the *Compass,* of *Gun-Powder,* and the *Circulation of the Blood:* But, I challenge any of his Admirers to shew me in all his Writings, a compleat Account of the *Spleen;* Does he not also leave us wholly to seek in the Art of *Political Wagering?* What can be more defective and unsatisfactory than his long Dissertation upon *Tea?* and as to his Method of *Salivation without Mercury,* so much celebrated of late, it is to my own Knowledge and Experience, a Thing very little to be relied on.

—*A Tale of a Tub,* Section V

Foreword

GREAT POETS are traditionally subject to the gleaning of minor critics; and since critical work is generally cumulative in character, every grain, however minute or discolored, is properly made welcome. Bibliographies exist to record the contributions; time and the educated reader serve to divide the grain from the chaff.

To these agencies the job of preserving and selecting trifles may safely be left. But the multiplication, during recent years, of critical theories and methods of interpretation has created a number of special problems. The critics, by intention at least, are not minor; and the theories which they put forward have now begun to jostle. They are no longer complementary, nor even disparate, but often directly contradictory. Thus we have seen established a number of images of a single author, images which no longer offer a fruitful multiplicity but a blurred confusion and sometimes a downright contradiction. Each of these images is rooted in philosophical presuppositions, with which it is often useful to quarrel; and each exponent of a new approach tends to present his figure of the great author as an exclusive version.

Sometimes he declines to consider opposed or alternative views because controversies are complicated and tiresome; sometimes his ignorance of other critics is a matter of principle.

Milton in particular, because it is generally agreed that he had a distinct character in his person and in his work, has been subject to varied interpretation. The Protean character of Shakespeare is unalterable; he has ended by strangling most of those analysts and speculators who have tried, by a laying on of hands, to reduce him to one single self. Even if someone should prove tomorrow that the Bard was a Catholic or a homosexual, I do not think the discovery would alter substantially our reading of *Hamlet* or *Othello,* creations which have a dramatic existence of their own. But Milton, though he may have "meant" fewer things than Shakespeare, meant them in a more personal, committed way; and the attempt to tie down those meanings to a finite number of ideas and feelings is not quite so obviously self-defeating as it is with Shakespeare. Thus we have had of recent years an increasing number of Miltons—Miltons, indeed,

> of every shape and size
> That critics could produce or cults devise.

These creations are now full-grown; they present to the searcher after John Milton a forest of choking luxuriance. If I interpret the contemporary prospect correctly, it calls out, not for more seed and more energetic cultivation, but for a firm hand on the pruning shears; not for more and newer insights into Milton, but for some secure principle of controlling and co-ordinating what we already know. The conservative essays which follow are a first venture in this direction.

That the task involves a steady reliance on the devices

of polemic has been both a satisfaction and an embarrassment. The rigors of the game provide a bracing stimulus to which Milton himself was not immune. They also tempt one to assume a peevish, ungracious, ungrateful role—to which also Milton was sometimes inclined. I have often regretted the choice of a subject which gave so little play to the gracious sentiments of generous appreciation; but the task as I defined it imposed its own rules. The better side of my own nature also asserted itself; and rather than seem to flog dead thoroughbreds or pursue subjects beyond the bounds of humane discretion (not to mention the reader's patience) I have imposed an arbitrary limit on polemic by limiting myself to one or two typical examples of each critical approach. The sort of criticism which I direct against the view of *Comus* put forward by Messrs. Cleanth Brooks and J. E. Hardy might easily be extended through all the minor poems into an assault on Mr. Arnold Stein's conception of *Paradise Lost;* from the Jungians an easy transition might lead to consideration of less imaginative followers of Freud and more imaginative admirers of the Devil; the critique of Mr. Leavis' and Mr. Eliot's comments on Milton's verse might spread through an entire bibliography of modern criticism. But enough is enough; *ex pede Herculem,* and literary critics need no more exhaustive anatomy. If somewhere I have spoken too harshly of my predecessors, I must beg their pardon and the reader's, with the plea that I have not sought occasions of easy triumph, but only such light as comes from the clash of flint on steel. Perhaps polemic is not always the best way of discovering new light; it is the best way I know to discover which of several pretended lights is genuine.

The obligations I have incurred are many and multiform; two in particular require distinct acknowledgment. An eminent Milton scholar, whose name is supposed (according to the regulations of a discreet publisher) to be shielded from my ken, was asked to read the MS before publication was decided upon. Gallantly setting aside several ungraceful references to his own work, he provided for the MS a critical reading so careful, so explicit, so just and searching, as greatly to enhance the presentation of a thesis which he can only have considered misguided. For the sake of so generous an antagonist, I can only wish that my blundering attack had been framed with enough art to set off properly the brilliance of his ripostes. In joining the heroic little band of women whose husbands have written on Milton, my wife deserves the assurance that this fate does not oblige her to read my book, or even Milton's. To have been present at the writing of this study has been a destiny in itself; for her sake, I can only hope that my next one has a less turbulent gestation.

Three of the essays, in somewhat altered form, have appeared in periodicals; "Reading *Comus*" in *Modern Philology* for August 1953; the first half of "The Text of *Paradise Lost*" in *Modern Philology* for November 1954; and "Empson and Bentley" in *Partisan Review* for March–April 1954. I am grateful to the editors for permission to reprint. To the editors of the *Oxford English Dictionary,* to John Bradshaw, compiler of the *Concordance to the Poetical Works of John Milton,* and to the indexers of the *Columbia Milton* I owe whatever eyesight remains to me. The teachers with whom I studied and the students whom I tried to teach, the books and articles I read with hearty agreement and admiration, those which put me to sleep, and those from which I recoiled in shock and horror—I have learned from them all, not least from those whom I may seem to have repudiated most vigorously. To rouse a sleepy, blinking prejudice, to exterminate a fair misconception, are always painful acts of self-discipline, likely to be begun in hostility and concluded in humility. In the course of writing I have worked through a good many pseudo-beliefs about Milton and will feel mostly gratitude toward anyone who can rid me of another.

In a famous passage Milton compares the search for truth with the attempts of Isis to collect the scattered limbs of Osiris. The recovery of Milton himself is a similar process, except that a dozen or so simulacra are already before us, all embodying much genuine material, some obscuring it with more dross and counterfeit. To break these images in the hope of releasing that truth which lies imprisoned within them has been for me a work of reverence, not blasphemy, justified only if it clears the way for a fairer perspective of the divine original.

Robert Martin Adams

Ithaca, New York
April 1955

Contents

A Note on Documentation

In order to obviate excessive footnoting I have included much of my documentation within the text, placing it between square brackets and making use, after a first citation, of the following abbreviated titles:

APP	Maud Bodkin, *Archetypal Patterns in Poetry* (London, 1934)
AS	Arnold Stein, *Answerable Style* (Minneapolis, 1953)
B & H	Cleanth Brooks and J. E. Hardy, *Poems of Mr. John Milton* (New York, 1951)
BCHM	George Conklin, *Biblical Criticism and Heresy in Milton* (New York, 1949)
BOE	Grant McColley, *Paradise Lost: The Birth of an Epic* (Chicago, 1940)
L & S	R. J. Zwi Werblowsky, *Lucifer and Satan* (London, 1952)
MLM	George Whiting, *Milton's Literary Milieu* (Chapel Hill, 1939)
MM & T	Denis Saurat, *Milton, Man and Thinker* (New York, 1925)

MRR	Harris Fletcher, *Milton's Rabbinical Readings* (Urbana, 1930)
MSS	——, *Milton's Semitic Studies* (Chicago, 1926)
MUDB	G. C. Taylor, *Milton's Use of Du Bartas* (Cambridge, Mass., 1934)
P & D	M. M. Ross, *Poetry and Dogma* (New Brunswick, 1954)
PLIC	A. J. A. Waldock, *Paradise Lost and Its Critics* (Cambridge, 1947)
PLIOT	Douglas Bush, *Paradise Lost in Our Time* (Ithaca, 1945)
PPL	C. S. Lewis, *A Preface to Paradise Lost* (London, 1952)
SCR	B. Rajan, *Paradise Lost and the 17th-Century Reader* (London, 1947)
SVP	William Empson, *Some Versions of Pastoral* (Norfolk, Conn., n.d.)
TGA	Maurice Kelley, *This Great Argument* (Princeton, 1941)
THV	Don C. Allen, *The Harmonious Vision* (Baltimore, 1954)

I have also used the following abbreviations of scholarly journals:

CJ	*Cambridge Journal*
ELH	*English Literary History*
ESEA	*Essays and Studies by Members of the English Association*
JEGP	*Journal of English and Germanic Philology*
JHI	*Journal of the History of Ideas*
KR	*Kenyon Review*
MLN	*Modern Language Notes*
MP	*Modern Philology*
PaR	*Partisan Review*
PBA	*Proceedings of the British Academy*
PMLA	*Publications of the Modern Language Association*

PQ	*Philological Quarterly*
RES	*Review of English Studies*
RR	*Romanic Review*
SP	*Studies in Philology*
SR	*Sewanee Review*
UTQ	*University of Toronto Quarterly*

In referring to Milton's poems I have used the form "IV, 708" to designate book and line numbers of *Paradise Lost* (1674 edition). Quotations have been taken from the Columbia edition except where, in discussions of textual details (Section III), Columbia has been augmented by the more elaborate apparatus of Harris Fletcher and Miss Helen Darbishire. *PL, PR,* and *SA* are of course stock abbreviations for *Paradise Lost, Paradise Regained,* and *Samson Agonistes.* Citations from the Bible are made by book, chapter, and verse, after the model "Genesis 1:3."

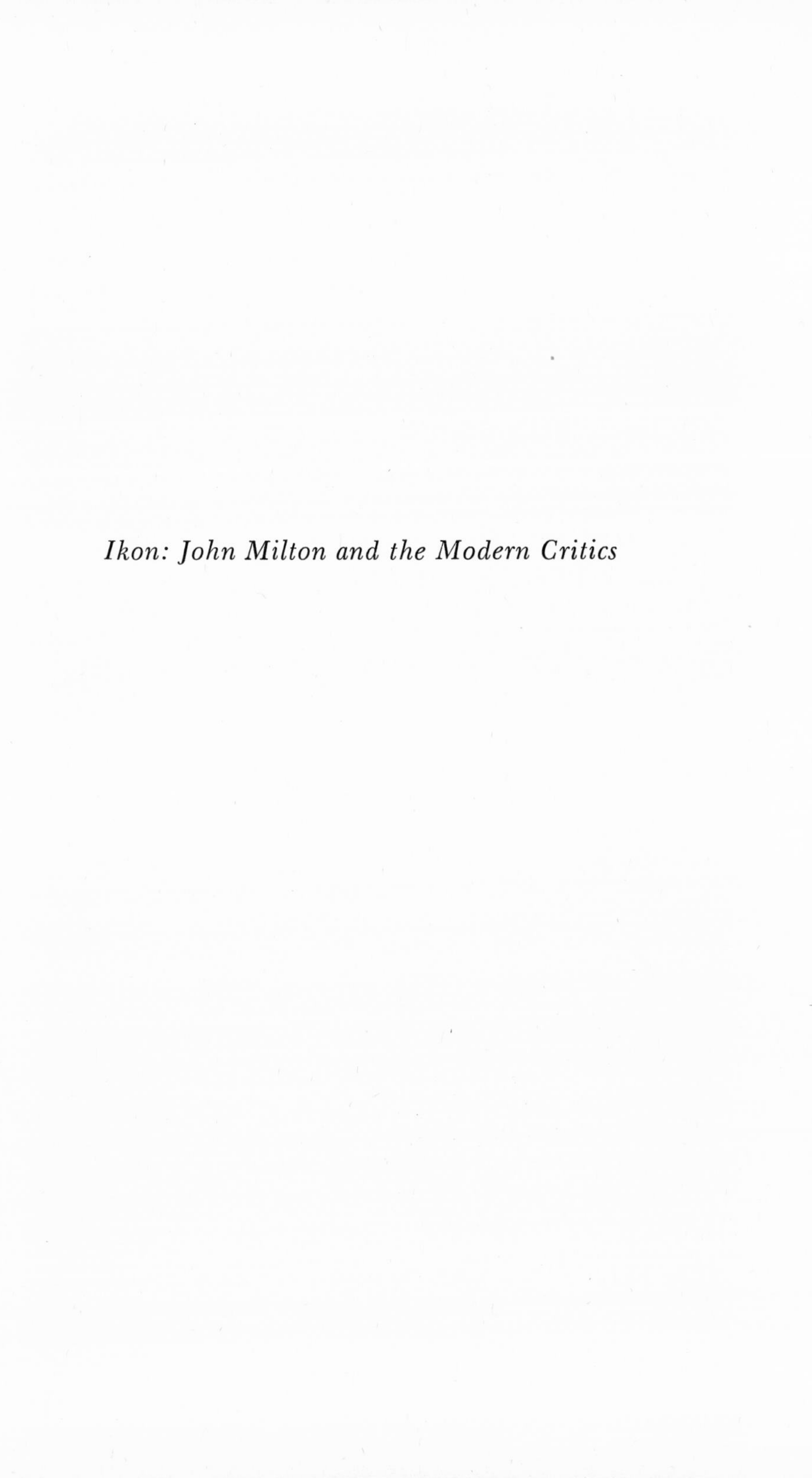

Ikon: John Milton and the Modern Critics

[I]

Reading *Comus*

ONCE upon a time *Paradise Lost, Paradise Regained,* and *Samson Agonistes* were the major works of John Milton; recent criticism has gone a long way toward replacing them with "Lycidas," *Comus,* and the poem "On the Morning of Christ's Nativity." It seems to me that this tendency has involved, as cause or as effect, a major overreading of the three early works, and of *Comus* in particular. By "overreading" I mean overloading the allegory, probing too deeply into the background of the imagery, and enlarging upon the incidental implications of secondary concepts at the expense of the work's total structure.

Overreading a literary work is best accomplished through line-by-line analysis, according to the familiar approach of *explication de texte.* The announced aim of this technique is to reveal the true dramatic form of the work of art; and with this aim none can quarrel. But unfolding the text line by line does not necessarily serve this end any more than methodically inspecting the bricks of a house gives one a notion of its architecture. We may therefore begin our consideration of *Comus,* not with line 1, but by asking what sort of literary work it is and then, in the broadest sense, what it is "about"—what themes it chiefly handles and what sort of impression it seems designed to make.

Though it is often described loosely as a play and sometimes as a poem, *Comus* is so much a masque that this was its original, and for a long time its only, title. Mr. Don C. Allen has argued recently that *Comus* is not a masque because

> it is much longer than the masque as written by Jonson or Daniel; its cast of speaking characters is much smaller; its locale of action is much less fantastic; its plot, though not exactly more elaborate, is more tense; its theme is more serious; it is totally wanting in humorousness; and its emphasis is more on dramatic crisis than on spectacle, dance, costume, and even singing [*The Harmonious Vision* (Baltimore, 1954), p. 31].

But Mr. Allen himself does not use these criteria seriously, or at least consistently; for example, he holds that *Arcades* is a true masque, though it has even fewer speaking characters than *Comus,* lacks humorousness entirely, and is only 109 lines long—far shorter than the masque as written by Jonson and Daniel. Besides, a work of art does not forfeit its position within a genre by differences of this sort; otherwise one might prove, by comparing *Macbeth* with *Everyman,* that Shakespeare had not written a play. In short, if we are not so strict as to correct the author in his very declaration of intentions, "masque" may continue to describe Milton's effort.

Now the masque is a form of literature designed primarily for public recitation and performance. Its major functions are triple: to voice a compliment, to present a moral allegory, and to provide occasion for a spectacle. Each of these requirements lays one more demand on a verse statement which is unalterably public in character; consequently, the "Dorique delicacy" which Sir Henry Wotton remarked in *Comus* was widely recognized as a notably successful style for masques. Simplicity wedded to elegance—this was the style at which the most successful writers of masques generally, and the author of *Comus* in particular, aimed. It is a matter of history that masques were not written in the metaphysical manner; even masques by poets like Carew and Townshend, who were occasionally given to conceited verses, never stray far from the strict Jonsonian style. Consequently a preliminary doubt may be felt, simply on the score of *Comus'* form, that techniques appropriate to reading a metaphysical poem will quite apply here. The unity of a metaphysical poem often lies in a progression of ideas and feelings which must be explicated out of the imagery; as a masque, *Comus* would be expected to possess a much more obvious unity.

This is not to say that wit- and word-play were under a ban or that secondary meanings and patterns could not be included anywhere within the main outlines of the masque; Milton, like Shakespeare, might well be expected to enrich a traditional form with such secondary elements. But one cannot lightly suppose that the writer of a masque would deliberately violate any of the major purposes of the genre to include secondary elements; still less that he would purposely conceal any major part of his statement where it was not easily available to a single hearing by an informed, attentive listener. The history of the writing of *Comus,* so far as it is available from manuscripts, supports this assumption. Whatever Milton had to say in *Comus,* he did not alter it radically in the course of composition; whatever main shape the masque had, it evidently had from the beginning. The textual alterations which are preserved aim at a greater clarity, a less pedestrian statement, a more exact propriety; not one of them is aimed at deepening or elaborating the allegory or symbolism, at adding new overtones to the imagery or harmonizing old ones.[1]

A formalist argument of this sort is, of course, inevitably general and abstract; the fact that Milton was writing a masque is no evidence that *Comus* is like all other masques or that it contains nothing but what is common to all masques. But so long as *Comus* can be read consistently and satisfyingly on the level of a masque for public performance, I think readings which depend entirely on a close analysis of the metaphorical overtones must be held suspect and kept subordinate. They may reinforce and enrich the more accessible meanings when they can do so without strain; they may be called on to mediate conflicts or to fill explicit gaps; but when they are not congruent with those more accessible meanings, the suspicion must persist that they are not significant. Milton at the time when he wrote *Comus* could not foresee that it would be "explicated" or even that it would be published; publication of a masque was unusual, and "explication," so far as it was practiced at all, was called "parsing" or "construing" and reserved for classic authors. We do Milton

[1] One set of alterations in l. 995 is devoted to removing an explicitly Judaeo-Christian symbol; the only other changes which seem even indirectly significant on the latent level have to do with ll. 356–58, where Milton removed a Proserpina-Lady comparison from the Younger Brother's speech, probably because it was too blackly diabolic in tone, perhaps also because the Proserpina-fertility connection did not fit well with the Lady's chastity. The fourteen lines which Milton removed from the prologue and rewrote for the epilogue were dramatically inappropriate in their original spot, a fact for which they made explicit and doubly awkward apology. Mr. C. S. Lewis has summarized the direction of Milton's revisions as rejection of the colloquial, the dramatic, and the technical in favor of poetic chastity, smoothness, singleness, and didacticism [*RES,* VIII, 170–76].

no more discredit in urging that he did not write a masque for the Earl of Bridgewater to "explicate"—unlovely word! —than we do to Ovid in suggesting that he did not conceive the *Ars amatoria* as a devotional handbook for nuns. One can explicate Milton's masque and allegorize Ovid's treatise, but only at a sizable risk to one's understanding of the "true dramatic form."

The risk of overreading *Comus* may be great; to assess the actual damage we must consider the poem's specific content and the violence which has, in fact, been done it by overreading. Since the publication of Mr. A. S. P. Woodhouse's classic account of its "argument," *Comus* has been generally supposed to concern the relations between "virtue" and "grace" [*UTQ*, XI, 46–71]. The virtue with which it deals is variously defined as continence, temperance, chastity, or virginity; whatever its character, Milton may be taken as saying of this virtue either that it co-operates with and leads toward grace or that it is distinctly inferior to grace and insufficient without it. How one reads the masque depends on how one makes these definitions, and vice versa. But on one point there is general agreement; the masque is built around a single central and important incident. Like Milton's tragedy and both his epics, *Comus* has a temptation at the center of it. The Lady, lost in a dark wood and separated from her brothers, is tempted by Comus, who is a magician and a sensualist; if she succumbs by drinking of his cup, her head will be turned to that of a beast. But she is rescued by her brothers, who (guided by an Attendant Spirit and protected by a certain herb which he has given them) drive off Comus, invoke the water nymph Sabrina to release their sister from enchantment, and escort her to their father's court.

The central episode of this story is clearly the temptation; the sort of allurements which are dangled before the Lady and the sort of energies which enable her to withstand those allurements must determine in very large measure the allegorical meaning of the masque. Secondary emphases may be altered by secondary elements—by the destination which the young people are supposed to be seeking, by the debate which the two brothers carry on while they are looking for their sister, by the prologue or the epilogue. But we shall not go far wrong if we look first at the central dramatic conflict of the masque as a means of approaching its intellectual and emotional content.

The relation of Comus to Circe determines a good deal of the significance which attaches to the seducer. In his prologue the Attendant Spirit describes Comus as the son of Circe by Bacchus [ll. 46ff.]; and, while Bacchus remains largely in the background, the maternal side of Comus' genealogy is several times emphasized throughout the masque. When he hears the Lady singing, Comus is reminded of his mother and the sirens [ll. 251ff.]; when the Attendant Spirit provides the brothers with a countercharm for Comus' enchantments, he compares it to

> that *Moly*
> That *Hermes* once to wise *Ulysses* gave [ll. 635–36].

The fate of Comus' victims is akin to that of Circe's; he is armed, like Circe, with a cup and wand; like Circe, he offers his victims food, revelry, and (latently but climactically) sexual enjoyment; the virtues which are invoked against him are the virtues of temperance, which Comus calls "lean Abstinence." It may be worth emphasizing that Milton has inverted the sex relationships of the original Circe story—perhaps to conform to the acting personnel at his disposal, perhaps to avoid too close a retelling of the old story, perhaps for more elaborate psychological reasons. In any event, the part of the fatal temptress, the deadly damsel, is here assumed by a male, the part of the shipwrecked mariners by a wandering lady; and from this fact derive some of the tonalities, and some of the incongruities, of the story.

For Comus is a seducer who makes remarkably few and feeble efforts to seduce; though he possesses the traditional enchanting devices of his mother, a glass and a wand, he never brings them explicitly into play. Instead of offering the Lady his magic brew while she is wandering alone, unsuspecting, and thirsty in the forest, he brings her into a palace, lets her see his troop of "oughly-headed Monsters," and only then, when she is thoroughly aroused and suspicious, tries to argue her into drinking of the cup. His wand is said to have power to "chain up [the Lady's] nerves in Alablaster" [l. 659], but so far as he enchants her at all, it is with a certain magic dust which blears her vision and with an anointed chair which holds her motionless. The wand and the cup, though much in evidence, never exert an active compulsion; and the seduction of the Lady, though unmistakably threatened, never develops into a real possibility. All this means, I suppose, is that the decorums of female innocence had to be very cautiously manipulated in the immediate proximity of symbols which folklore had rendered instinct with sexuality and which were controlled by the lascivious son of one (Circe) who was widely taken as a type of the strumpet.[2]

If the allegorical character of Comus is clear enough (he is Sensual Indulgence with some overtones of priapic fer-

[2] But Renaissance mythographers were not all orthodox Freudians, and Alexander Ross in his *Mel Heliconium* (London, 1642), pp. 96–97, interprets the rod of Circe as an instrument of punishment with which one who drinks of the cup is whipped. See also George Sandys, *Ovids Metamorphosis Englished* (Oxford, 1632), p. 481, where the rod reversed is said to symbolize discipline.

tility, black wizardry, and pagan sophistry), the forces which the Lady opposes to him are by no means simple. Some of her strength is her own, some is her brothers', some is the Attendant Spirit's. Her own strength is itself a complex element; when alarmed, she invokes

> The vertuous mind, that ever walks attended
> By a strong siding champion Conscience [ll. 210–11],

and, in addition, implies that if need were, a special guardian would be forthcoming from heaven. The Elder Brother adds a third element to these two; aside from her natural virtue and the "strength of Heaven," the Lady possesses

> a hidden strength
> Which if Heav'n gave it, may be term'd her own:
> 'Tis chastity, my brother, chastity [ll. 417–19].

The special power of chastity to defend itself against witches, ghosts, fairies, goblins, and wizards is not only the subject of set speeches by the Elder Brother, it is verified in the central action of the masque. Comus is able to surprise the Lady and assail her; he cannot enthrall or hurt her. And without the visible help of heaven she rebukes him until he acknowledges

> that I do fear
> Her words set off by som superior power;
> And though not mortal, yet a cold shuddring dew
> Dips me all o're, as when the wrath of *Jove*
> Speaks thunder, and the chains of *Erebus*
> To som of *Saturns* crew [ll. 799–804].

This "sage and serious doctrine of virginity," which the Lady says she will not reveal to Comus but which suffices to dazzle him anyhow, is said by Mr. Woodhouse to represent a religious aspect of the doctrine of mere earthly chastity enunciated earlier by the Elder Brother. But there is little evidence for this in the text: the Lady uses the "Sun-clad power of Chastity" as a synonym for the "doctrine of Virginity" [ll. 781, 786]; and the Elder Brother not only describes chastity as "Saintly" and "sacred" but uses "true Virginity" as a synonym [ll. 452, 424, 436]. The point has been elaborated in a different context by J. C. Maxwell [*CJ,* I, 376–80]. Thus Mr. Woodhouse, recognizing a possible confusion, is forced to appeal "to the intellectual frame of reference, supported as it is by the autobiographical passage in the *Apology*" [*UTQ,* XI, 56]. Here, it seems to me, the text is in danger of slipping away from us entirely. Valid support for ideas which are only adumbrated in a text may always be sought by appeals to related material; but here we are asked to import bodily, without any textual authority at all, ideas expressed by Milton in another context eight years later and ideas expressed by people other than Milton. This procedure seems unwarranted. Deliberately or otherwise, the text makes no distinction between chastity and virginity; when she rebukes Comus, the Lady does not describe chastity as a lesser virtue than virginity or make explicit reference to any specifically Christian sanctions for either virtue; and one reason for this reticence, aside from possible uneasy feelings on Milton's part about devotional celibacy, may be sought in the social implications of the particular masque he was writing.

For the fact is that in *Comus* Milton faced a rather delicate problem of tact. To make the Lady fully self-sufficient would be to eliminate the Attendant Spirit altogether as a functioning element in the story; but to make her virtue wholly dependent on heaven's assistance would scarcely be an overwhelming compliment to pay her. One simply does not tell an earl's daughter that she is chaste only by the grace of God. Thus Milton rather carefully, as it seems to me, manipulates his story to show that female virtue, while possessing defensive powers of its own and not by any means to be supposed vulnerable, much less defective in its own nature, does enjoy a special protection from heaven against such special menaces as Comus. And for this reason it is only after she has given a convincing demonstration of her own moral self-sufficiency that the Lady receives, even indirectly, the help of heaven.

What is the nature of that help? In attacking Comus with drawn swords and dispersing his "rout," the two brothers rely largely on their own powers; perhaps for this reason they are not fully effective in releasing their sister and must invoke the further interesting help of Sabrina. But the brothers are protected against Comus' magic by an herb named "Haemony" which the Attendant Spirit has provided for them; and the argument has been developed by Mr. Edward LeComte from a hint in Coleridge, and avidly accepted by Messrs. Brooks and Hardy, that haemony is a symbol of heavenly grace.[3] This identification rests partly on the name which Milton invented for the herb and partly on some of the things he says about it. The word "haemony" seems to derive primarily from the name for Thessaly (Haemonia), a land particularly rich in magical associations. It may also bear, through its close association with moly, an affinity to the Greek adjective *αἵμων*, "bloody." For one myth regarding the origins of moly relates it to the fate of the giant Pikolous, who, after the fateful war with Zeus, fled to Circe's isle, attacked her, and was himself attacked and slain by her father, Helios. From the drops of blood which Pikolous shed in the struggle with Helios, moly is said to have sprung, hence one possible origin of the name

[3] LeComte, "New Light on the 'Haemony' Passage in *Comus*," *PQ*, XXI, 283–98; Cleanth Brooks and J. E. Hardy, eds., *Poems of Mr. John Milton* (New York, 1951).

"haemony" and one possible argument, based on its origin in the blood of a god, for its character as a symbol of grace.[4]

The other reasons why haemony may be considered a symbol of grace derive from the things Milton causes Thyrsis (or the Attendant Spirit) to say about it. Haemony, he says, was shown him by a certain shepherd lad, "of small regard to see to" but skilled in herbs:

> Amongst the rest a small unsightly root,
> But of divine effect, he cull'd me out;
> The leaf was darkish, and had prickles on it,
> But in another Countrey, as he said,
> Bore a bright golden flowre, but not in this soyl:
> Unknown, and like esteem'd, and the dull swain
> Treads on it daily with his clouted shoon,
> And yet more med'cinal is it then that *Moly*
> That *Hermes* once to wise *Ulysses* gave [ll. 628–36].

The contrast between "another Countrey" where haemony flowers, and "this soyl," where it does not, is said to represent the contrast between heaven and earth; virtue thus reaches its final perfection in heaven, and indeed the total dependence of virtue on grace is said to be figured in the fact that "the flower is not only the final perfection of the plant, but the source of the seed" [*B & H,* p. 213]. Furthermore, Mr. LeComte declares that Milton's description of haemony is not unlike that of an herb named "rhamnus," which is mentioned in John Fletcher's *Faithful Shepherdess* (a recognized source of *Comus*) and further described in Gerard's *Herbal* under the popular name of "Christ's Thorn."

[4] Two more elements which scholars have, perhaps, been too dignified to throw into the etymological pot of "haemony" are possible puns on the hymen, guardian of virginity, and on harmony, the unruptured state of nature. Milton could have learned of Pikolous from Eustathius' *Commentaries,* a book known to have been in his library.

There are several difficulties with this interpretation. That the plant grows "in this soyl" but flowers "in another Countrey" is no great invention for Milton to have made on his own. Homer gives to moly (upon which haemony is obviously modeled) a white flower and says simply that it is hard for men to dig; but Pliny gives it a "florum luteum," a bright yellow flower, and reports that it grows in the districts of Pheneus and Cyllene in Arcady. Milton, who wanted to make use of it in Wales, may well have accounted for its being unknown there by saying that it grows there but flowers elsewhere. The notion that he gave it the name "haemony" as a way of referring not only to Pikolous' blood but to Christ's seems ingeniously esoteric; could Milton really have expected the Earl of Bridgewater and his guests to make on their own the not-even-suggested connection with Eustathius' *Commentaries,* and, supposing they made it, could he have doubted that the equating of Christ with a monster caught in the act of rape would have caused them anything but disquiet? Scarcely less extravagant is the assumption that they would all have read Fletcher's masque and Gerard's *Herbal* and would remember that the rhamnus misprinted in Fletcher was the same as the Christ's Thorn described in Gerard and that Christ's Thorn bore a vague resemblance to haemony.

Difficulties of this sort spring up on all sides as soon as one relaxes one's determination to ignore them. For instance, the simple shepherd lad of small regard to see to is a distinctly casual receptacle for divine grace. Perhaps his pastoral, swainish humility makes him an appropriate figure, but the early and persistent assumption that he is Milton himself or Milton's boyhood friend Diodati militates against his being the agent of grace. To open the door for immodest comparisons of this sort is a Shelleyan, not a Miltonic failing. If haemony is grace, there is another gross, immediate breach of tact in Thyrsis' declaration that in this country it is

> Unknown, and like esteem'd, and the dull swain
> Treads on it daily with his clouted shoon [ll. 633–34].

An audience of country gentlefolk would scarcely have been edified by this thought, particularly the clerical members of it; nor does it conform in the least with Milton's convictions as expressed elsewhere. One does not offhandedly tell the members of a Christian commonwealth that grace is unknown to them, that they trample it underfoot; at least, if one is the sort of immodest fanatic who thinks such thoughts, one does not conceal them in an incidental phrase describing a mythical root. But a magic symbol of temperance, having its origin and power in earthly elements and implying a contrast between Arcadian virtue and modern grossness, would suffer no such disabilities.

Besides, the effect of haemony is not the appropriate effect of divine grace. Maybe it blossoms in heaven, but its virtuous effect occurs on earth and is earthly in nature. All Thyrsis has of the plant is the root (the root traditionally contains the potent element of moly); so that apparently virtue (the root and stalk) is good medicine even without grace (the flower). And haemony is not used in the story to bring anyone to heaven or even to Ludlow Castle, but to avoid the ill effects of lust. It does not release the Lady; it protects the brothers against the enchantments of Comus, who is, allegorically, sensuality. Only in the vague sense that God is responsible for all things and the source of all energies (including the diabolic) did Milton suppose one needed divine grace to avoid drunkenness, riot, and lust. But as for the notion that grace in the Christian sense was necessary to lead a chaste life, the pagan world teemed with evidence to the contrary.

In addition, Milton could not have expected an herb closely associated with and resembling moly to carry for any conceivable audience the allegorical significance of divine grace. This is not a matter of Miltonic origins and derivations but of general, accepted significance. The only evidence that Milton did not derive haemony from some cat's cradle of gods, blood drops, and vegetables involving Pikolous, Osiris, Mithra, Cerberus, Cadmus, Coelus, mandragora, rue, rhamnus, dittany, bryony, and garlic is the known quality of his mind and the principle of economy of assumption. But if he associated haemony with moly and did not explicitly indicate a new interpretation, it seems likely that he must have expected the conventional allegorical meaning of moly to be felt. Allegories of the Circe-Ulysses fable might involve physical, moral, or mystical principles in great profusion; but, while the literal existence of moly was still being asserted, allegorical interpretations of the plant were more restrained. The one most easily available to a cultivated, unprofessional audience equated moly with temperance, and it was expressed in explicit detail prior to 1673 (when Milton last published *Comus*) by such men as Andrea dall'Anguillara, Pierre Gautruche, George Sabinus, D. Giphanius, Arthur Golding, Alexander Ross, and George Sandys. The same view is directly implied by Roger Ascham, Fulgentius, Apuleius, Heraclitus, Eustathius, and Boccaccio. For all these representatives of a larger company, moly is temperance or prudence, period.[5]

[5] Anguillara, *Le Metamorfosi di Ovidio* (Venice, 1572), p. 198; Gautruche, *Nouvelle histoire poétique* (Paris, 1738), p. 316 (first English ed., 1671); Sabinus, ed., *P. Ovidii Metamorphosis* (Frankfort, 1593), p. 491; Giphanius, ed., *Homeri Odyssea* (Strasbourg, 1579), p. 279; Golding, *The XV Bookes of P. Ovidius Naso* (London, 1567), "The Epistle," ll. 276–79; Ross, *Mystagogus Poeticus* (London, 1647), p. 67; Sandys, *The Relation of a Journey* (London, 1632), p. 308; also *Ovids Metamorphosis Englished* (Oxford, 1632), pp. 475, 479–81;

There is, to be sure, another allegorical view of the herb, which equates it with divine favor. This view might be found explicitly in Natale Conti, who speaks of the "divina clementia . . . quod per munus Ulyssi a Mercurio datum intelligitur," or in J. Spondanus, who gives a choice of two readings, in which moly may stand either for ethnic magnanimity or for Christian faith.[6] But the religious interpretation is a minority one, easily available to scholars, indeed, but by no means popularly diffused. To the degree that Milton could count on the members of his audience being familiar with any allegorical significance for moly or a molylike vegetable, it was likely to include, if not consist of, the notion of temperance. If he intended a more exalted or particular significance—above all, if he intended that meaning to be exclusively received—he would be unlikely to leave his hearers without a pretty broad hint as to what it was. There is no such hint in the text.

Finally, certain sanctions for the interpretation of moly as temperance may be drawn from Milton's writing before and after *Comus*. Elegy I to Diodati expresses the hope that Milton, with the aid of divine moly, will be able to avoid the fleshpots of London. Are we to suppose the poet so

---

Ascham, *The Scholemaster,* ed. D. C. Whimster (London, 1934), p. 68; Fulgentius, *Mythologicon,* ii, 12; Apuleius, *De deo Socratis,* cap. xxiv; Heraclitus, *De incredibilibus,* cap. xvi; Heraclitus (Ponticus), *Allegoriae Homericae,* cap. lxx; Boccaccio, *Genealogiae deorum,* IV, xiv; Eustathius, *Commentarii in Odysseam* (Leipzig, 1825), I, 381, calls moly an allegory of παιδεια but adds that it enables Ulysses to partake of Circe's pleasures with σωφρον. Note also that Mercury, the bringer of moly, is the god of prudence; see, e.g., H. M. Servius, *Commentarii in Vergilium* (Göttingen, 1826), I, 390. Cf. an interesting analogue in Marvell, "Upon Appleton House," ll. 355–60, where a prickly plant stands for conscience.

[6] Conti, *Mythologiae* (Geneva, 1651), pp. 566–67; Spondanus, ed., *Homeri quae exstant omnia* (Basel, 1606), *Odyssey,* pp. 142–43.

deeply sunk in cant and self-importance that, as early as the age of eighteen, he would consider himself in a state of grace? Temperance is a virtue which turns up with particular frequency throughout the Miltonic canon; it is the subject of Michael's lecture in Book XI of *Paradise Lost* and a major theme of *Paradise Regained,* Book II. "How great a virtue is temperance," cries the *Areopagitica,* "how much of moment through the whole life of man?" Milton here makes none of those reservations which Messrs. Brooks and Hardy would make for him—that virtue is wholly dependent on grace, that it is radically defective in its own nature, that it achieves full flower only in the contemplation of grace. Miltonic temperance is no such passive, contemplative virtue. As Milton's whole life indicates, as well as the history of the causes which he supported, virtue was for him an active, wayfaring, warfaring quality. And temperance, which enables a man by his own inner election to act or to refrain, to combine experiences and to direct them, is the very model of an active Protestant virtue. "Wherefore did he creat passions within us, pleasures round about us" (says the *Areopagitica* again), "but that these rightly temper'd are the very ingredients of vertu?" *Comus* itself emphasizes the concept of temperance at both the beginning and the end; the Attendant Spirit in his prologue says most people partake of Comus' drink "through fond intemperate thirst" [l. 67]; and the final song declares that the Earl's children have come

> To triumph in victorious dance
> O're sensual Folly and Intemperance [ll. 973–74].

If, on the other hand, one takes haemony to represent heavenly grace and the need for grace as a central theme of the masque, one must impute to Milton the artistic folly of introducing the climactic symbol and climactic idea of the poem in a subordinate clause four hundred lines from the poem's end and of never mentioning it again.

Lastly, if haemony is a symbol of grace, yet cannot be used to release the Lady from Comus' magic chair, what shall we make of the power which does effect that release —that interesting, troublesome creature, Sabrina? Brooks and Hardy, happy to find her a water nymph, eke out a suggestion of the waters of baptism and so convert her, not without a subdued scuffle, into another symbol of grace. But a sense of economy, if nothing else, will cause us to balk at these duplicated symbols. If Sabrina is merely what she seems to be, the genius of the shore and the patroness of virgins, her influence is one step above that of temperance and one step below that of grace itself, and her function in the masque is secure. But to make haemony grace, and Sabrina more grace, and the vision of the epilogue still another aspect of grace is to destroy the very possibility of variety and development within the masque. I cannot feel that any allegory is worth the price in nonsense that one must pay for this one.

Professor Woodhouse, less undiscriminating in his response to imagery, does not try to see grace behind both haemony and Sabrina, but he does conclude for Sabrina as such a symbol and so (presumably) against haemony [*UTQ*, XIX, 218–23]. But if we bear in mind the difficulties [emphasized by R. Blenner-Hassett, *MLN*, LXIV, 315–18] which Milton faced in converting his nymph from the somewhat tainted figure who appears in Geoffrey, I think we shall feel that he did enough simply in making her a chastity symbol. If she were a symbol of Christian grace, would it not be unreasonable to invoke her by means of a long list of explicitly pagan deities [ll. 866–83]? Would it not be absurd to let her sing about willows, osiers, and cowslips, but not a word about God or grace or divine power, and so to dismiss her to Amphitrite's bower without a single hint dropped as to Christian grace? When Spenser dipped the Red Cross Knight into the Well of Life, he made the action awkward and arbitrary in itself and added an explicit moral comment. But Milton did neither of these things; neither haemony nor Sabrina is marked unmistakably as the vehicle of grace; and there is no better reason to suppose that Milton intended either identification than to suppose he intended both.

So far as there is an allegorical meaning for haemony, then, one need not look beyond temperance. But an important reason for Milton's introduction of haemony is not allegorical at all; it has to do with the demands of his story. He cannot have the young men rush in and skewer Comus on their literal, material swords because natural powers cannot be allowed to overcome supernatural ones and because the Attendant Spirit, who has already announced that his function is to convoy the good, cannot be left unemployed. Milton clearly needs haemony in order to balance black magic with white; but as for a suggestion that he is trying to tell us that "Grace and Virtue are essentially the same" or that "the plant symbolizes Virtue in a state of awareness of its own imperfection, expecting perfection only in heaven" [*B & H,* p. 212]—these are pure extrapolations. One might as well argue from the statement that "the leaf was darkish, and had prickles on it" that the Lady herself was thus afflicted or that virtue on earth is not merely difficult but essentially forbidding in its aspect. This Milton simply did not believe; he would not have felt Spenser to be a sage and serious poet if he had. He would not have written those many passages on the beauty of virtue which stud his work. He would not have been a Renaissance humanist but a Coptic monk.

If, then, the masque is not preaching the insufficiency

of virtue without grace, there is no reason to suppose that the Elder Brother is the object of all that criticism which Brooks and Hardy impute to Milton. A priori, it is hard to see why Milton should have undertaken, in a masque which is essentially complimentary, to expose the adolescent heir of the Earl of Bridgewater as a pompous, pedantic fool; and, in fact, the evidence that he intended anything of the sort is remarkably slender.

For example, the Elder Brother's first speech is said by Brooks and Hardy to exemplify naïveté because he asks the moon to "disinherit Chaos" [ll. 330–33], and Comus has "already (on sound traditional authority) used the moon as the symbol of his sovereignty" [*B & H,* p. 205]. But the Elder Brother has not heard Comus talk about the moon; in fact, he has no reason for supposing that such a creature as Comus exists. The identification of Comus with the moon rests on line 116,

> Now to the Moon in wavering Morrice move,

though there seems no reason why one should not, by the same logic, identify Comus with the stars too, on the basis of lines 111–12:

> We that are of purer fire
> Imitate the Starry Quire.

But in fact there is no reason to identify him with either, for the moon is Cynthia's chariot as well as Hecate's and is associated with chastity as well as with witchcraft. As for the Elder Brother, he asks both the stars and moon for light and then says that if neither is forthcoming, he will follow a light from a house. Why this should be considered abysmal innocence is not clear. He wants light from stars, moon, or a dwelling, and an audience which is expected to find these requests naïve might well be advised what other sources of light a dark wood usually affords.

Brooks and Hardy make much of the supposed naïve confidence which the Elder Brother expresses in his sister's safety, as if Milton wanted us to consider him a brash and overconfident theorizer. But in fact he holds to the doctrine of virtue's self-sufficiency only with a very distinct qualification, which Brooks and Hardy do not so much as mention. He will not be alarmed that his sister is lost and alone,

> Not being in danger, as I trust she is not [l. 369].

If Milton intended us to consider him naïve, this reasonable restriction completely undermines the poet's dramatic purpose. The Elder Brother does not take an obviously unreasonable position in saying,

> Vertue may be assail'd, but never hurt,
> Surpriz'd by unjust force, but not enthrall'd [ll. 588–89],

since, as we have seen, this principle is dramatically fulfilled by the Lady and Comus in the temptation scene; and when Thyrsis is first heard approaching in the distance, the Elder Brother is notably aware of the various ills against which he and his brother must be on guard [ll. 482–84].

In two other passages Brooks and Hardy find the naïveté of the Elder Brother expressed in an absolute opposition of good and bad. He is so much against Comus that he forgets vice may be alluring; and the audience, in hearing him, is expected to realize this limitation of his character.

> Som say no evil thing that walks by night
> In fog, or fire, by lake, or moorish fen,
> Blew meager Hag, or stubborn unlaid ghost,
> That breaks his magick chains at *curfeu* time,
> No Goblin, or swart Faëry of the mine,
> Hath hurtfull power o're true Virginity [ll. 431–36].

Of this language Brooks and Hardy say that "it represents good and evil in abstract terms of white and black rather than light and dark. . . . The 'Goblin,' the 'Faëry,' the 'Hag' are merely items in a catalogue of evil *things,* the use of the word *thing* taking from them whatever quality of 'thing-ness,' of tangibility, they might have had" [*B & H,* p. 208].

This argument involves several strained, not to say mistaken, assertions. "Thing" as used of spirits comes with particular force; being creatures of several different spheres, neither wholly alive nor altogether dead, they can be referred to only by a slippery, noncommittal word like "thing."

> *Marcellus:* What! has this thing appear'd again tonight?
> [*Hamlet,* I, 1, 21.]

That the passage lacks all tangibility and is "completely abstract" [*B & H,* p. 208] seems so lamentable a misreading that I can only appeal in silent amazement to the lines themselves.

Another example of the Elder Brother's supposed naïveté is found in lines 601ff., where, in expressing his detestation of Comus, the Elder Brother is said to make of him "a 'simply' frightful creature, attended by such obvious bogies as Harpies and Hydras," so that the audience is intended to see in the Elder Brother a sort of "moral-philosophical Hotspur," illogical and immoderate [*B & H,* p. 211]. Against this view we may appeal to dramatic probabilities. Thyrsis has told the Elder Brother that his sister is entrapped by a sorcerer living "within the navil of this hideous Wood," a person skilled in witcheries, who offers to travelers a "baneful cup" which transforms them into "the inglorious likenes of a beast." Comus and his rout are called by Thyrsis "monstrous" and are compared to "wolves or tigers"; they are "abhorred" and "barbarous," and Comus, once again referred to, is a "damn'd wisard" [ll. 519–70]. After all this, the Elder Brother would have no dramatic existence at all if he were not fairly indignant at his sister's seducer—and such a seducer! He proposes direct action against the enchanter, and this idea, while inadequate, certainly is not held up to mockery. It is inadequate to the occasion, which is extraordinary in ways that only Thyrsis can suspect, but perfectly "natural" in its immediate contexts. The idea is natural in the situation in which the Elder Brother is involved, and natural in relation to the audience, which expects and sympathizes with impetuous faults in young men whose sisters are threatened with rape. A display of perfect decorum and a philosopher's wariness about all conceivable dangers would, under the circumstances, forfeit the sympathy of the audience forever.

Thus three central elements of the masque may be seen to fit together on the earthly plane without notable inconsistency or incongruity. The spiritual energies of the Lady's virtue suffice to repel Comus without any divine backstiffening. The brothers are able to approach Comus armed not with grace, but with temperance; and the doctrine that chastity or virginity possesses special powers for its own defense is enunciated by the Elder Brother without any such backlash of ironic commentary as Brooks and Hardy have imputed to Milton. The machinery of magic is invoked to protect the Lady and her brothers, and its connection with chastity may even have been, in Milton's mind, a conviction more integral than the word "machinery" implies [see the discussion in Tillyard's *Milton* (London, 1930), Appendix C]; but in the masque it serves moral ends which can be perfectly well understood on the secular plane.

Where, then, is heaven, and where in the masque does heavenly influence intervene? Obsessed with theological ultimates, Brooks and Hardy locate heaven at least three times over. The Attendant Spirit is for them a heavenly messenger because he comes from somewhere near Jove's court [*B & H,* pp. 189, 192]; but then they say flatly that the "father's . . . court, in the play, symbolizes heaven" [*B & H,* p. 226]; however, when the Attendant Spirit, speaking the epilogue, says he is leaving the court for a new sphere, this, too, seems to be heaven [*B & H,* p. 228]. Is it possible that he should leave heaven to go to heaven? No, it seems that the Earl's court has only "played" for a time at being heaven [*B & H,* p. 230]; and thus heaven is unmade as blithely as formerly it was made.

But, in the first place, there is little reason to suppose the Attendant Spirit a proper angel. Milton's manuscript refers to him as a "daemon," and daemons, as Burton will inform us, were not angels but tutelary spirits.[7] The Attendant Spirit goes to some pains to make his nature explicit:

> Before the starry threshold of *Joves* Court
> My mansion is, where those immortal shapes
> Of bright aereal Spirits live insphear'd [ll. 1–3].

He lives before—that is, outside—the threshold, and he lives where spirits are ensphered; these two facts place his home among the planets, where "Il Penseroso" assigns the residence of daemons:

> And of those *Daemons* that are found
> In fire, air, flood, or under ground,
> Whose power hath a true consent
> With Planet, or with Element [ll. 93–96].

[7] "Some indifferent *inter deos et homines* as heroes and daemons which ruled men and were called genii" [*Anatomy,* part 1, sec. 2, mem. 1, subs. 2]; cf. also Augustine, *De civitate Dei,* Books VIII and IX; and Apuleius, *De deo Socratis,* "Daemones sunt genere animalia, ingenio rationabilia, animo passiva, corpore aëria, tempore aeterna."

He represents the interests of heaven, he is a messenger of heaven, he has supernatural powers and supernatural knowledge; but his real business is on earth, and it is by no means so general a concern as one usually attributes to ministers of grace. He exists, by his own account, to provide a special protection for specially virtuous people against specially pressing perils [ll. 15–17, 40–42, 78–82]. Theologically he is a guardian spirit, dramatically a master of ceremonies; in neither capacity does he determine the events of the story, exercise any superhuman power other than his wisdom, or attempt more than the release of virtue to establish its own destiny.

The Attendant Spirit does not come from heaven, and there is no more reason to suppose the young people are going there. The court of the Earl of Bridgewater at Ludlow Castle is doubtless a good place to arrive, and heaven is no doubt the final destination of the good; but the Earl might well have been startled by the imputation that he was God the Father. The Attendant Spirit's account of the presidency of Wales [ll. 18–36] offers no allegorical significance to the scrupulous eyes of Brooks and Hardy; here, if anywhere, one would expect the symbol of heaven to be made explicit. But the allegory seems to rest entirely on two lines in which Comus tells the Lady that he has seen her brothers and

> if those you seek
> It were a journey like the path to Heav'n,
> To help you find them [ll. 301–03].

And that a hyperbolical cajolery in the mouth of a notorious deceiver should be taken as a positive statement of fact about an unrelated matter seems a queer sort of syllogism.

No, heaven appears in the masque just where it ought to appear, as the epilogue to a story which concerns primarily the trials of this earth. The Attendant Spirit departs to that "vaguely located mansion from which he has come" [M. Y. Hughes, ed., *Paradise Regained, The Minor Poems,* etc. (New York, 1937), p. 268], a mansion not to be equated with the Christian Paradise, but symbolized by a series of pagan heavens, the islands of Hesperus, the Elysian Fields, the garden of Adonis, and the retreat of Cupid and Psyche. Whatever else these heavens represent, they are not the Christian Paradise, either symbolically or otherwise;[8] for the Spirit can fly or run only

> to the green earths end,
> Where the bow'd welkin slow doth bend,
> And from thence can soar as soon
> To the corners of the Moon [ll. 1013–16].

His heavens are of the spheres, and of the lowest spheres at that, the earth and the moon. But in his final statement to the audience he urges:

> Mortals that would follow me,
> Love vertue, she alone is free,
> She can teach ye how to clime
> Higher then the Spheary chime;
> Or if Vertue feeble were,
> Heav'n it self would stoop to her [ll. 1017–22].

Here at last is the Christian heaven, unmistakably. It is not seen or described, as it should not be; it is merely indicated as an aspiration. Its position is "higher than the Spheary chime," above that music of the spheres which echoes and complements the saintly choirs, but is distinct from and inferior to them. "In any case," Brooks and Hardy assure us, "it is clear that the final attainment is not made without

[8] Note particularly the MS changes of l. 995, where Milton rejected successively "manna" and "Sabaean" dew for the strictly pagan "Elysian" dew.

the assistance of a power higher than Virtue's own" [*B & H,* p. 233]. What it is clear from is not apparent; all the poet says in the body of his direct declarative assertion is that virtue can teach mortals to get to heaven. No doubt Milton, like all other Christians, understood the efficacy of another power; but his silence here is more compatible with the emphasis that grace supplements virtue than with the negative assertion that virtue is inadequate without grace. The properly Miltonic mortal actively climbs toward grace, he does not passively wait to receive it. And if long-range consistency matters at all, one might point to that striking series of lines in *Paradise Lost* [III, 309ff.], in which Milton applied the doctrine of merit to Christ himself.

The last conditional couplet of *Comus* confirms, even as it expands this notion:

> Or if Vertue feeble were,
> Heav'n it self would stoop to her.

Taking it for granted that throughout the masque virtue has been shown as feeble and heaven as stooping, Brooks and Hardy are thoroughly embarrassed by Milton's use of the conditional in line 1021; they say Milton chose this construction "only to emphasize the paradoxical nature of the situation proposed, not to leave its existence in doubt" [*B & H,* p. 233]. This bit of critical patter may be worth a moment's examination. There is nothing "paradoxical" about virtue's being feeble or heaven's adjusting itself to this weakness. Even though the notion of "virtue" may include either goodness or potency, morality or strength, there is no impression of paradox in line 1021, because virtue in the first sense can obviously be feeble, and virtue in the second sense obviously cannot. When a word has two senses, the fact that one of them is nonsensical in context and the other platitudinous does not suffice to make a paradox. But even if a tiny germ of paradox were apparent at the farthest reach of one reading of "virtue," a conditional construction would not serve to emphasize it. The last word of line 1021, "were," is crucial here; and, to parse its grammar out, it is a third person singular subjunctive form used in a subordinate clause to indicate a condition contrary to fact. By writing the last couplet in this form Milton can only have intended to convey that if virtue were feeble (which he did not think she was and had not represented her as being), heaven would stoop like a falcon to help her. But in what sense virtue could be "free" if her only function, or an indispensable part of her function, were to be lifted aloft like a limp rabbit in the claws of an eagle is not clear. Active virtue is a norm in the masque; passive acceptance of grace is an exception. A glistering guardian *might* come to aid virtue "if need were" [l. 218], but such an appearance is exceptional and auxiliary. Spirits perverse have access to earth, says *Paradise Lost,* and can tempt or punish mortals,

except whom
God and good Angels guard by special grace [II, 1032–33].

If it has any moral meaning at all, *Comus* intends something much closer to "the Lord helps those that help themselves" than to Caliban's notion of the deity, or Holy Willie's. The point is made perfectly explicit in Aurelian Townshend's *Tempe Restor'd* (1631), which tells a similar story, with several close verbal parallels, and in which the Lady Alice Egerton had already taken part as a masquer:

He finds no helpe, that uses not his owne
[A. Townshend, *Poems and Masques,*
ed. E. K. Chambers (Oxford, 1912),
p. 85].

Though it may have this incidental result, the real trouble with overreading is not that it imposes a rigid pattern on the literary work. Ardently as Brooks and Hardy have struggled to interpret *Comus* according to their own lights, the total effect they present is not of an intricate architecture but of an ingenious, perverse chaos. When Milton wrote that virtue alone is free, it appears that he meant to say that virtue alone is dependent; why he did not say this instead of the contrary remains mysterious. When Milton wanted to refer to Christ's Thorn, he hid it behind the name of rhamnus, which he hid behind the name of moly, which he hid near the name of haemony; and he was so crafty about making us think of Christ's Thorn that he never mentioned it, as a result of which three hundred years had to elapse before anyone could so much as suspect his intention. There may be carelessness in this sort of thinking, or confusion, but it is principled carelessness and confusion. The trouble is not with the critics, who are men of ingenuity, not even with the particular interpretation of *Comus,* which is wrongheaded, but with a way of interpreting it, with an image of the creative mind which produced it. Milton's was not a sly, furtive, random, cryptic mind; he did not work, like some very great artists of another breed, in indirection, innuendo, and pastiche. For every beauty which one uncovers on esoteric assumptions (and it is both odd and significant how little Brooks and Hardy make of beauty, how indifferent they seem to be whether they uncover an anagram, a pun, a grotesque fault in taste, or a relevant harmony), one sacrifices a half-dozen of the larger elegancies for which *Comus* really exists. The fault of overreading is pervasive, it corrupts everything and will sacrifice even its own best perceptions for the glare and tinsel of a bit of false wit.

This is especially noticeable when, as frequently happens, Brooks and Hardy succumb to an obvious, jangling antithesis such as Milton had within his grasp and deliberately chose to forego. The double significance of "virtue," a word which may connote either "strength" or "goodness," opens the way to many puns, all of which, though Milton passed them up, Brooks and Hardy strive strongly to foist back into the poem. Another opening for a pun occurs in one of the concluding songs:

> Heav'n hath timely tri'd their youth,

says the song; and Brooks and Hardy must forthwith wrench Milton into a timely-timeless antithesis [*B & H,* p. 227]. Heaven has tried the youth of the young folk in the world of time; it will reward them in the world beyond time. No matter that neither Milton nor any contemporary ever uses "timely" in any such sense; no matter that the death thought involved in "going to heaven" jars on the jubilation of homecoming. We must have the antithesis at all costs.

One useful device for creating antitheses where Milton never intended them is to treat him as a nineteenth-century poet flavored with nineteenth-century transcendental philosophy. For instance, Thyrsis prefaces his account of Comus by saying that though "shallow unbelief" and ignorance" refuse to admit it, the supernatural beings described by poets do exist [ll. 513, 518]; and for Brooks and Hardy this comment imports "the dependence of poetic truth on belief" [*B & H,* p. 209]. Why they do not add that poetic truth also depends on knowledge is all too obvious. But, in fact, Milton did not think that poetic truth depended on belief; he nowhere distinguishes poetic truth from other varieties or asserts, as Blake and Keats were to do more than a century and a half later, that a strong conviction about any matter makes it true.[9] So also in line 10,

[9] *The Marriage of Heaven and Hell,* conversation with Isaiah; Keats to Benjamin Bailey, November 22, 1817.

where the Attendant Spirit mentions the crown that virtue gives

> After this mortal change, to her true Servants.

Brooks and Hardy read the phrase "mortal change" as "the constant change which makes mortal existence a death-in-life" [*B & H,* p. 189]. But a doubt or two may creep in as to whether Milton really intended a comparison between the Earl of Bridgewater's children and the Ancient Mariner. For one thing, he never uses the phrase "mortal change" or anything like it to describe life; but he does [*PL,* X, 273] use the same phrase of death, as well as a variant, "thy mortal passage" [XI, 366]. Not having read *Die Welt als Wille und Vorstellung,* he did not think of change as aimless or delusive, and nothing in his life or writings suggests that he considered mortal existence a "death-in-life." As a matter of fact, whether "mortal change" refers to life or death does not particularly matter, so far as the argument over virtue and grace is concerned. But Brooks and Hardy cannot resist the chance for a quibble; they must assume that Milton wrote "after this mortal change" by way of saying "after this changing mortal life," at the expense of a tautology, in defiance of the words' most obvious connotations, and for no other visible reason than to bemuse explicators.

Mr. Don C. Allen, in an essay already referred to, carries this position to its logical conclusion. Having urged that *Comus* is not a masque because it lacks formality and ritual, nor yet a play because it lacks suspense and character alteration, he adds that it is written in a patchwork of styles. When he has completed his indictment with the charge that *Comus* is intellectually muddled, Mr. Allen has ample reason to dismiss the entire production as a series of faulty compromises, "a mélange of various tendencies and styles that never merge into anything intensely organic" [*THV,* p. 32].

About Mr. Allen's need for something "intensely organic" I am not sure that anything can be done; "organic unity" as an exclusive wholesale criterion of critical judgment is a cant phrase out of eighteenth-century Germany, dependent on a sort of muzzy metaphysics with which neither Milton nor any modern critic except conceivably Sir Herbert Read is in genuine sympathy [see, for fuller discussion of these points, James Benziger, *PMLA,* LXVI, 24–48]. But some unity can be introduced into a reading of *Comus* by forgetting that the villain presents "a modified Neo-Epicurean argument" to which the Lady replies with a mixture of "stoic statements" and "the quasi-Christian concept of virginity" [*THV,* pp. 36–37]. Sly, sensual seducers are not usually held to such strict account for the exact framing of their arguments according to philosophic schools, any more than are virgins defending their virtue. If Comus is a bad man and the Lady a good girl, we shall not find their "ethical premises" mixed at all, even though our modified Neo-Epicurean had, at first sight of his victim, been charmed into standing for a moment, stupidly good.

Another device making for unity would be to disregard those elements of what Mr. Allen calls "the pre-texts" which Milton did not specifically invoke. "Comus is, of course, the son and heir of Circe and the brother of Ariosto's Alcina, Trissino's Acratia, Tasso's Armida, and Spenser's mistress of the Bower of Bliss" [*THV,* p. 33]. Of these five familial relations, four and a half are gratuitous attributions of Mr. Allen's; all Milton says is that Comus is a son of Circe. It is odd to suggest that Milton was "attempting to unite all these motifs with their diverse interpretations"; it is a great deal odder to blame him for not following "the traditional working-out of the pre-text" [*THV,* p. 33]. If he was really trying to unite five different moral allegories, on five different themes, the least one could grant Milton, it might seem, would be the right to modify his story a bit. And if he altered Geoffrey of Monmouth's account of Sabrina, the changes may indeed "bother those who have the original history in their heads" [*THV,* p. 35] so firmly that they cannot get it out; but these people would be bothered, too, by Shakespeare's liberties, in *Hamlet,* with Saxo Grammaticus.

Mr. Allen urges further that the theme of *Comus* "is not unspottedly Christian" because some pagans believed in the virtue of chastity [*THV,* p. 38] and that the time of the action is confused as between pre-Christian Albion and the Christian present. But, on the first point, few poems of any age have been so immaculately, not to say vindictively, Christian as to celebrate no virtue of which any pagan ever partook; nor am I aware that they have suffered from their contamination. The critical criterion is an odd one indeed. What the argument points toward is the idea that *Comus* is not a particularly Christian poem. This may or may not be true; the feeling, if not the machinery of the poem, is far from pagan. But even if *Comus* is not specifically Christian, neither is Donne's "Extasie" or Marvell's "Garden"; and what this has to do with the merits of these poems as poems is by no means clear. On the second point, it is true that *Comus,* being a pastoral, takes place in a world outside time; so does "Lycidas," where the poet communes now with Phoebus, now with St. Peter and compares young Lycidas now with Orpheus and now with a Christian saint. So too in Spenser's *Shepherd's Calendar,* where Christian and pagan mythologies are cheerfully scrambled into a panegyric of Queen Elizabeth. If an indeterminate date in time, involving a confusion of mythologies, mars *Comus,* surely it mars a great many other works as well. No doubt Mr. Allen can reconcile or adjust his various critical opinions without much trouble; what is interesting is his explicit recognition of the fact that, in searching for something "intensely organic" (i.e., in which the decoration is structural), he has been led to make hash out of *Comus.* It is no accident; the same principles followed with the same deadly consistency would make hash out of almost all the poetry written by John Milton, or for that matter by most English poets.

The examples could be multiplied, but conclusions are privileged to generalize. The readings of *Comus* which emerge from a close analysis of the imagery, unchecked by a larger perspective on the poem's literal architecture, may yield a series of flashing, fragmentary insights but are unlikely to co-ordinate them into a coherent whole. For good or for evil, much of Milton's imagery is strictly decorative; his overtones exist to be realized and forgotten, not to be exalted into general principles and large-scale structural devices. In point of fact, brightness and coolness do not happen to be "associated with Virtue throughout the poem" [*B & H,* p. 225]; but even if they were, the fact would be of dubious structural significance. Milton did not compose *Comus* in cools and hots any more than in lights and darks, louds and softs, wets and drys, or thins and thicks. He made use of these qualities as occasion required, but he did not attribute allegorical or general significance to them without explicitly indicating it; their role is decorative and subordinate, not structural and primary. Any reader who chooses may, of course, impose an allegorical significance on any element he likes; but only at the risk of having to drop it when it no longer fits. In certain sections of the masque, for example, no radical harm ensues from associating Sabrina's aquatic habits with a cool, cleansing virtue.

But if water-equals-virtue be made a constant equation, the brothers' search for virtue—"som cool friendly Spring" [l. 281]—then becomes responsible for the Lady's entire plight. No doubt any respectably energetic allegorist can invent in a few minutes half-a-dozen ways of getting over, under, around, or away from this difficulty; I am convinced that it would be far less distracting and far closer to the main lines of Milton's intent to let the water-virtue connection quietly disappear the minute it ceases to help our understanding of the images and begins to make demands on its own account. It should remain on the fringe of our minds, not in the center. If this critical outlook implies a low estimate of *Comus* as a tissue of images and implications, some consolation may perhaps be found in the sleazy weaving of all the fabrics hitherto produced from these materials. *Comus* as a masque presenting a clear story, a simple allegory, and a graceful compliment embroidered with a fluid imagery seems to me worth ten fretworks of strained conceit and forced interpretation. Perhaps when the critics have learned a little temperance in the application of their Byzantine ingenuities, we shall be able to enjoy without apology the simple beauties of obvious commonplaces set in musical language.

[II]

The Devil and Doctor Jung

ONE of the most striking of recent approaches to literature is that which labels itself Jungian; it is also one of the most puzzling, simply in the matter of its extent. For the alternatives with which one is faced do not involve simply those differences, experienced by every major theory, between advocates and antagonists of the complex as a whole. Some people think Marxism an invention of the devil himself, others treat it as a substitute scripture; but at least both parties are in substantial agreement about the dimensions of their topic. In addition to sweeping disagreements about its merit as a theory, the explorer of Jungian criticism must cope with differences, most striking when they involve critics whose general attitudes of approval or disapproval are broadly similar, as to just what they are approving and disapproving. Is the Jungian influence that of a vocabulary, that of a philosophy, or that of something halfway, like a critical theory? Suppose it a sort of theory, a working hypothesis; is it central or tangential, say, to the question of literary value? Some materials toward a tentative answer to these questions may be derived from considering the treatment which John Milton has undergone at the hands of the Jungians. The materials are copious enough to be representative but not overwhelming; and they run something like a gamut.[1]

At one extreme is the use or abuse of Jungian ideas which consists of borrowing nothing more than a vocabulary, and not even a total vocabulary at that but just a favorite word, preferably "archetype" or "archetypal." Mr. Arnold Stein, for example, seems to assert that in encountering Milton's Garden of Eden we experience "from the perspective of Satan and from our own, that of fallen humanity . . . an archetypal state that cannot be known to us directly" [*AS*, p. 53]. Why archetypal states cannot be known to us directly may be a little open to question. Since Jung defines them as the "psychic residua" of common experiences, one would think they ought to be fairly accessible and getting clearer all the time; in point of fact, it is the premise of a full-blown Jungian like Miss Bodkin that archetypes are available to all of us. Directness is the essence of her method. But Mr. Stein quickly equates his concept of archetypal memories with the "Neoplatonic" notion that "memory is the province of the soul" [*AS*, p. 53], quite careless of the fact that, while Neoplatonic ideas are supposed to exist independently of human experience and to draw their sanctions from another sphere of reality, archetypal memories are supposed to be derived from human experience, to be summary complexes of existence in this world. Still, it is useful to see how little "archetypal" can be made to mean.

[1] Arnold Stein, *Answerable Style* (Minneapolis, 1953); C. S. Lewis, *A Preface to Paradise Lost* (New York, 1952); Richard P. Adams, "The Archetypal Pattern of Death and Rebirth in Milton's Lycidas," *PMLA*, LXIV, 183–88; Maud Bodkin, *Archetypal Patterns in Poetry* (Oxford, 1934); R. J. Zwi Werblowsky, *Lucifer and Satan* (London, 1952).

Elsewhere, the word seems to mean something more, or at least something more explicit. Mr. C. S. Lewis, in describing the approach to Paradise, mentions rising tiers of trees, and adds incautiously that "as in dream landscapes, we find that what seemed the top is not the top" [*PPL,* p. 48]. For Mr. Stein this observation imports "that the sequence of Satan's entering Paradise resembles a dream" [*AS,* p. 56] and not only so, but "the dream has qualities reminiscent of an archetypal return," partly because of the "hairie sides" of IV, 135, and partly because the experience described is "real-unreal" like a dream. Discounting the charming circularities here, one may observe that the physiological overtones of "hairie sides" do not disturb Mr. Lewis, who notes with satisfaction that the earth in IV, 228, has pores to absorb water, and veins; and they please Mr. Stein by providing a sort of justification for the adjective "archetypal." Paradise, though both gentlemen are too nice to say so right out, is evidently a womb.

Now it may well be that Milton, with *The Purple Island* in his immediate background, would not have been frightened by these overtones; but the timid modern reader is likely to find himself badly scared by the implications which suddenly overwhelm Satan's entry into Paradise. There was only one entry "on th'other side" [IV, 179], but this did not bother Satan; "due entrance he disdain'd," jumped over the wall, and landed on his feet within. If we are not yet rid of the womb overtone, some of the more sensitive of us are going to be slightly queasy at this point. "Que diable allait-il faire dans *cette* galère?" As for the Paradisal hydraulics which in a later passage move Mr. Stein [*AS,* pp. 65, 67] to such ecstasies—"the waters below and the waters above; growing things are blessedly in the center, thirsting downward for darkness and earth and water, thirsting upward for light and sky and water"—if we have no womb overtones to reckon with, the situation is pleasantly representative of a turnip patch, though not much more exalted than that. But if we start with one big dark river which later divides into four and try to work the details in with certain elementary features of the urogenitary system in the human female—if we find ourselves trying to imagine what Gabriel is perched on, supposing Paradise to be a womb—I think we will soon find ourselves regretting the whole concept of an "archetypal return" and be happy to drop it.

Vox (archetypes) *et praeterea nihil;* at its most primitive, this is what the Jungian approach tends to become; and when it does achieve a discovery, the new element is sometimes intrusive or disturbing, sometimes irrelevant. Mr. Lewis speaks in a vague romantic vein of Milton's not creating or describing Paradise but "drawing out the Paradisal Stop in us" [*PPL,* p. 47], as if readers were so many Hammond Electric Organs. If this is what happens when we read Book IV, it is clear that modern readers are all subject to the sort of Stock Response of which modern criticism has labored for twenty years to make them all suspicious. Perhaps it would be good for poetry, as Mr. Lewis in his capacity of public moralist urges elsewhere [*PPL,* pp. 53–56], if readers' responses were more stock than they are. Offhand, it is not easy to think of any major social advantages which would derive from confusing Sir Richard Blackmore's handling of the Paradisal Stop with John Milton's. But, however things ought to be, the actual fact is that Milton's epic has earned its reputation by appealing to readers with many different backgrounds and hence, one supposes, many different stops. A student of literature, particularly, may be pardoned for thinking that this indicates some quality peculiar to the poetry as well as something which is generally true of all humanity. Many people appreciate Milton's description of Paradise who do not believe that Paradise exists or ever existed; few people who believe that Paradise exists or ever existed find themselves touched by Sir Richard Blackmore's manipulation of this stop. Surely the sort of one-for-one relation between subject and literary response which Mr. Lewis seems to defend is not only untrue to the experience of a sensitive reader but perilous to the very existence of sensitive readers.

In an early effort at Jungian analysis, Mr. Richard P. Adams some years ago displayed a remarkable sensitivity to a water-and-vegetable modulation which he found in "Lycidas." Various forms of vegetation are, indeed, mentioned in the course of the poem; and while it seems a little special to remark that "no less than fifty lines, out of a total of 193, are concerned with water in one way or another" [*PMLA,* LXIV, 185], it is certainly true that something like this number mention, in one way or another, something more or less moist. But that these vegetables and moistures have a significance is not clear. Animals and minerals and dry things are also mentioned in "Lycidas"; are they all significant too? Of the vegetable life mentioned by Milton, three plants, the rose [l. 45], the hyacinth [l. 106], and the violet [l. 145] were once reputed to have sprung from the blood of a mortal or a deity, and these plants might be considered emblems of immortality. But Milton makes reference to the origin of only one of these three and mentions a great many others, for instance wild thyme, white thorn, the rathe primrose and her many companions, which do not have mythological origins and are not symbols of immortality. Even in the one place where Milton does touch on the mythical origin of a plant, he is not eager to dwell on that origin; his intention is quite different. In point of prosaic fact, he is describing the bonnet of Camus:

His Mantle hairy and his Bonnet sedge,
Inwrought with figures dim, and on the edge
Like to that sanguine flower inscrib'd with woe [ll. 104–06].

There is a significant parallel between the mourning for Hyacinth and the mourning for Lycidas; but as for a promise of rebirth or a symbol of immortality, there is no such thing, perhaps because Milton is still asking questions about Lycidas' death and will not be concerned, till a good number of lines have passed, to suggest rebirth or immortality or anything of the sort.

As for the fifty watery lines, several are said to involve the themes of death and rebirth, notably, says the advocate of archetypes, those in which the legend of Alpheus and Arethusa is mentioned [ll. 85, 132]. But Arethusa and Alpheus are not primarily, or even ordinarily, symbols of immortality or rebirth; [2] they are patrons of pastoral poetry, as is made evident when Arethusa is invoked along with smooth-sliding Mincius and Alpheus along with the Sicilian muse. And the real reason for invoking them is to prepare for and return from the two voices of a higher mood by which the pastoral mode of the poem is interrupted. Just why Milton should have been concerned to weave rebirth and fertility themes into a part of his poem which is concerned with very different topics is not clear; and in fact the sort of evidence which is adduced would also serve to prove that a casual reference to Deiphobus converts *An Apology for Smectymnuus* into an argument against the

[2] Renaissance mythographers and allegorizers of Ovid did not usually interpret the Alpheus-Arethusa myth as a fable of death and rebirth. Conti has an interesting interpretation in which Alpheus is the maculate soul and Arethusa shining virtue; Ross in his *Mystagogus Poeticus* adds no fewer than eight others, some extremely farfetched; but none of them involves the idea of death and rebirth, unless this is latent in the concept of baptism.

Resurrection. To be sure, if one looks into almost any poem which possesses a good deal of natural imagery (poems like Spenser's "Epithalamion," Jonson's *Sad Shepherd,* Fletcher's *Faithful Shepherdess,* or Sannazaro's *Piscatoriae* come immediately to mind) one can find images, archetypal or otherwise, which have been used in one mythology or another to represent the forces of death and rebirth. But as for any evidence of Miltonic intention in the use of these images in "Lycidas," it is very much to seek. Certainly the Orpheus image, where the hope that the spirit may survive physical death is deliberately invoked, does not create the same impression as the many casual references to flowers. Milton emphasized the image of Orpheus as the Muse's son, made its purpose evident if not quite explicit, and urged it on the reader in a quite unmistakable way. This, indeed, is his common practice; when he wants us to think of an abstract idea, he emphasizes it. Thus, though he mentions amaranth in "Lycidas," he does not apply to it, and would not have wanted us to apply to it, the epithet "immortal" which he uses in *PL,* III, 353, because in the earlier poem the flower is supposed to be suggesting grief, not joy; a temporal fading, not an eternal bloom.

It is true that if we read lines 157–63 in a certain way, they will seem to provide a vague, rough parallel to an incident in *Beowulf*—which Milton had not read, and which is making, in any case, a rather unexpected appearance as a myth of death and rebirth. But here again, one scarcely sees how the parallels with *Beowulf* are any more significant than those with *20,000 Leagues under the Sea* or *Toilers of the Sea* or, for that matter, *Tom Swift and His Submarine*—except insofar as the most farfetched and seemingly unrelated parallels are supposed, by a kind of tacit default, to be evidence of "archetypes." This is the sort of logical leap from evidence of similarity to a conclusion of common origin which has brought discredit on so many studies of literary influence. Archetypes have, to be sure, this special advantage that, as they are supposed to be buried deeply in the psyche, the less explicit evidence for their existence appears, the more influence may safely be imputed to them. Hence, in addition to accounting for remote similarities, the word is sometimes invoked to give these similarities esthetic value.

Nothing in fact would be nicer than a quantitative basis for esthetic judgment, a correlation between the wide diffusion of a form, image, or concept, and its literary merit; and this is what archetypes offer to provide. But some of the special pitfalls of the undertaking are suggested by Miss Bodkin's experience with the scene of Satan's final retribution in Book X of *Paradise Lost*. Discussing the passage in which Satan is transformed to a serpent, she declares that "critics have remarked the poetic power of Milton's language in this strange passage of the punishment of Satan—a sign, one conjectures, of the significance in the poet's own feeling of the imagery employed" [*APP*, pp. 234–35]. The critics here referred to seem to be Miss Edith Sitwell and Mr. Lascelles Abercrombie. Few other commentators have shared their enthusiasm for the passage, and at least one, the late Professor Waldock, referred to it irreverently as a cartoon scene [*Paradise Lost and Its Critics* (Cambridge, 1947), pp. 91–92, 133–34]. Thus it appears that, though archetypes are invoked to explain effects too complex or profound for a merely esthetic accounting, the very question of where they are to be observed depends, in the first instance, on an esthetic judgment of no minor difficulty. Only a peculiar cause can produce a certain effect, which can only be recognized by people who believe in the peculiar cause; it is an esoteric argument all around.

One is sometimes hard put to see what Miss Bodkin's observations on Milton's muse and Milton's Eve are directed at, since two or three brief and passing mentions of the muse can scarcely exercise a major influence on the readers of a 10,000-line epic, and little more is proposed about Eve than that she combines three classic feminine roles—mother, seductress, and innocent. But Miss Bodkin takes a more interesting position on Satan, accepting the traditional division between the splendid figure of the first two books and the degraded villain of the later books but urging that it is precisely this variance, this transition from high to low estate, that qualifies Satan as tragic hero. The trouble here is that the criterion for a tragic hero is strikingly reduced. King Claudius, too, in *Hamlet,* first appears before us in flourishing estate, later appears as corrupt, and is finally punished. But to read the play with Claudius as tragic hero is obviously wrongheaded; his major action in the play is not one with which the audience can sympathize, there is no clear line to his development, he is not in fact central to the drama, as a tragic hero should be. And so with any reading of Milton's epic which puts Satan at the center of it. Satan is a member of the supporting cast, and one sign of this is the fact that he largely disappears from the poem in Books V, VII, VIII, X, XI, and XII. Moreover, while he is on-stage he does not develop consistently in any single particular direction; after being a toad and a schemer in the middle of Book IV, he is heroic "like Teneriffe or Atlas unremoved" at the end; at one point he is the spokesman for a diseased and strikingly human conscience, then again he is personified evil; at one point he is an audacious solitary adventurer, at another a jocosely complimentary sophist. He is, at any given juncture, whatever it suits the needs of man's story to have him; and in the crucial scene of temptation in Book IX, the focus is not and cannot be on him, because he is making no new discovery, suffering no new loss, adventuring no new hope. The fall of mankind is mankind's tragedy, not the devil's—so far as it is a "tragic," i.e., unhappy, experience. But of course the observation is familiar that Milton viewed the fall as in some sense fortunate; and though this point can be pushed too far, the long series of falls and recoveries which Michael foretells is undeniably supposed to culminate in the Second Coming.

Thus Miss Bodkin seems at odds with Milton in offering to read *Paradise Lost* as tragic in any extended sense (the poem is epic, not tragic); and even more so in supposing that Satan is the protagonist. But these difficulties are as nothing to those assumed by Mr. R. J. Zwi Werblowsky, who undertakes to explain in Jungian terms both the success and failure of *Paradise Lost* as a whole. The terms of this truly portentous problem are interestingly defined by Mr. Werblowsky. He feels that though *Paradise Lost* is "a great poem, if not one of the greatest," it is not "a perfect or at least successful work of art"; it is in fact a failure [*L & S*, p. 27]. It is a failure because it is not self-sufficient, or perhaps it is not self-sufficient because it is a failure. Anyhow, it is a failure because it is "full of unrelieved discord and unhealed splits" [*L & S*, p. 28]. This is an interesting critical criterion, which one would very much like to see applied to *Madame Bovary, Hedda Gabler, The Trial, The Misanthrope,* or for that matter *Prometheus Bound.* But whether they make the poem a great poem or a failure (Mr. Werblowsky, planting his feet grimly just this side of nonsense, seems determined to have them do both), certain vital themes are responsible for its peculiar (insofar as it *is* peculiar) character. Chief among these themes are those imported from the collective unconscious with the Prometheus archetype and inharmoniously though splendidly incorporated in the figure of Satan.

In approaching this Satan-Prometheus relation, which is most energetically enforced by Mr. Werblowsky and Miss Bodkin, it may be useful to bear in mind that the portrait of Prometheus presented in Aeschylus' drama is radically incomplete. Of an original trilogy we possess only a single part, probably the second. One may argue that the survival of this particular play, as well as the loss of the other two, was a significant accident; Prometheus the great rebel was preserved because men were fascinated by him, while the play of reconciliation was lost because men were not interested in it. But this argument, though it might be plausible if we were dealing with a text widely dispersed and popularly known, has little bearing on a text existing in a single copy. Unless the operation of archetypal patterns is more mysterious than one can well imagine, they could have little influence, say, on the survival of *Beowulf,* a single copy of a text which for hundreds of years no man living could read. And so with the Medici MS of Aeschylus; a good deal of its survival must be attributed, not to the pervasive power of its theme, but simply to coincidence and luck. The archetypes permitted a once-popular play to dwindle to a single MS lying for a couple of centuries unread even by scholars; one scarcely sees how they could have saved it from serving as a pie-plate or brass-polisher had a determined baker or Florentine housewife happened to lay hands on it. Thus the mere survival of the text is not in itself evidence that the Prometheus figure possesses archetypal, or even a shallower, cultural (*archetypische* or *kulturtypische*), significance.

It is impossible for anyone to tell what figure of Prometheus was presented in Aeschylus' total trilogy; impossible, therefore (even supposing that, like all good Jungians, one is somehow intimately and authoritatively acquainted with all the archetypes), to know how accurately Aeschylus' figure mirrored the presumed archetype from which it, presumably, drew its energy. It is impossible, even, to argue on the basis of verbal parallels that Milton was acquainted with Aeschylus' play at all, since he mentioned the playwright only two or three times in his entire career, and all the passages in which *Paradise Lost* is supposed to parallel *Prometheus Bound* appear, on closer inspection, to be unrelated or commonplace [J. C. Maxwell, *RES,* III (N.S.), 366–71]. But nothing is easier than to show that Mr. Werblowsky has radically misrepresented the image of Prometheus which Greek mythology has transmitted to us. Mr. Werblowsky asserts that "the order of Zeus is perfect, regulated, and static. His world has measure and limits, and every being is assigned its place" [*L & S,* p. 57]. Prometheus, on the other hand, is described as a rebel as well as a clever, tricky figure intent on evading or overstepping the bounds set by Zeus [*L & S,* pp. 57–58]. Now the Prometheus figure of Aeschylus contains many elements exactly contrary to this notion. Prometheus is the wise counselor and the son of Themis, who is the goddess of Justice; Zeus, on the other hand, is the usurper and tyrant, the raw new king whose rule is maintained only by force. Prometheus is the conservative, not the rebellious figure; he is not the trickster —he complains of being tricked. He has stolen fire, indeed, and invented the arts, but only to prevent men from being destroyed altogether, and the story of his tricking Zeus out of the best part of the sacrifices is not even referred to. Moreover, Aeschylus' Prometheus is not a heaven stormer like the other Titans, or Nimrod, or the builders of Babel, so much as a "fore-thinker," a "far-seer," one who anticipates and looks into the future. What he anticipates is the slow purification of injustice through the passage of time and the inevitable working of retribution, climaxed by the appearance of a substitute sufferer. Battles in heaven are no part of his program.

As for the Zeus figure delineated by Aeschylus, he is quite as much afflicted with *hubris* as Prometheus is. He is a lawless, brutal figure, concerned chiefly with the present moment of his power and careless of retribution; the rough, foolish arrogance of Force is matched by the foolish arrogance of Hermes, the other partisan of Zeus; and the whole image of Zeus as a fresh, roughshod, ignorant tyrant is underlined by the pathos of Io, whose account of how Zeus raped her is more eloquent than any protestations of Prometheus about his own motives. Finally, to take an episode from outside Aeschylus' play, the whole story of Pandora, Prometheus, and Epimetheus (a fable not so much as mentioned by Mr. Werblowsky) casts Zeus in the role of trickster and Prometheus as the farsighted exponent of wisdom. Certainly it would seem advisable, if we wish to attribute to a single archetype the undeniable fascination exercised by Aeschylus' Prometheus and Milton's Satan, that we decide what characteristics these figures, and their archetypal original, really possess.

Now if one looks at the matter distinctly, it will be apparent that the similarities between Satan and Prometheus do not amount to much more than this, that they are antagonists of the reigning deity who excite a measure of admiration. Their enmity for the deity is founded on different motives and expressed in different ways. Satan is active, causing others to suffer, Prometheus is passive, suffering himself; Prometheus is tempted by Pandora but avoids temptation, Satan uses Pandora (Eve) as a device to tempt Adam and succeeds in his aim; Satan attacks man as a surrogate for the deity, Prometheus is a surrogate for man, attacked by the deity; Satan is all but explicitly an agent of the deity (His Majesty's loyal opposition),[3] Prometheus eagerly anticipates the end of the Olympian dynasty; in direct contrast with the deity, Satan carries out many acts of destruction, Prometheus is the great creator in contrast to Zeus, who is malicious and destructive; Satan is proud and ambitious and is thrown into a dark, hot hole in the ground, Prometheus resents the pride and ambition of another and is nailed to a high, cold mountain peak; Satan is passionate, irrational, linked with the forces of the unconscious and the sensual appetite, Prometheus is rational, foresighted, wise. Both Satan and Prometheus are, or claim to be, gods, both are at enmity with ruling gods, and both produce in the reader an emotion of recognizable sympathy; but other common characteristics are notably few and not particularly significant. If there is a common archetype behind both figures, he is a faceless, shapeless, characterless shadow.

What this archetypal figure, the lowest common denominator of Satan and Prometheus, actually amounts to is something like a stock figure, the brave rebel, who takes his place with other stock figures like the melancholy lover, the disobedient son, the greedy parasite, the braggart soldier, and so on. These figures undeniably have a general appeal and are found widely diffused in the literature of the world. A number of common experiences are summarized in them, their quality is evident to the most untutored capacity, the simplest sort of abstraction is capable of producing them; whether one wants to call them "archetypes" or some equally pretentious name is plainly a matter of taste. But one thing is clear; a literature wholly composed of these stereotypes would be largely devoid of that unusual

[3] Stock passages are I, 210–20, and VI, 690–92; but see also the oddly ambiguous locution of the Lord in III, 180, and the perfectly explicit words of Satan himself, *Paradise Regained,* I, 358ff.

literary energy which archetypes are often invoked to explain. In fact, one need not phrase the matter in the conditional at all; there are plenty of treatments of the Prometheus theme so tritely flat or conventionally bombastic as to make it abundantly evident that this particular archetype flourishes only in conjunction with literary talent of a high order. Why, then, cannot critics hold the literary talent responsible for the literary product, without the *ex post facto* benediction of an archetype?

At first glance it seems pleasant to think that by hooking up a fable with independently existing and widely experienced psychological processes one can achieve an explanation of its emotional impact and so of its popularity. If it can be shown that stories involving *hubris* mirror the emotional experience of birth and are intimately tied up with homosexuality, this will no doubt explain at once the special impact which these stories carry. Everyone has been born, and the adjective "latent" does wonders for homosexuality. But fables as such do not enjoy, in literary circles, any significant popularity or unpopularity. Not very much time is spent in weighing the Prometheus myth against the Oedipus myth or the Ulysses myth. The individual work and the individual author seem to be the most practical units of discussion and analysis, because to most critics it appears obvious that literary effectiveness involves much more than a successful choice of subject. As for the idea that archetypal energy makes Satan and Prometheus successful literary figures, it is impressive only as long as one does not compare it with the inversion that Satan and Prometheus are such successful literary figures that they have been called "archetypal." No doubt it is a principle of rational thought to explain the obscure by the less obscure; and certainly the wellsprings of literary energy are obscure. But they are no more obscure than the wellsprings of archetypal energy, rather the contrary. Through careful analysis the reasons why a specific literary work has a specific effect may become less dark; but it is precisely this sort of careful analysis that the appeal to archetypes discourages. Mr. C. S. Lewis speaks of pulling the "Paradisal Stop" on a reader organ; Miss Bodkin describes how the reader's mind, "swayed by the rhythm of [certain] lines, surrenders to their imagery" [*APP*, p. 233]. No doubt ecstatic surrender to a poem will teach us a great deal; the best judges have frequently felt that other mental actions may also be of advantage to the critic.

Suppose, however, we do decide that the qualities of the minds experiencing a work of art are ingredients contributing to its total effect; it would seem advisable that we take all the psychological factors into account, not just a few—those, for instance, which are tied up so intimately with the matter of genre. A play is not the same thing at all as an epic; a Greek playgoer, especially, was by no means in the same frame of mind as a reader of a Renaissance humanist epic. At a collective Dionysian ceremonial devoted to the emotional purging of a tightly knit, homogeneous community, *hubris* must have carried a great many special tones and overtones; one might anticipate that a national epic would have very different overtones and a Christian epic overtones more different still. One of the first differences is that while one can often take the speeches of an epic hero at their face value, there is no dramatic figure, whether protagonist, antagonist, or chorus, of whom this can safely be said.[4] The hero of a tragedy pushes a sort of typical guilty behavior to its limit and then suffers, as surrogate for the audience, an imagined penalty. The epic does

[4] Mr. Werblowsky, for example, seems clearly in error on p. 57, where he takes at their face value the shortsighted comments of the chorus on Prometheus' farsightedness.

not have such a figure or such a pattern of psychological reaction. Epic heroes are more directly exemplary; perhaps for this reason they have a tendency to be priggish, cold, and dull. But not even the supreme antagonist in an epic —Hector, Turnus, Caesar, Argantes, or Agramante—carries the load of guilt feelings which attaches to a tragic hero. Epic "villains" are not deep offenders, they are scarcely offenders at all; typically, they are possessed of bravery and virtue which, however genuine within their own limits, are not quite of the right sort. They test the hero's character to the utmost so that we can see him as an unflawed diamond; and in order to perform this testing with conviction, they themselves are made just less than crystalline in the perfection of their powers.

Now it needs no emphasis to establish that Satan is neither a Hector nor a Turnus, though like both of them he is a brave and inventive warrior, a chieftain and strategist of note. His character was to a large extent determined before Milton appropriated him into the epic, so that he is not and could not be an epic antagonist pure and simple. But it may be worth remarking that the "difficulty" in his character which the Prometheus archetype is invoked to explain, that Satan is not Satanic enough, is precisely the sort of difficulty which might arise from the fact that he was for the first time appearing as the supreme antagonist in an epic poem. It flows from the general function of foils and antagonists that if they do not possess some of the inferior virtues, the fact that they lack the culminating few which the hero alone possesses will not be remarked.

To be sure, most of the great epic poems (Lucan's alone excepted) do not open with an extended description of the antagonist's activities, while the hero lurks in the wings. On the other hand, no previous epic had faced quite the same problem as Milton's, of giving narrative shape to the history of the world from the Creation to the Last Judgment while establishing a credible antagonism between Omnipotence and a challenger. On the stage, where physical battles with the Almighty are out of the question, Satan might well play a prowling, plotting Iago without any special build-up; he does so very neatly in Dryden's opera, where the conventions of the stage tacitly require that "omnipotent" should merely mean "very strong"; but in an epic he must have space to swell and preen himself, so that warfare on Heaven's wide champaign shall not invite our derision and disbelief. Satan may be a fool, as Mr. Lewis asserts [*PPL*, Chap. XIII], but a good deal of Miltonic ingenuity was expended in a great many areas of the poem to keep us from thinking so.

For all this, it is patently true that the fable as Milton received it did not allow much play for his feeling that in the conflicts of this world truth is generally represented by a persecuted minority. The whole story of Abdiel, leading as it does to that grand moment when, pointing to the Heavenly Hosts, he asks Satan to see his "Sect"—this whole story is an effort to compensate for a lack of sympathetic underdogs in the original fable. Another effort, not so often noted, involves the figure of Prometheus, but in a way scarcely recognized by Mr. Werblowsky.

For the fact is that the comparison with Prometheus that Milton wanted his reader to see, and deliberately emphasized, involves Adam, not Satan. Mr. Werblowsky has a vague adumbration of this idea when he says that "the Promethean myth can . . . point towards Christ as well as towards Satan" [*L & S*, p. 63]; and the truth is that it points right at the theater where these two forces join, at Adam. The last two books are largely concerned with an act of foreknowing, an act which is to strengthen Adam in the patient sufferance of evil which is his lot. After many revolutions and recoveries, at the end of an immense span of time, his redemption from suffering is foreseen when a substitute deity takes his place, and Satan, who has already tricked his unwiser self with a Pandora, shall finally be flung into the grave.

This interpretation of the relation between Prometheus and *Paradise Lost* has the peculiar disadvantage of corresponding, to some degree, with what seems to have been Milton's conscious intention. The only passage in *Paradise Lost* which mentions figures connected with the Prometheus myth (other than such stock properties as Jove, Titans, etc.) is IV, 714ff., where the Pandora figure is central and the Satan figure nonexistent. The total lack of direct comparisons between Prometheus and Satan is, in its own way, an eloquent feature of the poem; it adds credibility to the suggestion that for Milton the prototype of Satan is not the rebel but the tyrant. Satan is a tempter as well, in Books IV and IX, but he is a tyrant first and last. Satan perverts his followers, seizes the power and trappings of an oriental monarch, and proceeds with expedition to a series of unjust acts. He commits many acts of disobedience and trespass, but not of rebellion; except in Raphael's retrospect, he does not attack the Almighty or his warriors but for reasons of state concentrates on man the scapegoat, whom Satan himself recognizes to be guiltless. Like Zeus giving birth to Athena, he gives birth to Sin from his own head; and the very curious, cryptic vagueness of the catalogue in Book I with regard to the Ionian gods augments the possibility that he may be identified with Zeus on other levels —perhaps through the imagery of the thunder-blasted oak [I, 612ff.], or his own pretension to master thunder [II, 64–67], or via the roundabout fact that the name Prometheus, the far-seer, is a sort of kenning for the eagle, the bird of Zeus [S. Reinach, *Orpheus* (New York, 1930), p.

90]. If full identification seems extravagant, it may be worth remembering, at least, that in one of his aspects the ruler of Hades was often known as the "Zeus of the underworld," while Milton in addition refers to Satan as "Prince of the Aire," and the air is the particular domain of Zeus [X, 185; see also *PR,* I, 44ff.; and, for the triple Jove, *Comus,* l. 20]. These overlappings are haphazard enough and doubtless inconclusive; if Milton intended any sort of connection between Zeus and Satan, he intended it to be felt very peripherally indeed. But there are curious points of similarity between Milton's Satan and Aeschylus' Zeus which lend minor support to the contention that these characters have very much the same function in the stories where they appear.

Whatever one makes of the Satan-Zeus connection, Christ as the God who takes upon himself responsibility for the fault of man, and Adam as the man who anticipates becoming a God through suffering, obedience, and the assumption of his sins by a divine scapegoat are both distinctively Promethean figures. After Book II, on the other hand, whatever limited similarity has existed between Satan and Prometheus fades from sight. The quick-change artist of Book IV and the windy rhetorician of Book IX have nothing to do with Aeschylus' rock-pinioned god; and the jocose artilleryman of Book VI has more in common with Briareos, Nimrod, and Captain Quirt than with the thoughtful, foresighted Prometheus. By the time of *Paradise Regained,* Satan has been reduced to a mealymouthed scamp, a whining juggler of words and stage properties, a confidence man.

I except from these generalizations the first two books of *Paradise Lost;* and Mr. Werblowsky may urge, with Miss Bodkin, that these two books are precisely the ones which provide the problem. Satan is Satanic enough elsewhere;

it is only in the first two books that he is overly heroic. This represents a sizable modification of the problem; instead of discussing a whole myth or a single complete embodiment of a myth, we are asking why one part of a poem is different from other parts. There are many possible answers to a question like this. One particularly brilliant phrasing of an answer may be found in Arthur Barker's summary of the theory of the five-act epic [*PQ*, XXVIII, 21–23]. But in a more basic sense the question itself is its own answer. Surely it is a familiar literary device to start a long story with matters in one posture so that it may conclude with them in another. The principle behind the device is sometimes known as variety; its prevalence in seventeenth-century esthetic theory and Miltonic practice has been explored with great weight and leisure by H. V. S. Ogden [*JHI*, X, 159–82]. One could not judge the position of Achilles in the *Iliad* by his petulant appearance in the first books; why then should not Milton have given Satan one aspect in the first books so that his "true" appearance might have its proper impact in the later ones? If Satan does have two different aspects in the poem, Milton undoubtedly considered the second one "real" and "true." By way of heading his fifth chapter, Mr. Werblowsky quotes Mr. T. S. Eliot quoting Juliana of Norwich to the effect that sin is behovely; but I do not think Milton displays a mind unusually sympathetic to either T. S. Eliot or Juliana of Norwich. If we can trust his own allegory of sin, Milton would much have preferred to say that sin at first sight seems behovely but is actually disgusting. On these terms, the author's "editorializing" in the first books, which contrasts so oddly with Satan's splendid energy, is merely Milton's way of bridging the gap in the reader's mind between Satan's apparent attractiveness and his real corruption.

Professor Waldock has expressed resentment at this "editorializing" against Satan, feeling that the cards are stacked against the adversary; he urges that the Devil ought to be granted a more liberal interpretation of his acts and speeches. But *Paradise Lost* is not a sporting contest, and Milton is not cast in the role of umpire; he is bound to prepare his reader for the fact that Satan is the very Devil and will sooner or later act like the Devil. He editorializes against Satan, true, but for the reader's benefit; and while editorials in verse may not be the most artful way of handling misplaced feelings about Satan, they do represent Milton's best device to prevent the reader's being stood on his head by a sudden reversal of sympathies. As for granting Satan more fair play, a secular age makes the point with ill grace; if the epic concerned a theme that really offends the liberal ethos, if Satan were an aggressive anti-Semite or a dogmatic Marxist, we should feel that ample, perhaps excess, justice had been done him. Milton was in fact partisan, like his God; and he expected his fit audience though few to be partisan too, in the same way, for good and against evil.

The curious spectacle of Mr. Werblowsky quoting Professor Waldock with approval invites some further reflections on the complications to Satan's credibility posed by Milton's intellectual milieu. Mr. Werblowsky seems to feel that the excess energy which Satan derives from the Prometheus archetype flaws the poem; Professor Waldock objects to all the editorial restrictions with which Milton has attempted to control that energy. But the nature of things requires that any epic poem involving Satan treat him as a malignant power; and the more power he has of his own, the more malignant he must be presumed. The real difficulty has to do with channels of energy. When Satan is not cramped, like Dante's Devil, into one corner of a vast structure which by its very shape condemns him, his activities must condemn him, i.e., his power must be directed by his malignancy; it is just a necessary condition of portraying that sort of character. And when a story is traditional, so that the actions of the characters are already determined, an author does not have a great many ways, other than the overt editorial and the imputed motive, to express his views of a character. Because Milton's Satan is so free an agent (Milton's universe being so big and airy a space), the only way in which the poet can make us feel his badness is either to make him act badly or to tell us editorially of his wickedness. Milton, unable to do the former without resorting to melodrama or prematurely disclosing his story, makes frequent use of the latter device.

It is something of a commonplace that Dante does not have to tell his reader that sin is bad and sinners evil; he can greet Brunetto Latini with compassion or kick Filippo Argenti into the mud without elaborate theological explanations, because it is obvious from the very impersonal situation who is in the right with God and who in the wrong. In spite of this, sentimentalists still object to Dante's behavior, feeling that he makes himself repulsive by lying to Fra Alberigo or pulling Bocca degli Alberti's hair. But the price of almost any abstract system of justice is alienation of the sentimentalists. Milton's difficulty is that, not being able to count on an adequate abstract system in the reader's mind and not having one imbedded in the structure of his universe, he must establish or suggest one by whatever means are at hand—by lecture and editorial, by imputed motive, by soliloquy, by whatever sorts of pathos and sympathy the story allows him. Dante can raise a fine irony into a divine insight by writing over his Hell of ice, fire, and filth that Primal Love made it; even God's feelings are distinct from the system he has created. But Milton, lacking this sort of framework, has to make sympathy judgments do some of the work of ethical judgments. Satan does not sin against the divine nature by his very existence; his sin is a series of wicked actions. The reader tends to judge God, too, not by his cosmic works, which are sublime, not by the radiance of his religious essence, which is blinding, but by his lectures, his motives, and his actions, which till Book VII are appallingly petty. Quite aside from Prometheus archetypes, Milton's difficulty in establishing the inferiority of his Devil to his Deity may be ascribed to the decline, already amply evident in Milton's time, of theology as a discipline capable of accounting for the cosmos.

When we have exhausted our accounting of the literary, intellectual, psychological, and social factors which may have lent energy and confusion to Milton's portrait of Satan, the influence of archetypes may no doubt be accorded some consideration. In addition to Prometheus, of course, one might want to estimate the influence of such well-known culture types as Job, Jesus, Hercules, Gilgamesh, Set, Orpheus, Ea, Indra, Loki, and Iblis, not to mention the countless versions of the beautiful deadly woman (Eve-Pandora), the Deity, and the serpent. Such a study of interlocking and mutually opposed archetypes might well prove a fascinating venture into the six-dimensional geometry of the collective unconscious; one awaits its appearance with interest. Meanwhile, it is worthy of note that the Jungian critic typically concentrates on one archetype to the exclusion of all others. Miss Bodkin alone has several themes; she is also alone in possessing a presentable prose style, capable of asserting relatively distinct ideas in an orderly and coherent way. For the rest, Mr. Géza Róheim is hot on castration, Mr. Robert Graves on the Muse, and Mr. Werblowsky on the beneficent cosmic rebel. The historian of one archetype ordinarily pays very little attention to any other; the influence of each archetype is suspiciously limited to the book in which it plays, for the moment, a leading, indeed, a unique role. Without betraying an incurably suspicious mind, one may venture the suggestion that in the matter of archetypes a strong inner persuasion on the part of the critic may be doing duty for a rational survey of relevant facts. When we get a rounded account of the several archetypes, with a coherent explanation of their several sorts and directions of influence and just the least trace of evidence that this influence was actually exerted, they may perhaps be granted a more exalted role in literary analysis. For the present, however, and solely on the basis of their performance in the matter of Milton, it seems clear that archetypal influences deserve nothing more than a minor ancillary role in the discussion of literary works.

[III]

The Text of *Paradise Lost*

THE opinion is a little better than two centuries old that Milton was an exacting corrector of the proofs of *Paradise Lost.* With regard to Milton's other poems the question does not seem to have arisen at all, nor does the fact seem to have been immediately recognized with this one. Though he was a devoted picker of words and syllables, Patrick Hume, Milton's first commentator, had no notion that Milton's text was correct to the letter; he freely altered it in matters of spelling, punctuation, and capitals to accord with the casual practice of his own day, and he was known to dismiss a reading which troubled him as "a mistake of the printer." [1] No contemporary has preserved any testimony that Milton read proof on his poem with unusual diligence; in fact, Edward Phillips asserts that the poem, being written "by whatever hand came next," was very incorrect, when he first saw it, in its orthography and pointing.[2] Who cor-

[1] Patrick Hume, *Annotations on Milton's "Paradise Lost"* (London, 1695), notes on I, 469; III, 48; IV, 769; X, 989–90; etc.

[2] F. A. Patterson, *The Student's Milton* (New York, 1933), p. xli.

rected it, and how carefully, are questions which have been much mooted since Phillips' day.

1. *Emphatic forms*

The image of Milton as a scrupulous corrector of the press grew out of Dr. Bentley's efforts to emend the text and has flourished with varying degrees of fervor ever since. Scanning the Errata of 1667, those voluble Whiggish admirers of the poet, the J. Richardsons, father and son, found a direction to read in II, 414, "wee" for "we"; and this served as evidence that Milton, despite his blindness, was attentive not only to syllables but to letters.[3] The argument was weak, partial, and easily refuted by an appeal to the second edition, where the word is again spelled "we"; perhaps for these reasons, eighteenth-century editors remained for the most part unimpressed by it. Though many of them did remark and endorse Milton's habit of making apparently significant changes in commonly received spellings, they did not as a group concern themselves with a literally accurate text. In 1792 the overimaginative Capel Lofft put forward a version of Books I and II which undertook to restore some "lost" Miltonic spellings and punctuations and to explain others, including "hee" and "thir," as the product of a broad and conscious purpose. But it was not until the end of the nineteenth century that the devoted David Masson won anything like general assent to the existence of a philological or phonetic rationale, a set of general principles, behind Milton's variant spellings.[4] Masson was himself suspicious of "he-hee" (under which generic term I shall take the liberty of referring to "we-

[3] J. Richardson, *Explanatory Notes and Remarks on Milton's "Paradise Lost"* (London, 1734), p. cxxxii.

[4] David Masson, *Poetical Works of John Milton* (London, 1890), III, 42, "General Essay on Milton's English and Versification."

wee," "she-shee," and "ye-yee" as well); but he threw the whole weight of his tremendous influence behind the tendency to examine the text in microscopic detail for fragments of significance buried in the odd spellings. Many, if not most, of the twentieth-century editors have followed Masson's lead. Professor Grierson and Mr. Visiak, for example, base their editions on a close reproduction of the 1674 text, with only few and minor variations; Professor Patterson's *Student's Milton* and Canon Beeching's edition are almost as thoroughgoing in their devotion to the 1667 printing. The *Columbia Milton* ventures not only to follow 1674 printings *literatim* but to record all the variants between 1667 and 1674, as well as between the editions and the surviving MS of the first book. Finally, the facsimile version edited by Harris Fletcher carries reverence for the printed page to some sort of climax by reprinting both editions facsimile and collating a great many copies of each. Such pains have not very often been granted to the investigation of a printed book. A measure of the deepening concern with detail is the fact that whereas Bentley in 1732 recognized four differences between the first edition and the second and was rebuked in 1924 for his inadvertency by Mr. J. W. Mackail, who claimed to recognize thirty-three, Mr. Fletcher—boldly discounting dust on the type, bent rules, imperfectly inked commas, and the like—estimates the number of variations at something like nine hundred.[5]

But such painstaking pursuit of petty details must inevitably turn on itself. If editors are concerned with the trifling details of a text which is not grossly corrupted, the reason must be that they suppose Milton was interested in them, too; and if he was interested in them, it can scarcely

[5] Mackail, "Bentley's Milton," *PBA*, XI (1924), 69; H. F. Fletcher, *John Milton's Complete Poetical Works* (Urbana, 1948), III, 55.

have been for their own sake but because of those principles of pronunciation and emphasis which they are supposed to exemplify. Thus Miss Darbishire's new edition completes a cycle of editorial policy by asserting that Milton's texts, however accurately reproduced, do not carry out his intentions adequately and by offering to correct the text in accordance with the principles involved.

The venture is a bold one; before considering its details, however, let us return to the question raised by the Richardsons, of Milton's "he's," "we's," "she's," and "ye's." Why did Milton sometimes write these forms "hee," "wee," "shee," and "yee"? The usual explanation is that the unconventional form is emphatic; and so, under many circumstances, it may be understood:

> Mee mee onely just object of his ire [X, 936].

But sometimes the "emphatic" form occurs where there is no occasion for the emphasis:

> Oft he to her his charge of quick returne
> Repeated, shee to him as oft engag'd . . .
> [IX, 399–400].

"Shee" here requires no more emphasis than "he" in the line before; indeed, the "emphatic" form is sometimes used for unaccented words, as in Raphael's words to Adam:

> freely we serve,
> Because wee freely love, as in our will
> To love or not; in this we stand or fall [V, 538–40].

This observation, which could be many times repeated, raises the question of whether Milton intended anything by the distinction or whether he even made it. The fact is that the principle on which Milton, or his amanuensis, or his printer, distinguished "he" from "hee" is not an obvious one. Mr. Fletcher has attempted to distinguish systematically every "stressed" from every "unstressed" usage in the first edition but has been forced to resort, frequently, to making his attribution in the form of a query. What is more, a sizable number of Mr. Fletcher's attributions do not agree with the spellings of the text. "Ye" is duly recorded as "stressed" and "wee" as "unstressed"; and the contradiction is left unresolved. But if a principle is involved, rather than a vague tendency or a positive inconsistency, it should have some clarity. One should be able to decide, say, from a modernized text, which pronouns are properly emphatic. But the principle is too shy to give any such unequivocal evidence of itself; for a Miltonic principle, it has left a very muddled spoor indeed, and one further evidence of this fact derives from the differences between the two editions and the MS of *Paradise Lost,* Book I.

Neither Milton nor the 1674 printer left any evidence of any special feelings whatever about the way the 1667 printer handled "he-hee." They neither followed 1667 exactly nor changed it in any particular direction or according to any discernible system. In about fifteen instances, 1674 reduces "hee" to "he"; in about twelve instances it steps up "he" to "hee." (There is also some differentiation between "be-bee" which suggests a possible extension of the whole principle; did Milton distinguish an emphatic and an unemphatic way of being—*Sein,* perhaps, and *Existenz?* Reluctantly, one leaves this fascinating question to the Miltonic existentialists.) But the interesting thing is that the MS of Book I differs far more radically in the matter of "he-hee" from either of the printed texts than those texts do from one another. The MS is alone in using the "emphatic" form twenty-eight times. On a couple of occasions, the MS uses an "unemphatic" form which is restored in 1674 after being "emphatic" in 1667; on another occasion the "unemphatic" form of the MS, after being repeated in 1667, is made "emphatic" in 1674. The MS, however, is far more liberal than either text in using "emphatic" forms; and though the MS has been carefully corrected by several hands, presumably under Milton's direction, and microscopically examined by modern scholars, only one possible correction (and it is doubtful) of "he-hee" is recorded.[6] Either the copyist had this very delicate and exacting distinction down letter perfect (to Milton's satisfaction, at any rate, though not, one regretfully notes, to Miss Darbishire's) and understood it perfectly at a time when he was still subject to fairly massive correction on other scores; or else he followed his own head as to "he-hee," and the printer adopted as much of the copyist's mannerism as he chose. Milton's amanuensis, it is instructive to note, had a habit of doubling his "e's" and a general fondness for the extra "e" as in "paine," "doe," "availe," and "soone"; he had also a liking for the ampersand, which was not entirely erased even in 1674, and a tendency, not unusual in seventeenth-century handwriting, to double his "f's" for capitalization, as in "ffast," "ffavoured," "fforthwith," and "ffled." Some of these habits the printer corrected, some he left alone, and some he handled inconsistently, thus compounding his inconsistencies with those of the various amanuenses and their various correctors. But as for any consistent, systematic distinction between "emphatic" and "unemphatic" pronoun forms, until the dis-

[6] Helen Darbishire, *The Manuscript of "Paradise Lost"* (Oxford, 1931), note to line 749. Miss Darbishire takes the inkspot in question as a false stroke starting a new word rather than as a correction of "hee."

appearance from Book I of those twenty-eight extra "emphatic" forms is explained, I do not see how Milton can be saddled with any such intention.

Nobody has yet tried to argue that the "he-hee" distinction was systematically applied to the two poems which Milton composed after *Paradise Lost;* and the reason is perfectly clear, for *Paradise Regained* and *Samson Agonistes* could not be more random in their use of the "emphatic" forms. They do not entirely refrain from "hee" and similar spellings; such a *volte-face* might be evidence that Milton had principles about "he-hee" and changed them. But the late poems are not evidence that Milton changed his principles; they merely make obvious that he had never had any. They scatter "hee's" in sparse clusters, without any apparent relevance to the matter of emphasis, wherever the compositor of the moment happened to forget about correcting the copyist of the moment in a matter which neither considered of the least importance. *Paradise Regained* has five such forms and *Samson* eight, only one of which occurs in the last 1,467 lines. (The odd distribution suggests, though not conclusively, that the copyist or compositor may, in fact, have determined the spellings.) In each poem, no more than one or at the most two of the distinctively spelled pronouns would be considered emphatic if not spelled in an unusual way. But this, of course, is the whole explanation of the so-called "principle" of "he-hee"; as soon as one spells a pronoun with the double "e," it begins to look emphatic. In fact, there is no more reason to attribute significance to the "hee" spelling than to the occasional ampersand which creeps into all three poems.[7]

[7] As an experiment, if one scatters "hee's" with an absolutely arbitrary hand, using, say, the "emphatic" form for every third pronoun, he will be surprised at how many of the "emphatic" forms seem ap-

Miss Darbishire goes so far as to argue that some of the minor changes and variations in spelling and capitalization which are to be observed within the first edition itself were made by Milton's direction and represent significant alterations.[8] Since it is generally accepted that the entire first edition was printed off at once, the type distributed, and the sheets stored for binding as needed, this hypothesis puts blind Milton, his amanuenses, and his manuscript in the middle of a busy print shop, adding and subtracting "e's," changing small letters to capitals and vice versa, altering spellings, correcting type fonts, and breaking in upon the sweaty printers as the sheets were actually being run off, to loosen the forms and drag out or insert tiny bits of inky lead. Despite these fantastic pains, or more likely because of them, all sorts of wonderful errors passed unnoticed. Copies were printed off and bound up in which the printer, being momentarily short of capital "A's," had stuck a couple of inverted bits of type as the first letters of lines 563 and 566, Book I; nobody ever did catch the spellings "wilI," "aIl," "HelI," "meta!lic," or "Sarry" [I, 159; I, 600; II, 654; I, 673; III, 580] or the tetrameter line followed by a hexameter [IX (first ed.), 989–90]. Worse than these errors, most of which only eyes could have caught, are those which Miss Darbishire seems to have rightly distinguished in the fourfold substitution of "those" for "these" and vice versa [I, 71, 432; IV, 661; IX (first ed.), 72]; for these are sins against coherence and consistency

---

propriate. Mr. Fletcher's unworthy hesitation in deciding whether a form is properly "emphatic" or not has been sternly rebuked by Miss Darbishire, *RES,* II (N. S.), 386–89. "An editor must make up his mind"; it is a noble principle, but does it mean that he must make up his author's mind, too?

[8] Helen Darbishire, ed., *Poetical Works of John Milton,* I (Oxford, 1952), Introduction, xff., Appendices I, II, 309ff.

which an attentive ear could have noted. If Homer could doze while these camels passed by, why did he sit around the print shop pestering honest artisans about gnats which the labors of three centuries have scarcely been adequate to discern, and that dimly? Aside from its inevitable effects on the sanity of the printers, Milton's system of proof correction, if it was ever actually followed, must have made Samuel Simmons' shop a focus of amazed and incredulous attention in Restoration London. Miss Darbishire, one feels sure, would have accepted the situation with appropriate and praiseworthy reverence; whether a public with an acute sense of humor and a printer with several other irons in the fire would have been so understanding is another affair entirely. It may matter a bit that nobody concerned with the printing, except possibly Milton, could have had the least idea that an immortal epic was on Samuel Simmons' presses; and even Milton might have felt slightly graveled if he could have looked down the corridor of three centuries at Miss Darbishire and Mr. Harris Fletcher, with their intense concern for dim commas, ink spots, squabbled type, and high colons.

The fact is that of the changes made in the course of printing, the great majority and all those involving alternate readings of the text occur in only five of the forty-three signatures. Discounting the two signatures (Z and Vv) which were apparently printed in insufficient numbers in 1667 and so had to be totally reset and reprinted about two years later (Milton apparently never knew of these two reprinted signatures)—there are some dozen signatures, C, D, G, H, L, O, Q, R, S, Kk, Nn, and Oo, which show evidence of type reset in the course of printing; and, of these, only H, L, Q, S, and Oo show variations in the text which would be beyond the capacities, or indeed the function, of a printer's devil. An occasional change in the badly muddled line numbers, a bit of type dropped accidentally in the course of inking or pushed over during the printing process, an obvious misspelling or mispunctuation corrected—these are routine changes which might have been made or overlooked by anyone in the print shop. They have no more to do with John Milton than the mole on the neck of the tanner who cured the leather in which *Paradise Lost* was bound. But five signatures do show significant alterations. One cannot say blankly that only these signatures were corrected; but it is clear that only these sheets underwent significant correction while actually being run off; and, in point of fact, these sheets are the most thoroughly corrected ones of which we know. If the other sheets were corrected, there is no reason to assume that they were corrected any more (or less) carefully than these, which, we may conjecture, Edward Phillips happened to look over in the composing room or the printer's office.

Now the changes recorded in these five signatures are very moderate and largely unsystematic; they give evidence of no exalted sensibility and no fixed principles of either spelling, punctuation, or phonetics. There are, to be sure, five instances in the entire poem of "he" being changed to "hee" during the course of printing, and no instances of the contrary change. On the other hand, there is no evidence that in three of these changes any special emphasis was called for.[9] Miss Darbishire urges that in altering V, 160–61, from

> Speak ye who best can tell, ye sons of light,
> Angels, for ye behold him . . .

to

[9] The five passages are III, 97; V, 133, 160, 161; and X (first ed.), 32. Of these five passages only the last two place any particular emphasis on the form which we are told should be emphatic.

> Speak yee who best can tell, ye Sons of light,
> Angels, for yee behold him . . .

Milton has "delicately and truly indicated" the emphasis.[10] First let it be noted, any significance granted to "yee" in line 160 is granted at the expense of the truly dramatic word in the line, which is "Speak"; the second "yee" in line 161, might exist for purposes of emphatic contrast, with the earnest, accurate, but completely irrelevant overtone, *yee* behold him as *wee* do not. Or again, the "emphatic" form may have been added simply because the word happened to fall at an accented spot in the line, and the printer, a fellow without a great deal of experience in printing poetry stuff, thought in an unsystematic and disorganized way that poetic syllables ought to be long and short, as in Latin. The idea that he may have divided "long" from "short" syllables by a sort of mechanical scansion does not wholly explain "he-hee" or "thir-their" and I do not put it forward with any special conviction. It simply indicates that when one tries to discover the theories behind a performance as vague and casual as that of Samuel Simmons and his merry men, a vague and casual theory works about as well as a strict and elaborate one—sometimes better. As for the spelling of "Sons," if a capital "S" indicates a delicate and significant emphasis in line 160, a capital "F" added to the word "frame" in line 154 must be equally significant; one would gladly know what it signifies. But the fact is that any indications of capitalization which the surviving fragment of MS contains met with scant consideration from the printer. He put in capitals profusely where the MS had none, and he occasionally disregarded entirely the capitalization of the MS (see I, 265, "associates"). It is evident that in the matter of capitals (as in the matter of italic type, which the MS no-

[10] Darbishire, *Poetical Works of John Milton,* I, 297.

where indicates) the printer was given his head as a man of discretion and understanding. The consequences sometimes look significant and mostly do not; one can only conjecture what John Milton would have said of anyone who read his poem for the emphases contained in its capital letters—or, for that matter, in its spelling of "he-hee."

Like "he-hee," the topic of "thir-their" is at once much simpler and much less orderly than the exponents of an emphatic-unemphatic distinction suppose. The 1667 printer was slow to decide on a policy about spelling this word, which the amanuenses and correctors who prepared copy mostly spelled "thir"; hence he used the conventional "their" pretty generally through the first books, then gave up the effort at correction and switched to the less conventional "thir" for the rest of the poem, with occasional lapses when habit—his own or perhaps that of the amanuenses—overruled a very tenuous concern with consistency. The 1674 printer was, on the other hand, a little less slow in deciding to use "thir" throughout; hence there are a good many corrections of "their" to "thir" in Book I and a few more in Book III. On one solitary occasion [I, 499] the 1674 printer altered a 1667 (and MS) "thir" to read "their" in some copies; but it was not a significant alteration, and in the course of printing, someone changed the word to "thir" again, as "their's" were also altered to "thir's" during the course of printing at I, 71 and I, 478. After Book III the printer simply forgot about the whole thing, and followed 1667 through "their" and "thir" as they occurred. Now a thoroughgoing correction of "their" to "thir" is likely to look like a very principled undertaking because of one potent coincidence. The possessive pronoun third person plural generally falls, like other possessive pronouns used adjectivally, in an unaccented spot in a blank verse line. Thus the changes seem to provide evidence that Milton preferred to spell the unaccented syllable "thir" simply because most of them alter "their" to "thir" and most possessive pronouns are unaccented. But there are plenty of instances where the consistency breaks down—witness, for instance, I, 31; I, 348; and II, 800, where 1674 blithely corrects an emphatic "their" to "thir"; and, on the other hand, III, 118; III, 400; and VII, 453, where an unemphatic "their" remains even in 1674. Miss Darbishire has propounded three solemn laws governing the use of "their," viz., that it expresses (1) the emphasis required by an antithesis, (2) the emphasis required by the antecedent of a relative pronoun, or (3) the emphasis required by an objective genitive. Now if one takes the pains to disentangle from the second edition of *Paradise Lost* the twelve wretched "their's" which survived pruning (I discount here the three "their's" noted above, which were changed to "thir" in the course of printing), one finds that two of these three rules apply to only a single passage each—they are rules of a single instance; and six of the passages where "their" remains are covered by no rule at all.[11] Miss Darbishire, however, has not been so docile as to let this rather poor showing stand in the way of establishing some Miltonic principles. By hopping quickly from 1667 to 1674 to the MS and back, she can build up a very pretty case; and so we find her following MS and ed. 1 against ed. 2 in I, 383; ed. 1 against MS and ed. 2 in 384; MS and ed. 2 against ed. 1 in 388; ed. 1

[11] *Ibid.*, p. 287. The surviving "their's" occur at I, 267; II, 277, 362; III, 59, 118, 400; VI, 690; VII, 453; X, 242, 440; XI, 740; XII, 107. Of these instances, the first, fifth, seventh, eighth, tenth, and last fall under none of Miss Darbishire's rules. Only the third relates to her second rule; only the eleventh to her third. See also on the three rules Miss Darbishire's review of Fletcher, *RES*, II (N. S.), 386–89; and Appendix I to *The Manuscript of "Paradise Lost."*

against MS and ed. 2 in 391; and MS and ed. 2 against ed. 1 in 395. This is an elderly and useful device of scholarship; and, by patient application of it, one can discover not only Miltonic principles about "thir-their" and "he-hee," but also a secret cipher which says in so many words, "Francis Bacon wrote this book." But these are not the usual devices of rational demonstration; and I think Miss Darbishire's elaborate game of hopscotch will convince most people only that if principles for an emphatic use of "their" ever existed in anyone's mind, it was certainly not in poor blind Milton's.

Indeed, Mr. Harris Fletcher concedes, though only with the greatest reluctance, that, so far as he can see, at least half and probably two-thirds of the changes made between the first and second editions were the work of the compositor, or at least of someone other than Milton, his friends, and amanuenses [Fletcher, III, 57, 59]. I shall not inquire how, in the absence of all evidence except the alterations themselves, one distinguishes a Miltonic change from a mere Phillipsian or either from a humble compositor's change. But taking the simple estimate that someone other than Milton or his agents introduced 450 or 600 unremarked minor changes into the best text of *Paradise Lost* that we have, where does this leave the notion of Miltonic "principles" of spelling, capitalization, and italicizing? Presumably, if Milton attached the slightest passing importance to these "principles," he might, even through the mists of blindness, have recognized 450 departures from them; and if he did not choose to set them right, at least for the benefit of posterity he might have dropped a word to Phillips or someone else that Samuel Simmons was a meddling rogue. But not only is there no overt mention, in the whole career, of any such principles; there is no criticism whatever of behavior which directly subverted them if they existed—there is, in fact, no ground for supposing they entered Milton's mind either between the first and second editions or in the makeup of the first edition or at any point whatever.

It would have been very odd indeed if Milton had expected his readers to seek buried significance in every extra letter of his 10,665-line poem; for he was not a particularly careful speller, even among authors of his day. In the ordinary course of writing, consistency was not of paramount importance to him, and there is no conceivable rationale, either of buried significance, of philological origins, or of euphony, for a very great number of his spelling variations. For certain words Milton or his copyist does seem to have had a preferred, and unorthodox, spelling; for example, the form "warr" occurs forty-seven times in *Paradise Lost,* the form "war" only three times, and on two of these three occasions the MS of Book I reads "warr." It is perfectly clear what happened here; the printer took a little time to get used to the odd form and did not bother to go back and change his first miscorrections. But the interesting thing is that with seven years to alter his printer's errors if he thought them worth correcting, John Milton just did not bother; and the 1674 edition followed 1667 spellings of the word letter for letter. So, too, with "perfect-perfet"; the first two occurrences of the word in *Paradise Lost* are spelled "perfect," the next fourteen "perfet"; but once more Milton let the 1667 spellings stand in 1674, for no other conceivable reason than that he did not much care how the word was spelled. The alternatives are scarcely worth discussing. Either the variant spelling was the copyist's, or, if it was Milton's, he did not take the preference seriously; in either event, editors who venture to "restore" what Milton did not think worthy of restoration are simply foisting their own tastes on him.

The frequency of forms like "warr" and "perfet" provides evidence of a preference, however casual, on somebody's part for an unusual spelling; but many spelling variants in *Paradise Lost* are simply random. If Milton had read proof on his great poem letter by letter, he might have caught himself spelling as "Baume" in I, 774, a word which he spelled "balme" in II, 402; or as "hautie" in IV, 858, a word which he would spell "haughty" in V, 852, and "haughtie" in VI, 109. But, being the child of his age, he had no interest in such matters; he left trivia of this sort to printers and pedantic syllable pickers. Milton simply did not share that romantic reverence for the manuscript which, in the days when poets were publishing their fragments and dreams, would make poetry so inward and personal a thing—which led Keats, for example, to distinguish "faery" from "fairy" and "lily" from "lilly" ["La Belle Dame sans Merci," first and second versions]. These matters Milton left to his printer, probably because he had a more public notion than most romantics of a poem's existence and hence a more distinct sense of his own contribution as architect and rhetorician in addition to simple "sensibility."

Milton, then, left the details of his text to the printer; though he or his agent Phillips read proof carefully (by the standards of the day), neither one of them ordinarily read letters; and the evidence seems clear that if he checked proof at all, he usually checked it, not against the MS, but against memory and his own ear. This, after all, would be normal procedure for a blind author; with one voice reading proof, who should hold copy? To let a second reader hold the MS would have been to leave matters still at a distance from Milton, unless the whole poem were spelled out letter by letter. Milton may have given Phillips general charge of the proofreading and left the whole matter to him, as Phillips' own account implies. Or, at the best, Milton's reader may have held the proofs in his hand, with the MS by his side, while Milton made his corrections mostly by ear and occasionally asked to have the MS read to him or the text spelled out. This, indeed, is the sensible picture drawn by previous investigators like Professor Diekhoff and Miss Darbishire herself [*PQ*, XXVIII, 51]; how it jibes with an elaborate distinction between "emphatic" and "unemphatic" spellings one must leave to the authors of the latter hypothesis to unravel. The simplest solution is, I think, to dismiss the whole notion of "emphatic" and "unemphatic" spellings as a fantasy and a delusion. And when we have freed Milton from the mare's nest of picayune spelling problems in which he has sometimes seemed to be entangled, we may be able to ask some more general, and interesting, questions about the text of *Paradise Lost* and its deficiencies.

2. *Emendations*

In the first part of this essay, I argued that Milton was not an exacting corrector of the proofs of *Paradise Lost;* that though he had certain preferred and sometimes unconventional spellings, he did not distinguish emphatic and unemphatic forms of words like "we" and "their." Some of this argument depends on a conviction which I cannot quite formulate into a dogma and which had, therefore, best be phrased as a question: Is there any evidence at all that any polite English author of the seventeenth century—any poet, critical commentator, scholar, man of letters, or author more eminent than a vulgar numerologist or a semiliterate stargazer—ever at any time explicitly endorsed the technique of altered spelling as a device of interpretation or as a way of indicating emphasis? Some cloudy and confused speculations I am aware of regarding

John Donne's use of "she-shee"; but these are as recent and as shaky as the equivalent speculations regarding Milton. And they are subject to the same objection, that a printer and an author who were capable of conceiving and carrying out such a delicate and exacting distinction would have been most unlikely to leave the various gross corruptions with which the text is actually afflicted.

How gross these errors are and how far they merit correction are problems on which the ingenuity of emending editors has been exercised for better than two centuries. Stated in this form, the problem of emendation seems more considerable than it actually is. *Paradise Lost* is not a badly printed book. From the surviving fragment of MS one can see that the printer got a fairly clean piece of copy, which he followed after the fashion of the day, approximately, varying spellings and punctuations and supplying caps and italics in response to his taste and the availability of his type faces. But he did err—he was allowed to err—in a great many particulars, not all of which are insignificant; and while some of his errors were corrected in the errata or the second edition, others were not, and in the course of reprinting, still other errors were added. It is these reiterated or newly added errors which create the chief problems of emendation. The second edition of 1674 generally provides a superior text, not because of the now-challenged principle that the last form of an author's work best represents his established intention, [see Fredson Bowers, *MP,* XLVIII, 12–20], but on its actual merits. Discounting matters of punctuation and minor spelling variations, however, there are some forty-odd passages where the 1674 text as printed seems either inferior to 1667 or inadequate in itself. In the following list, the 1667 reading is pretty well recognized as a superior alternative. (In all tabulations of textual readings, I shall print the full line from the 1674 text, disregarding the italics of the original, using my own italics to indicate the questioned form, and adding the 1667 variant to the right in parentheses.)

1667 Clearly Superior to 1674

II, 483	Loose all *her* virtue; least bad men should boast	(thir)
II, 527	The irksom hours, till *this* great Chief return,	(his)
IV, 928	*Thy* blasting volied Thunder made all speed	(The)
VIII, 269	With supple joints, *and* lively vigour led:	(as)
IX, 213	Or *bear* what to my minde first thoughts present	(hear)
IX, 1019	Since to each meaning savour *me* apply	(we)
IX, 1092	What best may *from* the present serve to hide	(for)
IX, 1093	The Parts of each *for* other, that seem most	(from)
X, 550	Thir penance, laden with *Fruit* like that	(fair Fruit)
XI, 427	Nor sinn'd thy sin, yet from *that* derive	(that sin)
XII, 534	*Well* deem in outward Rites and specious formes	(Will)

By indicating that 1667 is clearly the superior reading in each of the above lines, I do not mean to suggest that the 1674 text has been universally discarded by modern editors. Of the eleven passages cited, the *Columbia Milton* reprints no less than six in the form which I suppose to be obviously inferior. But an overwhelming majority of modern editors follow the 1667 text—seven out of ten editors in all eleven passages, one other editor in every passage but one, and in no passage fewer than eight out of ten editors.[12]

[12] The ten modern editors, to whom this discussion will frequently recur, are: (1) R. C. Browne (Clarendon Press, fourth edition, 1875), 2 vols.; (2) David Masson (Macmillan, 1890), 3 vols.; (3) The Rev. H. C. Beeching (Clarendon Press, 1900); (4) A. W. Verity (Cambridge University Press, 1910); (5) H. J. C. Grierson (Chatto & Windus, 1925), 2 vols.; (6) Frank A. Patterson (Appleton-Century-Crofts, 1933); (7) Patterson, *et al.*, (Columbia University Press, 1931–38), 18 vols.; (8) Merritt Y. Hughes (Odyssey Press, 1935), 3 vols.; (9) E. H. Visiak (Nonesuch Press, 1938); (10) Helen Darbishire (Clarendon Press, 1952). Mr. Harris Fletcher's glittering volumes, being literal facsimiles, are irrelevant to my purpose. The editors following 1674 where it seems inferior to 1667 are as follows: (7) II, 527; IV, 928;

And, aside from the weight of editorial preference, there is in each passage specific reason for preferring the 1667 reading. (I shall not labor the point where modern opinion is unanimous.) In II, 527, Milton is describing how each bad angel

his several way
Pursues, as inclination or sad choice
Leads him perplext, where he may likeliest find
Truce to his restless thoughts, and entertain
The irksom hours, till *his* great Chief return [II, 523–27].

To read "this" for "his" is to shift the whole focus of the picture for a distracting moment, and to no advantage whatever. Adam's newborn cavortings are described in VIII, 269; he first looked himself all over, then

sometimes went, and sometimes ran
With supple joint, *as* lively vigour led [VIII, 268–69].

Altering "as" to "and" leaves Adam led by his supple joints, an uncommon and distracting guide; while the comma, of which Milton was not ordinarily profuse, also militates against "and." In IV, 928, to read "*Thy* blasting volied Thunder made all speed" would be to make Satan attribute mastery of the thunder to Gabriel when the precise point is that Gabriel had to be helped in battle by God's thunder. As for X, 550, one scarcely sees how it can be read as a pentameter line without the adjective "fair" prefixed to "Fruit." The 1674 reversal of "for-from" in IX, 1092–93, makes complete nonsense of the passage while providing no other recompense of any sort. In all the other passages, modern editions are unanimous in preferring the 1667 reading.

VIII, 269; IX, 1092, 1093; X, 550: (1) X, 550: (9) IV, 928; VIII, 269; and II, 527. In this last passage, Visiak emends both "this" and "his" to "thir" without warrant of either text or sense.

For a like number of lines, both 1667 and 1674 provide more or less acceptable readings, between which a correct decision is not always obvious (see table, p. 81).

Some of these disputed readings invite discussion, some are so trivial as almost to defy it; but before examining the passages in detail, we may well add another list, this one of passages where editors have in the past felt that both the 1667 and 1674 texts were faulty (see table, p. 82).

Finally, there is a special and distinct category of proposed emendation, involving the words "these" and "those" as both editions reproduce them in I, 71; I, 432; IV, 661; and X, 72; also an analogous confusion in regard to X, 397, where the editions disagree in the matter of "these" and "those."

From these lists certain limited consistencies in the editorial record appear at once. In every instance where there is a question between 1667 and 1674, the *Columbia Milton* (7) follows 1674; with equal consistency, Canon Beeching (3) and Miss Darbishire (0) follow 1667. In every instance but two, Professor Patterson's *Student's Milton* (6) follows 1667. Wherever any editor accepts an emendation, R. C. Browne and Miss Darbishire accept it too. Canon Beeching and the *Columbia Milton* accept no emendations at all; the *Student's Milton* accepts just one. For the rest, striking variations in individual editorial judgment are the only uniform rule.

Now it may seem a very simple matter to cast one's eye up and down these lists, which with modern apparatus are the work of a few hours to compile, and to decide between text and text, or text and emendation, according to one's tastes, tolerances, and more or less conscious editorial preferences. The qualities to be sought in a text (presuming the author's exact intentions to be unknown or unclear) are mostly matters of general agreement; they

Question as between 1674 and 1667 [13]

Editors				Editors
1245789	I, 530	Thir *fanting* courage, and dispel'd thir fears.	(fainted)	360
167	I, 703	With wond'rous Art *found out* the massie Ore	(founded)	2345890
179	II, 282	Of what we are and *were,* dismissing quite	(where)	2345680
7	IV, 451	Under a shade *of* flours, much wondring where	(on)	1234568890
79	IV, 705	Such was thir awe of Man. In *shadie* Bower	(shadier)	12345680
15789	VII, 322	Embattell'd in her field: *and* the humble Shrub,	(add)	23460
1245789	VII, 366	And hence the Morning Planet guilds *her* horns;	(his)	360
567	IX, 394	*Likeliest* she seemd, Pomona when she fled	(Likest)	1234890
579	IX, 922	And peril great provok't, who thus *hath* dar'd	(hast)	1234680
15789	X, 58	Easie it *might* be seen that I intend	(may)	23460
179	X, 408	If your joynt power *prevailes,* th'affaires of Hell	(prevaile)	2345680
1245789	XI, 651	But call in aide, which *makes* a bloody Fray;	(tacks)	360

[13] Numbers in the margins refer to modern editions (see n. 12, above), 179 in the left-hand margin indicating that Browne, Columbia, and Nonesuch follow the 1674 reading, 360 in the right-hand margin indicating that Beeching, Patterson, and Darbishire follow the 1667 text.

Both 1674 and 1667 in Doubt [14]

Editors		Texts	Emendation	Editors
123456789	I, 756	At Pandaemonium, the high *Capital*	(Capitol)	0
unanimous	II, 1001	Encroacht on still through *our* intestine broiles	(your)	
35679	III, 592	Compar'd with aught on Earth, *Medal* or Stone;	(Metal)	12480
35678	IV, 472	Whose image thou art, him thou *shall* enjoy	(shalt)	12490
unanimous	IV, 567	Gods latest Image: I *describ'd* his way	(descried)	
356789	IV, 592	Beneath th'Azores; *whither* the prime Orb,	(whether)	1240
unanimous	VI, 115	Should yet remain, where faith and *realtie*	(reality, fealty)	
unanimous	VII, 139	At *least* our envious Foe hath fail'd, who thought	(last)	
234789	VII, 321	The *smelling* Gourd, up stood the cornie Reed	(swelling)	1560
367	VII, 451	Let th'Earth bring forth *Foul* living in her kinde, *Fowle* (1667)	(Soul)	1245890
unanimous	IX, 410	To intercept thy way, *or* send thee back	(and)	
23456789	IX, 1183	Him who to worth in *Women* overtrusting	(Woman)	10
367	X, 989	Childless thou art, Childless remaine:	(*Print* "So Death"	
	X, 990	*So Death* shall be deceav'd his glut, and with us two	*on l. 989*)	1245890
unanimous	XI, 845	Gaz'd hot, and of the fresh *Wave* largely drew,	(Waves)	

[14] The six readings on which modern editors are unanimous have been questioned by earlier editors: II, 1001, by Newton and Todd; IV, 567, and VI, 115, by Bentley; VII, 139, by Thyer; IX, 410, by Bentley and Keightley; and XI, 845, by Keightley.

are plain good sense, sonority, metrical correctness, amplitude of meaning, and logical consistency; qualities to be avoided, if possible, are nonsense, bad grammar, dissonance, baldness of statement, awkwardness, and redundancy. Nothing, it would seem, could offer a clearer guide to textual decisions than these principles; one seeks good sense, good harmony, and good order, one avoids the contrary. But in gaining one of these virtues, editors are sometimes bound to sacrifice several others. A case in point is provided by IX, 394:

> To *Pales*, or *Pomona* thus adornd,
> Likest [1667] she seemd, *Pomona* when she fled.
> [Likeliest, 1674]

The editors divide between the texts 7 and 3, that is, if we count Professor Patterson twice in the unpopular cause of "Likeliest." And it seems very clear that "Likest," beloved of the majority, is indeed the neater form of the text. A comparison is being made, and "like to" in the sense of "similar to" is a natural locution. How then did the printer come to print "Likeliest" in the second edition? Miltonic misprints usually take the form, which one may note over and over in the table above, of dropping or altering a letter, occasionally of omitting a word. Of the emendations proposed above, only IV, 567, asks us to suppose that the printer erred in the direction of a more elaborate form; and even here the more elaborate form is the less uncommon word. Inherent probability suggests that a careless printer would be unlikely to print merely by accident a more elaborate form of a less obviously appropriate word. His eye might easily be seduced into "Likest" vice "Likeliest"; but seven editors out of ten have thought the contrary more probable. Professor Grierson points out, interestingly, that Spenser used the word "likely" in the sense of "similar":

> For Love is a celestiall harmonie
> Of likely harts composd of starres concent
> ["Hymn in Honour of Beautie," 197–98].

To be sure, Spenser used the word only once, and in a spot where he needed the extra syllable to eke out a melodious line; but in fact, as a check of *OED* will verify, the meaning of "likely" was undergoing a gradual change during Milton's lifetime from the idea of "similar" to the idea of "appropriate" and then to the idea of "probable." The change is marked by the dropping of the preposition "to." *X* is like to, i.e., similar to, *Y;* when *X* is like the nature of things in general, it is likely. *Comus* nicely illustrates the "appropriate" meaning;

> And in this Office of his Mountain watch,
> Likeliest . . . [ll. 89–90].

Thus if one reads Milton's IX, 394, "Likeliest," it becomes plain that one is faced with a sort of pun. Eve is like Pales or Pomona; she is also (like Pales or Pomona) a likely sort of female, the sort who is most likely to get in trouble with Jove, Vertumnus, or Satan. The word has a kind of sonority in this context which is not just due to its extra syllable; and though, for the modern reader, "Likeliest" makes hash of the plain sense, it may also enrich one's poetic perception of Eve's quality.

Did Milton intend this enrichment? In estimating the probabilities, we can scarcely fail to notice other instances of language used in the same way. An unchallenged reading, IX, 624, illustrates Milton's penchant for rich and witty speech. Here Eve talks of promised progeny who will

Help to disburden Nature of her Bearth.

In this context a conventional spelling, "birth," clearly robs us of a welcome, almost a necessary, overtone; Nature's "bearth" is the "burthen" that Nature bears, and an orthodox spelling eliminates the connection between two words that Milton plainly wanted in conjunction. A pair of similar puns elsewhere serves to bring out a mythological parallel between the sons of Noah and some classical deities and heroes. Milton mentions Iapetos, the father of Prometheus and Epimetheus, by a name, Japhet, which suggests Japheth, the third son of Noah [IV, 717]; he calls Jupiter Ammon by a name, Cham, that recalls the Latin form of Ham, another son of Noah [IV, 276–77].[15] On another occasion, describing the bridge built by Sin and Death from Hell to Earth, he refers to the "wondrous Art/Pontifical" of the builders [X, 313–14] and likes the slap at the papacy well enough to repeat it a few lines later [line 348, "this new wondrous Pontifice"]. And it would be superfluous to mention all the words, such as "fruit" and "stars," which Milton uses in both a literal and a figurative or metaphorical sense:

[15] Empson refers this passage to Raleigh, Marlowe, and a "wild gang of comparative anthropologists" supposed to cluster around the former [*Some Versions of Pastoral* (Norfolk, Conn., n.d.), p. 179], but the idea can be found as far back as Josephus, *De antiquitatibus Judaeorum,* I, 6. Indeed, Milton's own intentions in the matter are exaggerated if we suppose he made the puns defiantly or with any sense that they should stand out. Iaphet was a conventional spelling for the Greek name [see Jonson, "Ode to Himself," l. 27, and Hall, *Virgidemarium,* IV, iii, 6]; and Milton's handwriting, like that of the amanuensis who copied out Book I, made no distinction between "I" and "J". As for Cham, as it is a more striking departure from the conventional form, so it gets a line of explanation to soften, if not to obliterate the effect of a pun:

Whom Gentiles *Ammon* call and *Lybian Jove* [IV, 277].

Of Mans First Disobedience, and the Fruit
Of that Forbidden Tree . . .

Besides these more or less obvious puns, there are others in the poem, more deeply buried and less intimately related to Milton's major meanings; and a real critical question may be raised as to how far Milton intended the reader to yield them his attention. One may see a certain rationale for a half pun like that in IV, 1001, where either God or his heavenly scales may be the subject of the verb in the phrase "now ponders all events," since here the ideas of weight and reflection are almost equally balanced. But when Satan describes to Sin and Death the "buxom air" of the world, "imbalm'd/With odours" [II, 842–43], it is somewhat less evident that Milton intended the reader to feel the death overtones of "imbalm'd." By spelling "only" in the form of "onely" (as for example in III, 64, 79, 80), he may have intended to emphasize the idea of "one"; but when he concluded his description of Asmodeus [IV, 170–71] as

with a vengeance sent
From *Media* post to *Aegypt,* there fast bound,

it does not seem likely that he wanted to have the last three words bear two meanings, "there tied securely" or "hastening in that direction." And when the printer contributed a pun to II, 881, by misspelling the last word of the line,

Th'infernal dores, and on thir hinges *great,*

Milton showed his dislike by adding a correction ("for *great* r. *grate*") to the Errata. He may have wanted "aires, vernal aires" [IV, 264] to suggest both tunes and breezes; but he can scarcely have wanted any of the possible puns on "wine" or "harbor" to be felt when Gabriel remarks the approach of

> a third of Regal port,
> But faded splendor wan [IV, 869–70].

A set of positive limitations on Milton's willingness to disrupt plain sense for complex effects is suggested by a pair of passages which have evoked some discussion. Abdiel's battlefield reproach to Satan provides a notable crux:

> O Heav'n! that such resemblance of the Highest
> Should yet remain, where faith and realtie
> Remain not [VI, 114–16].

Both texts print "realtie," and all ten modern editors follow suit, though with different interpretations of the expression. Verity says that "realty" means "reality" and is found in that sense among other seventeenth-century authors; presumably, its only advantage over the usual form, used elsewhere by Milton, would be metrical. Other editors, deriving the word from Italian "leale" or "reale," give it the meaning of "sincerity" or "loyalty." One would like to think that Milton intended to make use of this charming macaronic ambiguity; Abdiel might thus be saying that though Satan looks divine, because he is not loyal his splendor is not real. On the other hand, this effect involves a greater reliance on Italian than Milton customarily admits; it is simpler to accept the existence, though verified by *OED* in only one other instance, of an English word "realty" used in the sense of "sincerity." Despite its weight, the macaronic pun is probably superior to the proposed emendation, "fealty"; but the separate word, however slender its existence, is plainly a better reading than the pun, partly because the impetus of a dramatic speech will not support such elaborate weight as the pun entails, partly because all Milton's overt macaronics involve classical tongues.

Finally, in I, 756, Miss Darbishire proposes to read "Capitol" for "Capital" in the description of Pandaemonium, so as to take advantage of the overtones of the Roman Capitol. In this emendation she goes against, not only the editions overseen by Milton, but a correction in the MS. The copyist originally wrote "Capitoll," and the word underwent alteration by a second hand to "Capitall." This second hand Miss Darbishire denounces as "officious and unauthorized"; and one understands her indignation, for the "Capitol" spelling would make something very specific in the poem which Milton, wilfully or otherwise, left vague. For the fact is that Milton never spelled the word "capital" with an "o" unless he had in mind specifically the temple of Jupiter Capitolinus at Rome. If he did not wish to identify overtly the temple of the devils in Hell with the chief temple of Roman paganism, and so to make Satan a mere mask of Jove, he was bound to avoid the pun which Miss Darbishire, supported by the great Theobald, obtrudes upon him. As for the "officious and unauthorized" hand, these are fine adjectives; but Miss Darbishire, who has carefully distinguished five hands among the correctors of Milton's proof, has no standing prejudice against this one and would be embarrassed to dismiss all his corrections as spurious. On the evidence, Milton went out of his way to avoid a pun which would have made one of his meanings too explicit altogether [cf. above, p. 54].

Thus one might establish a spectrum of Miltonic puns and ambiguities, ranging down from the most to the least functional; at the lower extreme one would place those puns which are inseparable from the language in its plainest and most literal use, at the upper extreme those which serve an obvious and distinctive purpose, which involve some change in the usual forms but no strained, extravagant, or undramatic connections, and which seem unlikely to be slips or omissions of the printer. How far one goes down this spectrum will clearly depend on the sort of poem one thinks Milton was writing, how far one supposes he wanted the reader to emphasize the large, vague, suggestive effects to which puns give rise at the expense of small, correct, literal ones, or none at all. And as to this, other evidence than puns enters in. For the moment, it seems possible that because it yields a complex of rich meanings without raising exorbitant difficulties, the appearance of "Likeliest" in the second edition at IX, 394, may be a significant alteration, expressing a genuine, and so presumably a welcome, Miltonic intention. The passage must be placed toward the respectable end of the spectrum.

The texture of Milton's verse is often entangled by verbal devices, some more superficial than puns, others more elaborate and deeply wrought. Satan discovering Eve is presented with a kind of verbal frippery compared to which a pun would seem pompous:

> He sought them both, but wish'd his hap might find
> *Eve* separate, he wish'd, but not with hope
> Of what so seldom chanc'd, when to his wish,
> Beyond his hope, *Eve* separate he spies [IX, 421–24].

This is a variety of ornate, artificial patterning of the language which complements, instead of distracting from, larger structural elements; but sometimes Milton strains and distorts grammar itself for special effects, and the choice between neat and extended grammar is involved in some of the questioned readings. In IV, 472, for instance, a daring but dramatic irregularity of grammatical agreement went uncorrected in both editions, though five of the ten modern editors have felt obliged to patch it up. In this passage the Deity muddles inextricably two simultaneous assertions while describing the mutual delights of Adam and Eve:

> follow me,
> And I will bring thee where no shadow staies
> Thy coming, and thy soft imbraces, hee
> Whose image thou art, him thou shall enjoy
> Inseparablie thine [IV, 469–73].

The peculiar virtue of "shall" is that both "hee" (with the object of "thy soft imbraces") and "thou" (with the object of "him") can govern it; and though some editors, sensitive to subject-and-verb agreements, have corrected it to "shalt," they have obviously narrowed Milton's meaning in the process. Still another passage, largely unquestioned, exemplifies the violence of which Milton's twisted yet functional grammar is capable. Adam in his first access of remorse calls out:

> both Death and I
> Am found Eternal, and incorporate both [X, 815–16];

and Verity defends "Am" by saying that the verb is attracted to the nearer and more important subject, "I." But "I" is not the more important subject; Adam is used to thinking of himself as immortal, but so far as he has known Death he has had every reason to consider it a momentary, an instant process. "I" is indeed closer to the verb, but English grammar does not make this a determining factor. "Am" is governed by a dramatic occasion, not by a rule of grammar. It is the discovery that Death is incorporate in his body that shocks Adam. Death is his body, is himself, by a kind of ghastly reverse incarnation; and the violence of the elision is conveyed by the wrench given the grammar. The best effect of "Am" comes precisely from the fact that it is not adequately "attracted" by the first-person pronoun, that its grammatical wrongness is dramatically right. This is the view of Miss Darbishire [*Milton's Poetical Works,* I, 305–06].

But the dramatic uses of grammar are sometimes less congruent with Milton's broad intentions and less valid in themselves. In IX, 922, for instance, the two editions offer us a choice between two versions of Adam's words to Eve on the occasion of her first confession:

> Bold deed thou hast presum'd, adventrous *Eve,*
> And peril great provok't, who thus hath [1674; hast, 1667] dar'd.

"Hast" is plainly the more consistent grammar, and the value of the alternative form must be great indeed to outweigh it. One might argue that Milton, by the sudden twist to third-person speech of "hath," may have aimed at a special effect, a sort of turning away from Eve, who after the first line is not any longer being directly addressed. Most of the speech is, in fact, a series of strikingly general reflections; and "hath" might carry the overtone, dramatically appropriate, of an address to God rather than to Eve. But on the other hand, this effect is not adequately achieved by "hath" alone; and if "hath" were properly supported by other, purely grammatical constructions, the ungrammatical twist would be intrusive and unnecessary. Thus we may establish, in the matter of dramatic grammar too, a sort of spectrum, from the accidental and inappropriate to the deliberate and functional. But there is not a norm for fractured grammar as there is for puns—or, if there is one, it is not so high; a grammatical conflict, as it is more glaring, must be presumed more deliberate than a buried pun. Hence, though the law it breaks is more rigorous, the break itself, when clearly established, must be supposed more purposeful.

Another sort of violence which Milton habitually did to English grammar is illustrated by the incongruity of "Wave" in XI, 845, with the plural possessive adjective of the following line:

> And the cleer Sun on his wide watrie Glass
> Gaz'd hot, and of the fresh Wave largely drew,
> As after thirst, which made thir flowing shrink
> [XI, 844–46].

Nothing could be neater than the emendation, rejected by modern editors though several times proposed during the eighteenth century, of "Wave" to "Waves"—unless it were a proposal to change "thir" to "her" in line 846. But neatness is obviously not the supreme value of Milton's grammar; for example, the Lord is almost painfully mixed up in his singulars and plurals when pronouncing his great decision:

> Let us make now Man in our image, Man
> In our similitude, and let them rule [VII, 519–20].

Or if this passage is considered suspect because of a Biblical model, Milton in his own person repeats the same incongruity in IX, 1183:

> Thus it shall befall
> Him who to worth in Women overtrusting
> Lets her will rule [IX, 1182–84].

In all these passages, the collective typical singular contrasts with and extends the more literal plural, giving the language its own sort of reach and range, as if one were simultaneously aware of the species and all the individuals in it.

Milton's apparent willingness in all these passages to fracture major rules of grammatical correspondence is evidently the product of an intense concern with the broad effects of language. However apt its effects, a single passage might be dismissed as an oversight and subjected to emendation, but the cumulative evidence of half a dozen passages points to a deliberate Miltonic intention. Modern editors seem, by and large, to have accepted this quality of Milton's style, at least in matters of grammatical emendation. In most instances, Milton's dramatic torsion of English grammar has triumphed without a struggle.

In some undetermined degree, then, we may assume that Milton sometimes misspelled words to accomplish fuller meaning, sometimes distorted grammar to gain a large effect. Plain sense was sacrificed here, but for a special purpose; an editor avoids emendation by accommodating himself to the special purpose in the degree that it seems to outweigh problems of plain sense. The issue is, more often than not, a straightforward one of balancing small, correct effects against large, imaginative ones, a smooth surface against an effect in depth. Much more complicated and ill defined are the problems of emendation where, without any apparent gain in depth or width of expression, Milton's text appears to have fallen short of plain good sense. In III, 592, for example, and VII, 139, genuine deficiencies appear which editors have been strikingly hesitant about correcting. The first passage describes Satan on the sun:

> The place he found beyond expression bright,
> Compar'd with aught on Earth, Medal or Stone
> [III, 591–92].

"Medal," the reading of both texts, is a patent misprint for "Metal"; lines 595–96 repeat the alternative in proper form:

> If mettal, part seemd Gold, part Silver cleer;
> If stone, Carbuncle most or Chrysolite.

There is no apparent reason why Milton in line 592 should have wanted the reader to think of medals, which are not distinguished ordinarily from a class of minerals like stone. The error, moreover, is of precisely the sort in which blind Milton would be at the mercy of a sleepy or indistinct reader. Yet only five of ten modern editors have felt a correction justified; and the same reluctance to break with the text on the score of deficiencies in the plain sense comes out even more strikingly in connection with VII, 139. In this passage the Son has just thrown Lucifer and his cronies out of Heaven; and God in his first speech is made to say,

> At least our envious Foe hath fail'd, who thought
> All like himself rebellious [VII, 139–40].

Taken at the foot of the letter, this speech minimizes the achievement of the Son and implies that there is another, more dangerous enemy who is yet secure. The speech might conceivably be ironic, if God's ironies were ever, in any other passage, wantonly ambiguous; but they are not. God's ironies, for example in V, 719ff., are always clear in themselves and are sometimes underlined for emphasis. Of course nobody is naïve enough to read the passage in its literal sense; everyone as he reads the line silently alters "least" to "last." Yet even the so-called modernized texts continue to print "least," and one wonders how editors who shrink from "last" as too radical an alteration can find it in their hearts to follow Bentley in so bold a change as that of "Foul-Fowle" to "Soul" in VII, 451.

This emendation, the most widely accepted of all those which have been proposed, aims at the elimination of a tautology, not at a correction of grammar, diction, metrics, or sense broadly construed.

> Let th'Earth bring forth Fowle [1667; Foul, 1674; Soul, emendation] living in her kinde.

The line as originally printed does seem to repeat the act of creating our feathered friends, an act which took place the day before and sixty-two lines above. Of modern editors, only Canon Beeching and Professor Patterson refuse to go along with Bentley in emending; both seem definitely committed to following a text supervised by Milton, without allowing any emendations at all. But in fact, the tautology in this particular passage can be eliminated without emending, if "Foul" or "Fowle" is taken as an obsolete form of the noun "Foal," meaning simply young quadrupeds; *OED* provides illustrations of these spellings. No doubt the Biblical text underlying the passage lends support to Bentley's emendation. Genesis, 1:24, reads, "Let the earth bring forth the living creature after his kind," and the Vulgate for "creature" reads "animam." In VII, 388 and 392, moreover, Milton paraphrases the Biblical "living creature" with the words "living soul." On the other hand, Milton did not follow the Bible passage any longer than it suited his convenience; for example, in this very passage he has altered the sex of the possessive, changing "his" to "her" for reasons which may or may not be significant.[16]

Whatever we may say against the emendation, it doubtless provides a more acceptable meaning than either of the original texts; but the issue is more evenly balanced than has sometimes been supposed. A nearby emendation,

[16] See also the curious parallels of V, 197, "Joyn voices all ye living Souls, ye Birds," and the Biblical expression, "let fowl multiply in the earth" [Genesis 1:22].

also by Bentley, has won much less acceptance, though the original passage offends against plain sense and decorum no less flagrantly than VII, 451:

> forth crept
> The smelling Gourd, up stood the cornie Reed
> [VII, 320–21].

Here only four editors of ten accept Bentley's emendation of "smelling" to "swelling." But the reading of the texts not only muddles the transitive and intransitive meanings of the verb "smell"; it ignores some fine precedents in Propertius and Virgil, flaunts a fact of botany (gourds as a class of vegetables do not smell), and achieves only a flat and ignominious statement.[17] These, however, are mostly elements of contrast lying outside the poem itself and so, to judge from the editorial consensus, less convincing than a gross repetition within the poem.

Dramatic propriety is a basis for determining readings less cogent than plain sense; though perhaps too tenuous to determine an emendation, it may provide interesting and challenging grounds for choice between alternate readings. For instance, in I, 530, there is a choice between

> gently rais'd
> Thir fanting [1674] courage, and dispel'd thir fears
> [I, 529–30],

and "Their fainted courage" of the MS and 1667. Though the present participle yields an easier and vaguer meaning, it would seem proper to make use of the more distinct sense of the earlier reading. The courage of the devils was not fainting when Satan raised it, but had fainted before and was now reviving. Yet the editors support, by no less a majority than seven to three, the undramatic reading of the second edition.

[17] Prop. IV, 2, 43; *Georgic* IV, 121–22. Cf. below, p. 156.

Other textual passages involving dramatic propriety are VII, 366; X, 58; and II, 282. In the first of these passages, the editors are disposed, again by a seven-to-three margin, to follow the second edition in applying the feminine adjective to the morning star:

> And hence the Morning Planet guilds her [1674; his, 1667] horns.

This is clearly preferable, to avoid inconvenient Luciferian overtones in the middle of the Creation. In X, 58, the Deity's speech to the Son and the assembled angels offers an alternative:

> Easie it might [1674; may, 1667] be seen that I intend
> Mercie collegue with Justice.

The issue amounts to a question of whom the Deity is actually addressing. "Might" implies a hypothetical observer or one far removed from the action, perhaps the reader of *Paradise Lost;* "may" is more appropriate if one supposes that the heavenly beings themselves are to appreciate the Lord's moral purpose. Thus it is a nice question whether Milton chose his verb to fit within the dramatic framework of the speech or to appeal to the reader outside of it; the editors are exactly balanced, and only the principle of following the later text in substantive matters lends weight to the reading of "might." In II, 282, we find Mammon suggesting that the devils consider things in the light

> Of what we are and were [1674; where, 1667], dismissing quite
> All thoughts of warr [II, 282–83].

Both readings make adequate sense in that they do not offend our notions of the physically and logically possible, but the consideration of where the devils now are is dramatically much more potent than the consideration of what they once were, especially since Mammon is advising that they forget all efforts to regain their former status; one of his arguments is that a close consideration of where they are will reveal that Hell is not so bad after all. Besides, the what-and-where locution was one that Milton used elsewhere [IV, 451–52], and the 1674 reading is not hard to account for by the dropping of a letter, which has been remarked before as an easy slip for a printer to make. On all these counts, "where" is pretty clearly the better reading; it is also the one preferred by seven of ten editors.

But the limits of dramatic propriety as a guide to emendation are quickly reached; and not one of the ten editors has seen any reason to alter "our" to "your" in II, 1001, though the dramatic logic of the change seems very cogent. Chaos speaks to Satan here, describing his situation:

I upon my Frontieres here
Keep residence; if all I can will serve,
That little which is left so to defend,
Encroacht on still through our intestine broiles
Weakning the Scepter of old *Night* [II, 998–1002].

The textual question seems to depend heavily on the character attributed to Chaos; he speaks either as an outsider disturbed by broils in Heaven, or as a fellow spirit aware of a sort of identity with Satan and God, or, finally, as the spirit of confusion, tumult, and discord, whose kingdom of its own nature is racked by "intestine broiles." The second reading is most easily disposed of. Chaos is not thinking of "the quarrels of us angels"; witness not only the resentful tone of "Encroacht" but all the rest of his speech, which is consistent in drawing a distinction between "your" fall and "our" empire. The third reading is logically possible; the weakness of old Night may be due to intestine broils within his kingdom, while the encroachment is

Satan's; because of our intestine broils you can encroach on us. But the only intestine broils which the reader has seen in Chaos' kingdom are just those which provide the most effective barrier against encroachment; the gates of Hell and Paradise are nothing as obstacles, compared with the turbulent confusion of Chaos. *Your* intestine broils, civil wars in Heaven, have led directly to an encroachment, the establishment of Hell; but there is no reason to suppose that *our* intestine broils have hindered our resistance to Omnipotence or led to any encroachments. On all these scores, the better reading would be "your," in accordance with the first view of Chaos' character as an outsider. But dramatic logic has not appealed strongly to the editors, and the text readings have been unchallenged since the eighteenth century.

In a couple of passages, a choice between variant readings of the texts seems to depend largely on the propriety or impropriety of the diction. For example, in XI, 651, Milton was describing the sad state of fallen man, when peaceful shepherds are attacked and fly,

> But call in aide, which tacks a bloody Fray.

So reads the first edition; the second alters "tacks" to "makes." If the change was the printer's, he would have been much more likely to err in the direction of the common word "make" than toward "tack," an idiomatic expression meaning "to join battle." But this is only one of two possibilities. Milton himself may have felt the expression "tack" as too low and professional for the heroic style; though he liked to name things, he did not revel in technical language, and often went to some pains to avoid it. For instance, in the passage describing the building of Pandaemonium, the vague magic of "rose like an exhalation" is substituted for more prosaic carpentry; and the wars in heaven are fought with a minimum of strategic terminology. In II, 1019, the poet used "Larbord," a term of art to which Drs. Bentley and Johnson objected, but he did not use many other expressions from the crafts and trades, and his diction is rarely quaint or mannered in the measure which conscious intention would lead us to expect. (An exception which, in the exact sense, proves the rule, is the comic effect achieved by "unhoord," "cash," "Burgher," and "Cross-barrd" in IV, 188–90.) Thus the second edition seems to supply a substantive and acceptable change. But the same logic leads us to support the first edition in the well-known crux offered by I, 703. Here we are offered a choice between saying that the devils

With wond'rous Art found out the massie Ore,

or that they "founded" it, as the MS. and first edition say. The ore has already been found, in line 690, so that the verb "find" is impossible here. "Founding" is a perfectly respectable metallurgical process; the question is simply which expression describes the melting of the ore most effectively. "Found out" might glance back at the Latin root of "found," *fundere,* with the meaning "pour out," thus avoiding the ambiguity of the purely English word, which means both to pour and to mold. On the other hand, this present tense would jar on the pluperfect in which the rest of the sentence is cast; and Milton, if he himself knew anything about the two processes of founding, surely did not care about making the distinction in any precise technical way. Thus *founded* seems to yield the less obtrusive and more appropriate locution; this is the general conclusion of a discussion summarized by Miss Darbishire in her note on the passage [*Milton's Poetical Works,* I, 289].

Among the proposed emendations are a couple of related passages where history and the changing language have created a confusion which would not have been apparent to the seventeenth-century reader. When the spellings "whether" and "whither" were interchangeable, IV, 592, was not burdened with the extra hesitation which the second spelling creates today:

> *whither* the prime Orb,
> Incredible how swift, had thither rowl'd
> Diurnal, or this less volubil Earth [IV, 592–94].

"Thither" adds an uncertainty, "or" sends us back to reread "whither" as "whether." Another such passage is IV, 567–68, where Uriel reports of Satan that

> I describ'd his way
> Bent all on speed.

Only the interchangeability of "descry" and "describe" kept this passage from sounding as queer to the seventeenth century as it does to the modern reader. Of course the safe, and cumbersome, compromise is to cope with problems of this sort in the footnotes; but it certainly seems like an uneconomical and distracting practice to continue, under such a clumsy patch, a form which not only misrepresents the author's plain intention and constant practice, but encumbers the poetry itself. If we were to form here another spectrum, ranging down from more to less permissible emendations, we might place "at least" and "whither" [VII, 139, and IV, 592] at the top of it, with "medal" and "describ'd" [III, 592, and IV, 567] somewhere down the line.

I do not think the remaining emendations and alternative readings offer grounds for any extended discussion or involve any significant principles. The only interesting thing about IV, 451, is that no fewer than nine out of ten editors are sure that the first edition should be followed in preference to the second:

> and found myself repos'd
> Under a shade on flours, much wondring where
> And what I was [IV, 450–52].

The second edition substitutes "of" for "on." Whether one locates Eve's flowers on the grass or in the trees could scarcely matter less, in itself. But it is curious that nine editors of ten are sure that Milton did not intend a reading which is inferior neither in sense, sound, coherence, nor propriety to that of the first edition. The trees of Paradise have flowers on them, and the very fact that Eve lies *on* flowers elsewhere may be a reason that Milton would have wanted her to lie *under* them here.

Two or three instances of minor miscellaneous inelegancy have been handled without much difficulty by the editors. The tetrameter line followed by a hexameter [X, 989–90] is so clearly a misprint that only Canon Beeching and Professor Patterson refuse to deviate from the printed text; while the violated concord of comparatives which the second edition imposes upon IV, 705, is approved only by the *Columbia Milton* and Mr. Visiak. With the proposal to substitute "and" for "or" in IX, 410, one reaches into the area of diminishing returns.

> To intercept thy way, or send thee back
> Despoild of Innocence, of Faith, of Bliss [IX, 409–10].

Satan of course both intercepts Eve's way and sends her back; but Milton may be describing Satan's intent, which would be either to intercept (i.e., to capture) her or to send her back. The "or" does not seem awkward enough to require replacement. We are offered another balanced choice in VIII, 322, which reads pretty adequately in the 1674 version:

> up stood the cornie Reed
> Embattell'd in her field: and the humble Shrub,

but the punctuation, of which Milton was ordinarily so sparing, speaks against a mere "and" in this line. A colon could not have been extracted from Milton by anything less than a change of verb and subject, which "add" [1667] provides. As for X, 408, which offers us a choice between "prevail" [1667] and "prevails" [1674], the normally Latin cast of Milton's grammar would lend authority to the subjunctive in an "if" clause. One must then suppose that the 1674 printer erred by adding rather than dropping a letter; but this is not a prohibitive assumption.

Finally, in the matter of the "these-those" changes, of which Miss Darbishire is the chief exponent, two of them involve merely a restoration of the MS reading, a reading which the printer, misled by an unfamiliar "e," muffed in 1667 and never was asked to correct. In both these passages the emendation "these" for "those" adds a certain useful immediacy to the passage; and the same logic would call for the same emendation in IV, 661, and for following the 1674 "these" in X, 397. On the other hand, in X, 72, the Son is speaking to the Father of man as a third and rather remote party, and, since he refers to Adam and Eve as "those two" in X, 82, had best be made to harmonize his speech both with itself and with the circumstances of its delivery. Though none of these emendations add significant meanings or alter major emphases, it is probably useful to have the text polished up in such minor details, particularly since the MS gives evidence that mistakes of this kind were not only possible but easy.

So much for those passages where conflicting texts have forced a choice, or where deficiencies, either real or supposed, have seemed to warrant an emendation. Not to labor an obvious point, the editorial record is a mixed one. There is no occasion for surprise that one editor should approve what another disallows; but one may, perhaps, comment on the evident impropriety of following fixed preconceptions, such as the universal superiority of either text or the infallibility of the two editions where they agree. Clearly, it is almost as extravagant to accept none of the proposed emendations as to accept them all. In dealing with individual passages, the editors have sometimes shown startling unanimity; they accept "on" in IV, 451, and reject "last" in VII, 139, as if the evidence were much more one-sided than it actually is. On the other hand, individual editors seem sometimes downright eccentric in their choices. What wayward impulse swayed the editor of the *Student's Milton* to accept "swelling" for "smelling" in VII, 321, while rejecting every other proposed emendation in the entire poem?

Whatever the achievements and deficiencies of the editors, however, they cast only an indirect light on the sort of poem that Milton intended to write. In composing a total picture, indeed, we find the editors at something of a loss, for Milton took so many liberties with English spelling, grammar, and diction, he fulfilled and defied so many different sorts of propriety, and his intention is so blurred by a few undoubted and many possible errors of the printer, that it is no light matter to describe the poet's authentic purposes. In the matter of puns and ambiguities, the record seems to indicate a probability that Milton intended many but not all of those which can be found in the poem. He did not mind enriching the texture of his verse with occasional verbal devices, but I do not think he concealed major meanings in them. It is well enough to play with Ham-Cham and Japhet-Iapetos; but the identification of Satan with Zeus-Jove should not be made to depend on a punning use of "Capitol" to describe Pandaemonium. Here we have a ceiling and a floor for the use of puns; by rejecting the insignificant and the oversignificant, we may get an image of Milton as a writer whose concept of the epic included certain incidental decorative effects to be achieved by puns and ambiguities, even at the expense of a certain unclarity in the plain, literal sense.

In the matter of grammar, the poet distorted English usage freely, sometimes for dramatic effect, sometimes for no particular effect at all, so far as one can judge. The result is discords and sometimes obscurities which are so frequent and apparently so deliberate that one dare not invoke emendation to remove them. In describing Death's weapons, Sin warns Satan that

> that mortal dint
> Save he who reigns above, none can resist [II, 813–14].

Here the sense is not obscured, though the grammar of the subjective pronoun is very dark. Elsewhere, to connect the grammar with the broad sense of a passage requires something of an effort. When the Lord speaks to the Son, telling him,

> Thou therefore whom thou only canst redeem,
> Thir Nature also to thy Nature joyn [III, 281–82],

it may take a little while for the reader to realize that "whom" is plural, on the model of Latin *"quos,"* referring to the possessive adjective "Thir." This is a strain, but to the athletic reader a welcome one, since the difficulty is capable of resolution. But a few lines later there is a less satisfactory difficulty when the Lord has finished his long speech of injunction and prophecy, and Milton describes the jubilation:

> No sooner had th'Almighty ceas't, but all
> The multitude of Angels with a shout
> Loud as from numbers without number, sweet

> As from blest voices, uttering joy, Heav'n rung
> With Jubilee, and loud Hosanna's filld
> Th'eternal Regions [III, 344–49].

Here one reaches down rather further to make sense of the passage. Bentley found a verb missing, and promptly changed "with" to "gave" ("the multitude of Angels *gave* a shout"), and this undeniably helps matters. To avoid the textual alteration, however, an alternative was put forward by Zachary Pearce and widely endorsed; it is to make a sort of absolute construction of all the words from "all" [344] to "joy" [347]. One might paraphrase: "No sooner had the Almighty ceased but—the Angels uttering joy with a shout—Heaven rung with Jubilee," and so on. More awkward English than this one cannot imagine. The absolute construction, if there is one, begins without punctuation or other warning at an extremely clumsy spot in the line, so that it leaves the last word and syllable dangling on the very end of line 344; it continues so long that one loses sight of the beginning of the sentence; and it does not reveal itself as an absolute construction till nineteen words after it has begun. Though these are not all un-Miltonic qualities, I do not think there is any passage in the poetry where they yield quite so unreadable an effect as this. So that after some groping one may well feel that a better way to read the sentence is with "the multitude of Angels" as subject, "rung" as the verb, and "Heav'n" as the object. Though it does not eliminate the violence done to English idiom, this reading may mitigate it; and the locution is within Miltonic reach, since he uses "resound," for example, as a transitive verb [III, 149]. But one does not lightly reach in passing through so many levels of tangled grammar, nor is any reading so satisfactory as to leave the mind fully at rest.

The fact is that Milton did not always distinguish carefully between the broad and the precise effects of language, so that his poem seems sometimes to exist on two levels, and it is not always easy for the reader to keep them both simultaneously in mind. Whether one likes it or not, there is a tendency for the reader to float or rumble along on the large meaning without paying much attention to the small, which may or may not be the grammatical one. Though it is generally possible to bridge the gap with an effort more or less conscious, though "sublime nonsense" is probably too strong a term to describe the effect which Milton's verse occasionally produces, still the gap seems undeniable. How many readers, skating across Adam's invocation to Eve,

> Sole partner and sole part of all these joyes . . . [IV, 411],

pause to reflect that "sole part" is, given the obvious meanings of both words, an Irish bull; and so—discounting a possible pun on another spelling of "sole" (Eve in her reply less than a hundred lines later will invoke Adam as "part of my soul," IV, 487), and considering but rejecting Pearce's proposal to insert a comma after "part," understand an "of me" in the same spot, and read "of" as meaning "among"—will assign to "part" meaning II 7A in *OED,* "share" or "portion." "My only partner and the only share I have in all these joys. . . ." In the end there is a sort of plain grammatical sense at the foot of the passage; but if anything is clear at all, it is that Milton wanted the jangle on "partner" and "part" even at the cost of possible, indeed probable, misunderstanding of the literal sense. Anyone who reflects on the number of readers who have accepted the passage without question must feel that it is precisely in spots like these, where the sense is too slight almost to bother with, that the attempt to discover or create a solid structure of plain sense breaks down entirely. One can emend Milton's text into plain sense; without emendation, one can almost always create for the text as it is given a plain-sense meaning which more or less satisfies one's sense of grammar, logic, and idiom. It is overwhelmingly clear that Milton did not compose his poem, or expect it to be everywhere read, for its plain-sense values.

So with Satan's third soliloquy, in which, reflecting on the possibility of meeting some spirit whom he might pump, he declares that

> A chance but chance may lead where I may meet
> Some wandring Spirit of Heav'n [IV, 530–31].

One way of making sense out of the locution lies through the assumption that "but" means "mere," though the question what chance is not mere chance is one to baffle students of probability; another device is to suppose that "but chance" is parenthetical, and to eke the line out with interpolations till it reads "a chance, and it can only be a chance, may lead," etc. A third way out, rather more painful, is through the assumption that "but" means "that," on the analogy of Latin *"quin,"* and that an auxiliary verb has been ellipsed. "There is a chance that chance may lead. . . ." But here again it becomes obvious that plain sense and coherent grammar are not everywhere an advantage to the reading of the poem, not even a matter of indifference, but on occasion a positive impediment. No meaning that one could conceivably discover at the far reaches of IV, 411 and 530, no set of grammatical connections that one could import, would be esthetically worth the distraction of discovering or importing them. In reading Milton's poem, evidently, one must have the restraint to subordinate effects of detail to those of structure, to pursue some curious inquiries and to refrain from pursuing others equally curious. And one must recognize further that in this poetic style some of the ornament is either not functional at all or functions in such a roundabout way as to create a counterpoint of complex and elaborate senses which may obscure, delay, and perhaps confuse, even more than they enrich, the broad and obvious effects of the style.

Milton's use of dramatic grammar provides evidence of his willingness to make considerable sacrifices in the verbal carpentry of his poem in order to achieve dramatic effects; and this is presumably a sort of evidence useful in determining the text in those four or five instances where dramatic and undramatic locutions are involved in alternate readings or a proposed emendation. I do not think any clear trend emerges from these passages. Perhaps the most striking observation one can make is that Milton, though the dramatic character of his intention is generally clear, did not have enough control of minor textual variations to carry out any policy with absolute consistency.

In the matter of diction, comparatively few problems arise. Though Milton had a tolerance for terms of art from which the eighteenth century notably receded, he did not seek them out as Shakespeare did, and he made less use of them in such incidents as the raising of Pandaemonium, the war in Heaven, and the story of Noah's Ark than one might have anticipated. His reliance on the classical tongues far outweighed his use of modern languages; in descending order of importance, one might list the influences on his diction as Latin, Greek, Hebrew, and Italian. He liked to list words, but not in any degree words peculiar to a craft or a dialect; he did not aim at particular but rather at general speech, and though he distinguished broad characteristics, as in the Great Consult, he was notably unconcerned with rendering the peculiar accents of any individual speaker. So far as this issue concerns alternate readings of the text, it seems that our search should probably be for the unobtrusive word.

The conclusions of this experiment in emending Milton must, then, be sharply tempered. While the poet dealt freely with many of the conventions of English speech in order to gain special effects, his control of the text and his interest in exact grammar can be shown in many small details to have been notably loose. Milton would seem to have aimed primarily at broad effects and to have been careless, either because he was blind or indifferent, of many minor correctnesses. There are some extraneous difficulties in the text of the poem which Milton did not put there, would not want there, and which modern editors have been oddly reluctant to remove. On the other hand, when one has done his best to redeem the text from the flaws and blemishes attributable to blindness, human nature, epic dimensions, and seventeenth-century printers, the poem still offers sizable difficulties as to the level on which it should be read. Though there are no passages which cannot be reduced or expanded into a sort of plain sense, there are many passages where the difficulties of this process are so great that one must presume the literal sense is not always felt and was not in fact intended to be felt. Indeed, this fair defect is so deeply rooted in the character of the style that one may doubt if it is rightfully called a blemish, no matter what one's esthetic principles or preconceptions. It is an infirmity consequent upon certain virtues, a roughness of detail which is a product of sustained devotion to the grand architecture of the poem. What Mr. Jacques Barzun cleverly calls the "principle of Preferable Error" [*KR,* XII, 88–89] complicates the critical and editorial situation to a degree which would be inconceivable if we were dealing with a carver of cherry stones. About the only useful general rules which emerge are that sweeping judgments are often misleading, that a more or less eclectic text of Milton is more or less inevitable, and that not all sorts of perfection can profitably be sought in one poetic achievement at the same time. With these tepid precepts of moderation the critical temper must, and no doubt will, be satisfied.

As readers, our problem is at once larger and simpler. When it becomes plain that we cannot remove the wart without disfiguring the Miltonic nose, there are two things left to do. We can look at the wart and nothing but the wart and call what we see Milton. Or we can step back a little and, in the full knowledge that part of what we see is undistinguished wart, try to balance our talents for criticism and appreciation in order to understand that poem which, when the worst has been said against it, may claim against all challenge, "with respect to design . . . the first place, and with respect to performance, the second, among the productions of the human mind." The tribute need not be perfectly accurate to impress us; that it is not ridiculous is enough.

[IV]

Empson and Bentley: *Scherzo*

EMPSON on Pearce on Bentley on Milton; one would hesitate to involve the Chinese puzzle any further, if it were not for the hope of clarifying it. Milton wrote the poem, Bentley emended the text, Pearce criticized the emendations, Empson to gain his private ends revived the debate.[1] But Empson's comments have been treated very much like Bentley's emendations, as a *faux pas* with just enough oblique cleverness attached so that one had better be careful. Professor Hanford has employed a classically Empsonian ambiguity in dealing with Empson. *A Milton Handbook* said in 1946, "It has remained for William Empson to declare Bentley superior both in sincerity and discernment to those critics who have found no aesthetic difficulties in Milton's poetry and who praise him for the wrong reasons." The tone of this phrasing is pretty clearly hostile; the expression "it has remained

[1] Milton, *Paradise Lost;* Richard Bentley, ed., *Milton's "Paradise Lost,"* (London, 1732); Zachary Pearce, *A Review of the 12 Books of Milton's "Paradise Lost"* (London, 1733); William Empson, *Some Versions of Pastoral* (Norfolk, Conn., n.d.).

for" implies that now we've heard everything, and the assumption that Empson is a defender of Bentley right down to his "sincerity" makes opposition easy. But in 1949, Professor Hanford's *John Milton, Englishman* planted a thick hedge by saying that some of Bentley's emendations had been "interestingly" defended by the "super-subtle modernist," Empson.[2] "Interestingly" here means "clever but unsound, though one doesn't know quite why"; "super-subtle" means "he reads very acutely" but also "what he pretends to see isn't really there," also perhaps "he conceals what is really obvious"; and "modernist" carries so many overtones of "faddist," "sensationalist," and "subverter of established truths," that one does not know how to attach the word to Mr. Empson. Certainly *explication de texte* is a curiously straightforward, old-fashioned device for a supersubtle modernist.

But Empson has written on Bentley, who wrote on Milton; he is, like Bentley, a challenging and rewarding critic because of his faults as well as his virtues, for he is equally rich in both. Most critics allow us to feel safe in one quarter or another; with Empson, anything can happen. Far from being supersubtle, he is wild but willing; he will cheerfully commit twenty absurdities for a chance at one insight. To read Empson hard is always useful and pleasant because his mistakes are as much fun as his perceptions. To read him any less critically than he reads his text is to invite disaster. For he is one of those guides to the waxworks who are so vehement and profuse that they

[2] James Holly Hanford, *A Milton Handbook* (New York, 1946), pp. 339–40; *John Milton, Englishman* (New York, 1949), p. 258. The earlier book is not without its own charming bifurcations, for example, Hanford scorns Bentley because only two of his emendations "have been adopted in the received text, while some five or ten additional ones are held by J. W. Mackail to be all but certain" (p. 340).

end by overwhelming both the exhibits and the visitors.

One picayune preliminary may dispose of a good many adventitious problems. Empson's account of Bentley is impressively inaccurate verbally. Though he makes some point of quoting originals, he seems to quote largely from memory, and inaccurately at that. It seems odd to have "thir" meticulously recorded for "their" when half a line has been silently dropped from the passage, or a key word altered to make hash of the sense. The more significant of these misquotations, which involve more than a queer spelling or a dropped preposition, are indicated briefly in the footnote.[3] Some quotations are provided with a notation of the source, others not, apparently at random; among those given, a number are significantly wrong.[4]

[3] Page 159, line 11, for "make no attempt to defend" read "have no intention to justify"; p. 160, l. 5, for "corrected" read "assisted"; p. 163, l. 17, for "visible" read "intricate"; p. 164, l. 10, for "who knew till then" read "till then who knew," l. 11, for "due" read "dire"; p. 165, l. 11, for "on" read "in," l. 21, for "and" read "am"; p. 166, l. 9, for "ye" read "you"; p. 167, l. 31, for "with" read "could"; p. 170, l. 16, for "touring" read "tow'ring," l. 34, for "they" read "it"; p. 173, l. 23, for "would have suspected that they could" read "would suspect they could"; p. 176, l. 4, for "let none admire; that soil" read "let none admire that riches grow in Hell; that soil"; p. 183, l. 12, for "Fairest star of night" read "Fairest of stars, last in the train of night." Errors of representation in connection with X, 580, and VI, 178, are noted in the text below.

[4] Page 150, line 16, for V, 602, read IV, 602; p. 158, l. 22, for V, 186, etc. read VI, 186, etc.; p. 166, l. 28, for V, 726, read V, 729; p. 167, l. 7, for V, 793, read V, 796, l. 14, for V, 832, read V, 837, l. 29, reference is made to the "stupidly good" passage IX, 465, to describe passages from IV, 362, 374. In a specially odd muddle on p. 160, ll. 3–4, Empson quotes IV, 785, which is not criticized metrically, with V, 786, which is, as if they were joined together in the poem and in the criticisms of it. Mr. Empson has declared, in answer to these criticisms, that since he is not a textual critic, inaccuracies of this sort do not really affect his argument [*PaR,* XXI, 698–700]; one can only regis-

In addition, Empson's prose is often involved to the point where not only significance but sense is in question; pronouns are deliberately double in reference, comparisons are carefully left incomplete, abrupt alterations of subject and jittery generalizations are routine.

Rather more disconcerting than these pervasive and sometimes purposeful slips is Empson's habit of attributing to Bentley or Pearce phrases and ideas of his own invention and of suppressing inconvenient thoughts which they actually express. He says, for example, that Bentley and Pearce agree in finding I, 745,

> Dropt from the Zenith like a falling Star,

quite impossible, because it alters the prevailingly iambic rhythm. In fact, neither critic ever discusses the line; they disagree about the metrics of I, 746, but only over the pronunciation of "Aegean," not over the iambic line. With regard to VII, 55,

> And Warr so neer the Peace of God in bliss,

Empson says Bentley emends "Peace" to "Seat" "because the text implies that the Peace of God was not incapable of being disturbed." The reason assigned is original with Empson; all Bentley says is that the accepted reading was "the Editor's fancied Elegancy." There is a special poignancy to Empson's invention of a motive for Bentley, because it is not an appropriate motive. A literal, devout mind would find it just as unseemly that God's Seat should be disturbed as his Peace. With regard to X, 581–82, Empson invents a silly argument for Pearce and denies that he has made any other, when in fact he has a couple of good

ter, with Professor Tillotson, one's conviction that "it matters horribly when a deflowered text is followed by an advertisement of its subtleties" [*Essays in Criticism and Research* (Cambridge, 1942), p. xvii].

ones. Not only does Pearce propose that "wide-encroaching" is a permissible adjective for Eve, and consistent with a similar usage in XII, 72; he suggests a repunctuation, by which the adjective would be transferred from Eve to Eurynome, where it would be still more appropriate.

These are depressing, pedantic details, of the sort which inspire pervading distrust of Empson in anyone who has checked him against an original. But his own generalizations often require more than a grain of salt. To support his own reading of Satan's speech [IV, 358ff., esp. 383], he invents a "key word" of Milton's, *all,* which he declares that the poet does not use "for any but a wholesale and unquestioned emotion." Disregarding compounds like "almighty," Milton uses "all" no less than eight times during the speeches of Belial and Mammon. Presumably their feeling is very wholesale indeed, and one would be hard put to find a retail passage in Milton.[5] In dealing with Pearce, Bentley, and the discussion which they centered on VI, 178, Empson fuddles a couple of issues strangely in "quoting them both on the 'sound' issue":

> God and Nature bid the same,
> When he who rules is worthiest, and excells
> Them whom he governs. This is servitude. . . .

Bentley emends "governs" to "rules" and "servitude" to "servility," the first alteration on grounds of "force and

[5] A subsequent publication of Empson's [*KR,* X, 597ff.] withdraws the original generalization but puts forward so many new ones that a volume would be required to cope with them. It is an odd argument which calls Milton an absolutist, an all-or-nothing man [p. 597]; which goes on to suggest, as if the ideas were perfectly congruent, that "his feelings were crying out against his appalling theology in favor of freedom, happiness, and the pursuit of truth" [p. 600]; and which concludes by urging that "all" may or may not be used as part of a buried pun on "fall."

rotundity," the second on grounds of dramatic coherence, because Satan's original accusation is of "servility." Empson clips off the Milton quotation after "governs," quotes Bentley in support of the first change, and then as a reply to Bentley misquotes Pearce on the second change, altering his words into complete nonsense.

"Bentley is always ruthless," Empson says, "about the large ornamental comparisons." But this is neither a full nor an accurate description of Bentley's position; a random glance shows plenty of elaborate similes which he accepts without question. For example, he does not criticize, except in minor details, the shield like a moon seen in a telescope [I, 286], the bad angels like a cloud of locusts [I, 338], the bad angels like a hive of bees [I, 768], the applause like blustering winds [II, 285], the rejoicing after the Consult like calm after a storm [II, 488], Satan like a comet [II, 708], Death and Satan like two black clouds [II, 714], Satan like a vulture on Imaus bred [III, 431], or Satan like a scout finding a metropolis [III, 543]. Bentley does have a more suspicious attitude toward metaphor than Milton does; one sign of this is that he likes natural comparisons but is impatient of anything which seems to involve unusual book learning, strained conceits, or a confusion of mythological systems. His poetic feeling is strikingly localized in natural objects, perhaps because he was himself a bookish man; but within his limits, he is perfectly tolerant of the most ornate comparisons.

Of Milton's loose grammar Empson says that he often uses "and" or "or" where the sentence needs more detailed logical structure, because he aims at both a compact and weighty style (which involves short clauses) and a sustained style with momentum (which involves long clauses). It is hard to say which is the most confusing part of this tangle, the fact, the motive, or the consequence. The basic fact is doubtful or worse; for Milton's grammatical looseness is more often a matter of the modifiers or the verb than of the connectives. Bentley devotes much of his energy to separating verbs from inappropriate subjects and to adding new verbs and new subjects where he thinks they are needed. By contrast, he spends little time strengthening connectives; and where he does, it is hard to see how a confusion of style as between long and short clauses is behind Milton's difficulty. A special Miltonic fondness for "or" as a connective perhaps derives from the frequently unresolved character of Milton's allegory, mythology, and cosmology. Sometimes he does not want us to inquire too closely into the ways and means of a process [IV, 804] or a mode of existence [X, 1001]; and he often wants us to keep in mind three or four swift, glancing comparisons at once [IX, 393–95]. But this balancing and aggregating of ideas and impressions is not a matter of long or short clauses, of compact or sustained style, since Milton, like Homer, Virgil, Dante, Lucan, and every other poet, knew that the epic manner involved both elements, according to the dramatic occasion.

Finally, Empson delights in bits and scraps of evidence wiredrawn in arbitrary directions to excessive lengths. This is not quite the familiar complaint that what Empson sees in a passage nobody else, including the author, could ever have seen. Whether or not one can see too much in a poem is, in emphasis at least, another question from whether or not one sees accurately. Empson does not always see accurately. To support the point that Satan was justified in thinking himself the equal of God, he cites Milton's own language in II, 108, as speaking of the angels as Gods. But Milton says only that the war Moloch denounces will be dangerous "to less then Gods," and the war is certainly dangerous to the angels, particularly the fallen angels, who are therefore less than Gods. The obvious sense of the passage is directly opposite to that which Empson gives it. His reading is often arbitrary in this way; and when the contrary sense is not positively indicated, it frequently is possible. With regard to XI, 102, the passage where God foresees that Satan may raise new troubles,

> Or in behalf of Man, or to invade
> Vacant possession,

both Bentley and Empson see "in behalf of" as implying Satan's good will toward man; but Pearce and the *OED* agree in making clear that the meaning of "with regard to" or "in the matter of" was common in Milton's time. Quoting IV, 268ff., lines which compare Paradise with Proserpina's Enna and the grove of Daphne, Empson undertakes to read the passage as a slap against Eve. Proserpina became queen of Hell—"became Sin, then, on Milton's scheme; Eve, we are to remember, becomes an ally of Satan when she tempts Adam to eat with her." Eve does of course help Satan to overcome Adam; created out of Adam, as Sin out of Satan, she has almost incestuous relations with her progenitor. So that there are Eve-Sin parallels; and the background holds a forbidden pomegranate to provide a direct Eve-Proserpina parallel. But Proserpina did not become Sin in any sense Milton would have recognized, because she could still come back to earth for six of the twelve months, and when she came, she brought summertime and the flowering of the earth; because she is never associated with the active seduction or punishment of sinners, but only with alleviating their misfortunes as a fellow victim; and because if she became Sin, there would be no reason for Ceres to look for her so long and so hard. Parenthetically, if Milton really intended to suggest sexual relations between Eve and Satan, it is odd that no least suggestion of snakiness attaches to Adam after the Fall. As for the parallel with Daphne, Empson suggests that because she resisted Apollo, Milton introduced her to the detriment of Eve, who fell to Satan. But note how this argument trips over the preceding one regarding Proserpina. Eve is like Proserpina, to whom something terrible happened; she is worse than Daphne, who came off fairly well. The interpretations could just as easily be reversed. Eve is better than Proserpina because at least she never had to marry Satan, and she is like Daphne in that, saved by divine favor, she was not really, irrevocably seduced. Of course, Milton is really comparing groves, not people; aside from lesser inexactitudes like the lack of parallels for Ceres and Adam, neither the Daphne nor the Proserpina fable represents exactly what happened to Eve, according to Milton's theology. She neither turned into a tree nor married Satan; and there is no more reason for supposing Milton wanted to suggest either alternative than for supposing he wanted to suggest both. Even if he had intended an exact and detailed correspondence of persons or stories as well as meadows, the slap at Eve would still be Empson's invention imposed upon Milton; the correspondence might just as well be complimentary.

If all these criticisms of Empson are correct, and if "Milton and Bentley" provides a fair sampling, our critic does not quote, cite, generalize, or read accurately, and the reader may well ask, "What's left?" Not much more, it would appear, than a faculty for muddling around in interesting places. This is partly a true bill. Bentley is an interesting place for Empson to muddle, and Empson's muddling is not at all unlike Bentley's. Both men have a preconceived pattern to impose on Milton, whose effects often depend on a willingness to sacrifice neatness in details for the large architecture, the deliberate multiplicity of reference. Milton is writing about the fall of man, the history of the world, metamorphosis, theogony, and contemporary politics, all at once. Bentley, with his enlightened concepts of correctness, does not like to see any author talking about two things at once; he is especially strict about questions of relevance, so that Pearce can often hoist him with his own petard by quoting classical precedent for a liberty which he denies Milton. In any event, Bentley denounces "irrelevances" which come from the romances as "romantic"; when they are geographical, he calls them pedantry; and when they are not quite congruent with the Bible story, he feels shocked. His notions of matter and spirit are rather more distinct than Milton's, and he does not suffer allegory gladly. Given these principles, grant him the authority of an editor, and almost all his emendations follow as a matter of course.

Empson also stretches Milton on a Procrustes' bed, but of a slightly different design. The violations of decorum which Milton evidently considered somewhere between the natural, the tolerable, and the necessary, and which bothered Bentley into the hypothesis of an editor, Empson treats as positive virtues. Whether Milton wanted an incongruity or was unable to avoid it or was unaware of it, Empson is eager to see an unintentional richness in the poem; and I suppose one sounds ungrateful or petulant in refusing to see what he has dug up with such spaniel vivacity. But the accumulation of his insights results in an agglomeration, not a structure, not even a structure with its lines of stress laid bare.

For however richly Empson's method works out in the most favorable circumstances, the price of these efforts is a multitude of disappointments elsewhere. For instance, Milton compares Satan flying through Hell [II, 634ff.] to a fleet seen in the distance, and Empson explains that he is "like a fleet rather than one ship because of the imaginative wealth of polytheism and the variety of the world." This may or may not be so; a couple of reasons rather more immediate and practical come easily to mind. (A single ship in Milton's vast perspective would be lonely and small, unwelcome connotations under the circumstances. A fleet, on the other hand, would bring to mind the spice and gold fleets of Spain, Italy, and Portugal, three rich, wicked, and powerful empires.) But if we must see polytheism and variety in Satan when he is compared to a fleet, what shall we see when he is compared to "Teneriffe or Atlas unremov'd"? Shall he then be monotheism and barrenness? Every successful excursion down the back alleys of an image implies a long series of unsuccessful or incongruous ones. If no image can serve a simply decorative end until we have exhausted all its conceivable thematic implications, reading an epic will be like panning for gold in thin territory, our chief emotional responses will be profound boredom and occasional mild surprise. In order to read an epic by the explication-of-images method at all, one must pick and choose and match images like a mosaic worker; even within the individual image one must somehow purge the unwelcome elements. Empson finds it simplest to ignore elements which do not serve his purpose, even—especially—when they do serve Milton's. He is enthralled by the subconscious motives which apparently enabled Milton to write an interesting poem in spite of himself. To judge from the account he gives of *Paradise Lost,* composing an epic must be something like standing guard over a basket of eels; you wait for one to start wriggling and then knock it over the head.

To say this much is not to deny the presence of subconscious or half-perceived elements in Milton's work; precisely because his structure is so large and his conscious resolve so exactly focused, there is a rare penumbra of half-glimpsed, half-developed conflicts on the outer fringe of his vision. But there is a limit to the profitable perception of these things; it is found where variety of effect gives way to monotony. If, when Milton seems to be describing the devils digging gold out of a hill, the garden of Paradise, and snakes climbing apple trees [I, 688; IV, 268; X, 556], he is really slapping at Eve, an extraordinary monotony settles over the poem; and the more ingenuity one devotes to the argument, the more repetitious its pattern becomes.[6] If we suppose ourselves obliged to keep in mind that Eve is to be identified with Sin, Eden, serpents, vines, Pales, Pomona, Proserpina, Pandora, Pyrrha, Ceres, Circe, and Pharaoh's daughter, large sections of the poem will consist of nothing but labored explorations and explanations; indeed, every epithet, every image, every assertion will be the occasion for an adventure in indirection. Now epic poetry read in this way cannot be epic; among the cardinal virtues of the proper epic are motion, magnitude, sustained narrative line, typicality of character, and clarity of emotional response. Milton, if he had expected his poem to be read by detailed analysis of the imagery, would certainly have written it very differently from the way he did. He would not have written an epic at all, he would have written a Euphuistic romance. As it is, he frequently employs the stock epithet, the conventional adjective, and the broad, swift, fluid techniques of impressionism, eked out with some

[6] Undeniably, if we make a supreme effort to think and feel counter to Milton's directives, we shall be rewarded with a strong, grotesque sense of ambivalence. On the other hand, this is not much of a reward to distribute over 10,000 lines of blank verse. Even Benin sculpture, to which Empson likens *Paradise Lost* [*PaR,* XXI, 698–700], would be rather dull stuff without a strictly irrelevant awareness of the shocking social milieu which produced it.

explicit allegory and versified sermonizing. His unit of thought and expression, within which images are fitted and arranged (and from which Empson vigorously extracts them), is the verse paragraph. He manipulates a double plot with some skill, integrating the fall of Satan with that of Adam, playing Satan against Christ as champions of their respective causes, gradually narrowing the limits of his theater and resolving the vast, awful lights and darks of his myth into the mingled earth colors of everyday. The peculiar qualities that Empson looks for in the poem are undoubtedly there, to some degree; and the fact that Milton did not intend them may not be particularly important. But there is something profoundly frustrating about a man who insists on investigating a giraffe as if it were a rabbit oddly botched in the making. The sort of discoveries that make it a brilliant incarnation of rabbit are precisely those which get in the way of its being a functioning giraffe. And when the entire animal kingdom has been reduced to the category of more or less successful rabbit, a natural monotony ensues.

Still, when all is said, Empson's passing point remains that there is a pastoral feeling about Milton's Paradise because Adam and Eve in their innocence are (like pastoral characters generally) both higher and lower than man as we know him, simpler and so more nobly representative. This is a useful corrective to Mr. C. S. Lewis' solemn correction of Sir Walter Raleigh's professorial flippancies; and perhaps the matter should be allowed to rest here. But it is hard to forbear the notion that Milton's pastoral feelings extend far wider than the boundaries of Paradise. There is a duality, whether one thinks of it as swainish or not, in Heaven's wide champaign and in the fields of Hell. Like Adam, Satan is above and below the human level; the grandiose ambassador of a gorgeous kingdom and a bestial element, he is a figure of comedy and yet of terror, a joke and an ogre. The angels too are figures of genre; Milton explains in elaborate, uncomfortable detail about their digestive and sexual functions because he knows that we, like Adam, are curious about these rare birds; they are at once odd specimens in this world and splendid ambassadors from another. God himself, with his arbitrary permissions and forbiddings, his vindictive punishments and elaborate atonements, has two aspects; one cannot imagine the splendidly laconic architect of the cosmos who presides over Book VII leaving such a muddy, serpentine track as Book XII describes.

One of the main directions which the whole story takes is away from the fabulous and mythical into the prosaic and everyday. The conventional, much-described decline of Satan is paralleled by a decline of God from the miraculous to the legal and then to the episodic level, a decline of man from a princely to a schoolboy figure, a narrowing of the theater and the issues from cosmic to psychological scope. The myth is brought down in the last books to its practical application, as Michael offers Adam a series of enlightened aphorisms to guide him through life. If Bentley finds nothing much to criticize in the last books, one of the reasons may be, aside from the critic's being bored and tired, that Milton had come down to writing the sort of poem of which he could approve, an enlightened poem in the sense that its discourse is literal, largely unadorned, and all on one rational level. If there is any passage in the poem of which Dr. Johnson could say, "The substance of the narrative is truth," and feel confident that he was referring to a single coherent area of thought and discourse, it is the prophecies of Michael. What this suggests is that the dramatic tensions of the poem parallel in their decline the decline of man from a dualistic, pastoral condition of humble rank yet typical importance to a literal, unsymbolic, unshadowed status. The ontogeny of the poem's structure recapitulates the phylogeny it describes; the prevailing melancholy which Mr. Tillyard notes in the final books is thus a function of Milton's feeling that the age of miraculous and mythical events, the age of sympathy, is over. This feeling, profoundly ambiguous since the Nativity Hymn, is now tinged with unqualified regret; what man has lost is hope as well as poetry, a chance of swift redemption as well as of picturesque error. Thus the telling of the myth culminates not in a mythical truth, but in a truth of the audience; not in the Second Coming but in things as they are, the human condition as the reader must know it. Relegated to that recital which for Adam concerns only a distant future and for the reader an equally remote past, the Second Coming is cramped into the farthest perspective of a vast and tangled panorama. It lacks all energy and dramatic significance; the true conclusion of the poem is in the languid movement of humanity, abandoned and aimless, which the last two lines present:

> They hand in hand with wandring steps and slow,
> Through *Eden* took thir solitarie way.

Bentley found this last distich altogether too mopish for Queen Caroline's taste; the adjectives especially troubled him.

> Why *wand'ring?* Erratic Steps? Very improper: when in the Line before, they were *guided by Providence.* And why *Slow?* when even *Eve* profess'd her Readiness and Alacrity for the Journey, 614: . . . And why *their solitary Way?* All Words to represent a sorrowful Parting? When even their former Walks in Paradise were as solitary, as their Way now. . . .

But it is exactly the "solitary" state of man that keynotes the passage. By the end of Book XII all the supernatural persons are withdrawn or reduced to attendant, symbolic roles. The Devil is in Hell, a snake; Sin and Death, losing even their allegorical personalities, have resolved into conditions of human existence; the angel faces, barricaded far away, are remote and "dreadful"; only man is left to carry on the story of history, and his significance is no longer pastoral. Indeed, he is no more than a wanderer, a seeker after significance; and if this aimlessness reflects on the guidance of Providence, so much the worse for Providence.

> THEN hand in hand with SOCIAL steps their way
> Through *Eden* took, WITH HEAV'NLY COMFORT CHEER'D.

Bentley wanted to do away with the pastoral elements in the poetry because they disturbed the character Milton was forced to assume. Empson muddles Milton's need to do away with them by suggesting a simple regret for Elizabethan hey nonny-nonny which is really a more complex and inclusive melancholy, for a lost synthesis of virtue and grace, for a series of organized stock responses, for an architecture of the emotions. Only compare Raphael's speech on Harmony [V, 469ff.] with the history of mankind according to Michael, the fine tact of "Lycidas" with that provincial contempt of the classics, that feeling for the Christian dispensation as not only supplementing but canceling pagan reason, which resounds through *Paradise Regained,* IV, 285ff.! *Paradise Lost* is one of the first pastorals to express nostalgia for the good old days when life was complex and harmonious instead of simple and disorderly.[7] Reading Empson, one cannot help feeling that the chaotic uniformity of his responses largely justifies the melancholy of Milton's conclusion.

[7] I paraphrase here Professor Stoll, who spoke long ago of a "decrease in the magnitude and increase in the complexity of both the emotions and the expression as we proceed through the great poem" [*UTQ,* III, 16]. Of the emotions, he is exactly right; of the expression, I think he might better say that it diminishes both in magnitude and in complexity.

[V]

Milton's Reading

ONE area where the researches of the past fifty years have produced notable results is in the attribution to Milton of possible literary experiences, the rediscovery of the books he read or may have read. Needless to say, the task has been a tremendous one. Milton put out his own eyes reading; simply to retrace his steps would require an equal sacrifice, and to read all the various attributions, alternatives, mutual critiques, and circumambient arguments would use up the eyes of Argus. But division of labor conquers all. The students of a certain area, the specialists in a certain author have brought their individual lights to the illumination of Miltonic texts; and a wilderness of possible sources for Miltonic phrases, ideas, and dramatic episodes has been laid open.

Aside from specific mention, the usual evidence that Milton read a given book is some similarity between a passage in it and a Miltonic passage. The objection is trite that in any specific context this logic ignores the possibility of originality on the part of Milton. A more general difficulty arises from the fact that whereas similarity may be evidence of influence, an equal or greater amount of dissimilarity is not usually considered evidence of lack of influence. Though Milton differs from Author X on 999 pages of 1,000, it is the thousandth page which will be cited to show that Milton "undoubtedly knew" or "may well have known" the work of Author X. The positive argument is thus presumed stronger than the negative, as in almost no other line of scholarly endeavor; and so the number of possible Miltonic readings and influences has steadily increased to a quantity which would make even the laborious Masson stare.

But while the aggregate of attributions has increased, the chance that any one of them is correct (beyond those for which there is explicit evidence) has, in compliance with a familiar law of probability, steadily diminished. For if we suppose that Milton was capable of only a given amount of reading in the thirty years of adult life before he lost his eyesight, that quantum—however generously we estimate it after discounting sleep, "gawdy days," domestic life and duties, labor in a vocation, and other necessary activities—is pretty well taken care of by the readings and rereadings of which he has left evidence. The total of those speculative readings which he "may well have undertaken" should not exceed the leisure time available to an already heavily overtaxed pair of eyes. After a while, the more little guesses we put forward, the less probable any of them look. The geographers, the classicists, the historians, the theologians, the astronomers, the cabalists, the lawyers, the humanists, the mythographers, the pamphleteers, the critics, the sermon writers, the politicians, the linguists, the Bible students, the antiquaries, the rhetoricians, the scientists, the tacticians, strategists, and explorers all have a claim on Milton's time which is legitimate—up to a point. But if each is allowed to ride his Miltonic hobbyhorse as hard as he chooses, we shall first of all have a Milton with no sense of discrimination at all, a bibliophilic Grangousier; and then we shall have either five or six separate Miltons, or a physical impossibility, or a solid mass of Milton surrounded by a mist of speculation which grows forever thinner as each new possibility is extended from a total amount of reading which can only have been so great. We know that Milton did not do all the reading he "might have done" by the same logic which teaches us that he did not write secretly in his spare time Hobbes' *Leviathan* or *The Pilgrim's Progress*. It was not within human possibility to do so much work of such different, and in fact incompatible, sorts. Any man with the furious, undirected energy to do all the reading attributed to Milton would not have had the discretion, let alone the time, to write *Paradise Lost*.

In point of fact, a spot check of Miltonic indexes and concordances makes it easy to place certain spectacular limits on Milton's knowledge of particular books, or at least on our knowledge of Milton's knowledge of particular books. There is no specific reason to suppose that he had read Montaigne, Plotinus, Cervantes, Villon, Ronsard, Rabelais, or John Donne. No doubt John Milton was a well-educated poet, and a well-educated poet of the seventeenth century, like a well-educated poet today, had looked into all these authors. But if Milton looked into them, they remained dead to him so far as overt and specific evidence will carry us. In the course of a long and busy life, during which he produced at least thirty volumes of poetry and prose famous for the weight of their learning and the complexity of their reference, he never once mentioned any of these men by name, never spoke the title of any of their works, never borrowed from any of their writings a turn of phrase, an item of fact, or a traceable opinion which he could not more easily have acquired elsewhere. These names do not occur in the lists of his reading; no marginalia survive to indicate that he ever perused their volumes, nobody ever recorded a conversation in which he mentioned them. And yet it is absurd to suppose that he was not acquainted with some of them, at least.

In estimating the degree of any man's learning, one must always deal with maximum and minimum possibilities; but the gap between the two is rarely so vast as with Milton, and it is not often the upper end of the scale which is left open to the blue sky. Nobody can defend, or for that matter advance seriously, the idea that Milton left somewhere in his life or works an explicit record of everything he read. He was in fact particularly chary of mentioning contemporaries, perhaps considering "his mention of a name as a security against the waste of time, and a certain preservative from oblivion" [Johnson, *Lives of the English Poets* (Everyman's), I, 60]. But it is also absurd to suppose that he read everything which has been assigned to him under some such rubric as "we may well suppose," or "it is perfectly possible that. . . ." There is in fact nothing impossible about any one of these individual assignments. Milton may have read Galileo and Bishop Wilkins, Copernicus and Kepler and Bartholomaeus Anglicus; he may even have been aware of all the commentators on Genesis: Ben Gerson, Ibn Ezra, Rashi, Grotius, Calvin, Pererius, Mersenne, Hammond, Mead, Cartwright, Paraeus, Rivetus, Wollebius, Philo, Josephus, Augustine, Jerome, and so on. (Scholarship has handsomely distinguished between commentaries on Genesis known to Milton and those of which he left no record [Arnold Williams, *MP,* XXXVII, 263–78], but there is no inherent improbability in his having known any one of those which he did not mention.) It is only when the duplications and repetitions start piling up beyond any conceivable necessity imposed by Milton's text; it is only when we start urging that Milton read all the originals and all the translations and all the populariza-tions, that he was simultaneously aware of the most minute scientific details of botanical studies and the most naïve of folk superstitions, that he imbibed with the same voracious lack of discrimination the vulgar astrological flimflam of Dr. John Dee and the serious astronomical treatises of Gali-leo—it is only when the image of Milton starts to resemble a neurotic magpie or a compulsive pack rat, that the need for some distinctions and discriminations makes itself felt.

As a matter of fact, it is not difficult at all to distinguish various degrees and modes in Milton's knowledge of books. After the very sizable list of books which he never men-tioned, never borrowed from, was never influenced by, was temperamentally alien to, and may well be supposed never to have read, there are those which he encountered in the course of his general reading program—books read, re-corded in various commonplace books, and perhaps even annotated—but never mentioned or used by Milton in the course of his literary career. Some writers, like Wyclif or Petronius or Apuleius, Milton mentioned by name but with no indication that he knew their books; the reference is perfectly general and conventional, having to do with reputations as a schoolboy becomes acquainted with them. Then there is a group of books which he used in the course of his literary career but consulted only for specific infor-mation required for a specific occasion; such, for example, are many of the volumes used to write *The History of Britain*. References to these books are concentrated in a single work or area but do not occur elsewhere. Books which were cited on several separate occasions were evi-dently more important to Milton; one may even suppose that the more casual, trivial, and numerous the references, the more considerable is the familiarity implied. Then there are the big books in Milton's life—Augustine, Homer, Ovid, Spenser, and so on; books which shaped his vocabulary, his diction, his very thought, repeatedly, throughout his literary career. And finally there is the Bible.

Though ranged in some such hierarchy as this, the books in Milton's life must clearly overlap in many particulars; the place of any individual volume in the hierarchy is a matter of the most delicate estimation. Most appealing and perilous of all is the area of speculation opened up by the existence of apparent contraries in the list of Miltonic readings. If Milton had the sort of mind to be strongly influenced by the urbanity of Cicero or the calm nobility of Virgil, could he possibly have given his serious attention to the naïve and superstitious Robert Fludd? If the prevailing cast of his mind was Stoic, does any presumption lie that he was relatively immune to significant influence from Epicureans or Skeptics? Is there such a thing as intellectual incompatibility, and does it apply to John Milton? These are deep waters, on which every adventurer is rash. Yet the reader may wind up, as a result of the writer's follies, with a clearer picture of Milton's literary interests and activities than could ever be achieved by venturing one safe little unverifiable guess after another about this or that possible source, influence, parallel, or analogue.

The question, in its essence, is one of evidence; and some of the most interesting issues emerge from consideration of a theory which has suffered, over the last three or four decades, variations of fortune which can only be described as spectacular. This is the theory that Milton was intimately familiar with, and strongly influenced by, medieval Jewish lore.

The theory registered its most spectacular advances during the decade from 1920 to 1930, under the impulsion of two publications by M. Denis Saurat and two by Mr. Harris Fletcher, in addition to articles by Mr. E. C. Baldwin and Miss Marjorie Nicolson.[1] And after the studies came the annotated editions, such as that of Professor M. Y. Hughes (1935), which appeared just as the tide was beginning to turn.

The common thesis of all those who advocated a Jewish influence on Milton was expressed with fine tact by Miss Nicolson, who said she was less concerned to establish "actual borrowing on the part of Milton than to indicate typically Cabbalistic strains in *Paradise Lost*" [*PQ*, VI, 2]; and with fine indiscretion by Mr. Fletcher, who said flatly that "wherever else Milton may have encountered [certain] ideas, the rabbis would have determined his use of them" [*MRR*, p. 135]. The circularity of this latter notion could scarcely escape comment; by assuming that the rabbis were responsible for Milton's phrasings, Mr. Fletcher undertook to prove—that the rabbis were responsible for Milton's phrasings. But however one dressed it up verbally, the point was to establish a significant relation between Milton and medieval Jewish writers and to do so primarily by the method of accumulating parallels.

The number of these parallels multiplied with lapin rapidity; their character became the object of prolonged and elaborate scrutiny. M. Saurat in a memorable passage declared that with only one exception (the idea of the non-existence of the soul) all of Milton's philosophy was in the

[1] Saurat, *La Pensée de Milton* (Paris, 1920), translated, augmented, and reprinted as *Milton: Man and Thinker* (London, 1925); Fletcher, *Milton's Semitic Studies* (Chicago, 1926), *Milton's Rabbinical Readings* (Urbana, 1930); Baldwin, *JEGP,* XXVIII, 366–401; Nicolson, *SP,* XXII, 433–52, XXIII, 405–33; *PQ,* VI, 1–18. See also such ancillary attributions as those of Kathleen Hartwell, *Lactantius and Milton* (Cambridge, Mass., 1929); R. H. West, *SP,* XLVII, 211–23; D. C. Allen, *MLN,* LXIII, 262–64, etc.

Zohar and conversely, that there was but one great idea in the *Zohar* (reincarnation) which was not also in Milton [*MM&T,* pp. 282–83]. This was splendid indeed, though it called for some demonstration. Among the many particulars which he adduced, M. Saurat placed greatest weight on the idea of creation by retraction [*PL,* VII, 170] and on Milton's Muse, Urania, as paralleling the third *Sefira* (*Binah:* Understanding) in the universe of *Atsiluth:* Emanation. Thus the foundations were laid; and when, in 1930, Mr. Harris Fletcher produced *Milton's Rabbinical Readings,* great architectures seemed in the making.

And yet Mr. Fletcher's book was not exactly congruent with M. Saurat's; on the contrary, much of what M. Saurat put forth Mr. Fletcher ignored; and sometimes the two seemed at actual odds, though the sharpness of these odds was muted by a notable moderation of mutual polemic. For instance, Mr. Fletcher, though he identified Milton's Muse with Ben Gerson's concept of Understanding as if this concept were distinctively Ben Gerson's, did not think it necessary to adjust his view with Saurat's interpretation of the Muse as the third *Sefira.* Could it be that as long as Milton was indebted to one rabbi or another, it did not greatly matter which? At any rate, Mr. Fletcher, with a somewhat greater show of precise and positive demonstration than M. Saurat had ventured, set forth three passages where Milton seemed to give specific evidence of having read the rabbinical commentators and added some thirty parallel passages in token of direct influence. And so, for a precarious moment, the structure of rabbinical readings attributed to Milton stood and glistened. Professor Tillyard looked upon the cornerstone of the structure and found it solid [*Milton,* p. 274].

The first attackers were hesitant and respectful, and they worked mostly from the Miltonic end of the problem. In

1934 Mr. G. C. Taylor, without denying that Milton consulted "some of the rabbinical readings noticed by Fletcher," [*Milton's Use of Du Bartas* (Cambridge, Mass., 1934), p. 13], reduced Saurat's central contention to a notable misinterpretation of VII, 168ff.

> Boundless the Deep, because I am who fill
> Infinitude, nor vacuous the space.
> Though I uncircumscrib'd my self retire,
> And put not forth my goodness, which is free
> To act or not, Necessity and Chance
> Approach not mee, and what I will is Fate.

By showing that Saurat gratuitously treated the word "retire" as if it described itself the act of creation instead of a limit placed by God on his own creativity, Mr. Taylor obviated any necessity of invoking the *Zohar* on this point. He suggested in a footnote, mild to the point of confusion, that the paradox of the fortunate fall had found expression outside the *Zohar* [*MUDB,* p. 45, note 1]; and then took a hasty step backward by suggesting that, after all, Du Bartas was himself a sort of cabalist [*MUDB,* p. 45]. Mr. G. W. Whiting in 1939 carried the campaign a step further by criticizing several other of Saurat's Miltonic readings and rehearsing about a third of the parallels set forth in Fletcher's last volume. He found several passages misread in egregious fashion; he found a good many commonplaces adduced without specific authority as evidence of rabbinical influence; but he found no solid evidence that Milton was influenced by the rabbis [*Milton's Literary Milieu* (Chapel Hill, 1939), chap. I]. Mr. C. S. Lewis, though he did not deny that Milton got the idea of creation by retraction from the *Zohar,* quickly rehearsed the rest of Professor Saurat's evidence and discarded it abruptly, pausing only to applaud Professor Saurat for raising such interesting questions [*PPL,* chap. XII]. Equally critical of M. Saurat and Mr. Fletcher—though he did not deny that "Fletcher has indeed rendered a service to Miltonic scholarship" [*This Great Argument* (Princeton, 1941), p. 111]—was Mr. Maurice Kelley, who found their interpretations at fault in one detail after another. Milton's Muse was not Ben Gerson's Understanding, or the third *Sefira* either; no more was she, as Mr. Whiting had implied, an element of the Trinity [*TGA,* pp. 109–18, 128–30]; creation by retraction was not a Miltonic doctrine [*TGA,* pp. 80–82, 205–13]; and, "all in all, . . . Saurat's synthesis [was] a misleading exposition of Milton's views" [*TGA,* p. 212]. But though he repudiated many specific details of Saurat's argument and one or two of Fletcher's, Mr. Kelley did not speak against the concept of rabbinical influence as a whole; on one occasion [*TGA,* p. 210, note 70] he even attacked the thesis of Saurat that Eve's soliloquy [*PL,* IX, 826–33] was borrowed from the *Zohar* [*MM&T,* pp. 283–84] by urging that Fletcher had more convincingly attributed it to Yosippon [*MSS,* pp. 132–35], even though Fletcher in the meantime had attributed it again, this time to Rashi [*MRR,* pp. 206–07].

But in 1949 Mr. George Conklin laid an ax to the roots of the whole rabbinical theory by arguing energetically that there is no real evidence of Milton's ever having been a capable reader of rabbinical Hebrew [*Biblical Criticism and Heresy in Milton* (New York, 1949)]. That Milton knew Biblical Hebrew is not in question. But though Fletcher sometimes argues from the unquestioned fact that Milton knew the Hebrew text of a particular passage to the further presumption that he knew the rabbinical commentary as well, this is by no means an automatic consequence. As a matter of fact, there is a major gap between rabbinical Hebrew and Biblical Hebrew, to cross which might well be the work of several years. Mr. Conklin urges that Milton never spanned that gap.

His arguments are not absolutely convincing. Though it is true that Milton could have acquired from Schindler's or Buxtorf's lexicons some of the information which Fletcher says he got from the rabbis, Mr. Conklin still has not explained the turns of language by which Milton implies to the reader of the *Apology for Smectymnuus* that he has read the rabbis and the Targums. If he had read no deeper than Schindler's commentary on a single word in the original Hebrew text, then surely he was guilty of a sort of intellectual pretension, not to say dishonesty, in writing a casual phrase like "as the Rabbines expound," and another phrase out of *"Ionathan, or Onkelos the Targumists,"* from whom he pretends to quote directly. Besides, Mr. Conklin invokes, to explain half a page of the *Apology,* no less than four books, the lexicons of Buxtorf and Schindler, Weemse's *Christian Synagogue,* and Hottinger's *Thesaurus Philologicus.* There is no specific evidence that Milton knew any of these books. There is, to be sure, no specific evidence that he knew the Buxtorf Hebrew Bible either, though we do know that he had and read a Hebrew Bible which may as well have been Buxtorf's as anyone else's. But it is not clear, in any event, that acquaintance with four books in English and Latin constitutes a lesser presumption than acquaintance with one Hebrew Bible, from which Milton might have deciphered, with difficulty and perhaps with help, crucial passages of the rabbinical commentators.

This possibility is notably enhanced by the passage from *The Doctrine and Discipline of Divorce,* in which Milton, for the only time in his career, cites specific rabbis on a substantial point of interpretation. Mr. Conklin is not ungrudging in his handling of this evidence. No doubt Drusius cites Rashi and Kimchi on the point at issue; but Milton cites Kimchi and two other rabbis, Ibn Ezra and Ben Gerson, and he gives the actual words of Ben Gerson. If he obtained any major part of this information from Drusius, he was certainly dealing in bad faith with the reader by pretending to have it from the original; and he could not possibly have obtained it all from Drusius. No doubt Milton's point was already well proved out of Grotius, the Septuagint, Josephus, and "the Chaldean" (Mr. Conklin apparently accepts Milton's use of the Targum in this particular spot, though he argues against it in discussing the passage from the *Apology*). But if the citation of rabbis was strictly unnecessary to his argument, this fact emphasizes, instead of diminishing, their availability to Milton. To say that "it is not likely that Milton learned rabbinical Hebrew solely for the purpose of adding two sentences to his divorce tract" [*BCHM,* p. 65] is to make a merely rhetorical point. If he ever approached the rabbis, Milton approached them seeking serious answers to major religious questions. This was the way in which he approached all the exegetes and commentators; and he has left, in the foreword to the *Christian Doctrine,* a record of how he was disappointed by "wretched shifts," "formal sophisms," "quibbles," "misconstruction of Scripture," and "the hasty deduction of erroneous inferences." A student of Milton's reading should be aware that a man does not always approach a book for the things that he finds in it. On the larger issue, it may be worth noting that all the specific evidence for a Miltonic interest in rabbinical commentators dates from a period of a few years in the early 1640's, when he was furiously busy rethinking his religious, political, and domestic situation—when he was searching for authorities to use in controversies and trying to reconcile contradictory authorities in the interests of his own peace of mind. Outside this period, Milton's references to Hebrew materials are neither precise nor spontaneous; by the time of the *First Defence* they are infrequent and uniformly contemptuous; and throughout the rest of the career, this tone is never altered.

Thus it seems safe to presume, on this much-mooted question, that Milton had, at one time in his career, a little more acquaintance with the rabbinical commentators than Mr. Conklin will allow; but it seems even safer to presume that they had far less influence on him than Mr. Fletcher has tried to establish, especially in connection with *Paradise Lost*. For the real objection to the theory of rabbinical influence on Milton the epic poet is the imbecilic role in which it casts John Milton. Unfortunately for M. Saurat's theory, since *Milton: Man and Thinker* was published, the *Zohar* has been translated into English. It reveals itself as a tangled, confused, elaborate mass of mumbo jumbo. The rabbinical commentators are, with one exception, untranslated; they deliver, unless every reporter does them an injustice and the samples available in English are utterly unrepresentative, an enormous lot of mystical and strained interpretation, a great many dusty, often puerile legends, and some technical points of grammar and philology. Did John Milton construct an epic poem by pulling out of this great black bag such materials as are noted in the fourth chapter of Mr. Fletcher's last book? A gigantic commonplace, that the universe is surrounded by a crystalline sphere, could have been picked up from a thousand sources more immediate and explicit than the rabbis. Milton's major heresy, that the universe was not created *ex nihilo,* seems; as Mr. Conklin argues, far more likely to have been philological than philosophical in origin, based on nothing more than Milton's literal understanding of the word "created" in Genesis 1:1. The words "play" in *PL,* VII, 10, and "brooding" in I, 21, might have been derived from the Hebrew text without any commentators or from other sources (one from the Vulgate, the other from the Tremellius Bible); the "compasses" of VII, 225, might have been derived from the King James version; the presence of two auxiliary spirits at creation might have been authorized by the plural "Elohim" in Genesis itself, by Proverbs 8:1, or by Philo and a thousand years of Christian Platonism; and the idea that the earth was hung on a center which does not exist in reality is based on a misreading of Milton's VII, 242—the supposed parallel does not actually exist, either with the Hebrew text or with the rabbinical commentary.

A good many of the twenty items of evidence which make up Mr. Fletcher's fifth chapter are equally inconclusive and picayune. That Milton says worms crawl on the ground is undoubted [VII, 480–81]; but neither he nor anyone else ever had to go to Rabbi Rashi to learn this fact. Though Rashi says that birds were created from mud and Milton says they were hatched in "tepid Caves and Fens and Shoares," this is scanty evidence of borrowing. Milton could not in decency have the Lord roaming His countryside building nests in trees; the birds hatched out on the ground, and if they were near the water, it was because in Genesis 1:20, God said, "Let the waters bring forth abundantly the moving creature that hath life, and fowl that may fly above the earth. . . ." A whole group of Miltonic passages alleged to be from Rashi's commentary on Genesis may thus be dismissed as matters which Milton would have had no difficulty in gathering from the original Biblical text, whether he read it in English, Latin, Greek, Hebrew, or Low German. Of this order are passages like VII, 334–37, which directly paraphrases (except for one detail which is not in Rashi's commentary either) Genesis 2:5. So also with VII, 309–16, where Rashi has only one minor emphasis, even more minor in Milton, which is not to be found in the original passage, Genesis 1:11, 12. In describing the creation of Adam, Milton says that the Lord made man outside the garden and then put him in it; Rashi says this too, but so does Genesis 2:7, 8, 15. The idea that Adam and Eve were vegetarians in Eden is so plain in Genesis 1:29, and so closely involved with the very idyllic character of Eden itself that one scarcely sees any necessity of invoking the rabbi on this point. As for Milton's assertion that before God's edict,

> over all the face of Earth
> Main Ocean flow'd [VII, 278–79],

it hardly seems beyond the intellectual powers of John Milton to deduce this from Genesis 1:9, without rabbinical aid.

Almost as evanescent as these cobweb correspondences with the acts of creation are certain other ones involving Adam, Eve, and the Serpent, as well as the Father and Son. Milton agrees with Rashi, it cannot be denied, that Adam and Eve had sexual relations in Paradise; but Augustine agrees with both of them, and adds a great deal of peculiar and particular speculation of a very refined nature [*De civitate Dei,* XIV, 22–26]. Not much can be made of the idea that Milton owed to Rashi the jealousy which he represented as motivating Satan; for though Rashi makes this suggestion in his commentary on Genesis 3:1, the idea is also in Augustine [*De civitate Dei,* XIV, 11]. It is perfectly true that Milton in V, 600ff. had the Lord announce to the "Empyreal Host" the begetting of that Son who in V, 837–38, is said to have created

> All things, ev'n thee, and all the Spirits of Heav'n
> By him created in thir bright degrees.

But though Mr. Fletcher thinks this contradiction is explained by Rashi's notion that the cosmos was created all at once and the various parts produced as needed, it is clear that if Milton had really had Rashi's idea in mind, he would have known how to express it better than by writing a flat, unexplained contradiction. By substituting "revealed" for "begot" in V, 603,

> This day have I begot whom I declare,

he might have avoided all confusion. That he did not adopt this easy expedient is no doubt evidence of a sort that he did not have Rashi's concept in mind. Still, the passage as written undeniably invites confusion. When we have disposed of a rabbinical influence, the question of why Milton used "begot" in V, 603, does remain. It has been profusely and, one hopes, finally answered by Mr. Maurice Kelley [*SP,* XXXVIII, 252–65], who in concord with a clutch of earlier critics attributes to "begot" the metaphorical sense of "exalted" or "glorified." The few objections which remain are chiefly artistic in nature, most easily answered by declaring the crucial "begot" an artistic oversight akin to the triple repetition of "stood" in VI, 579–81, or an ill-advised influence from Psalms 2:7.

For two passages derived by Mr. Fletcher from Rashi's commentary, there does seem to be no satisfactory original in the Bible or in any of the obvious literary sources. After naming the creatures, Milton's Adam expresses discontent with his single condition and is then quizzed by a playful Deity about his need for a helpmeet, while the Bible shows God having the first idea about man's need for woman. Milton also asserts, like Rashi and Yosippon, that one of Eve's motives for giving Adam the apple was to ensure that she would not die while he lived and took another wife

[IX, 827–30]. Hints for these passages are not found in obvious sources; without bothering to look in more recondite places, let us suppose that for these two incidents there is no possible influence other than the rabbis; are we now obliged to presume that this influence was actually exerted? The character of these two passages is such as to make it particularly doubtful that Milton was influenced by anyone at all. Both incidents involve the attribution of a motive to characters of the Bible. Adam and Eve as anyone discovers them in Genesis are outline figures, to whom Milton was obliged to attribute a good many motives and speeches in order to fill them out to human shape. He was not hesitant about doing this; a good deal of what he would have described as the poem's "invention" consisted of finding appropriate motives and language for a sequence of events given by his authorities. Especially in this matter of the relations between the sexes, some of his deepest feelings came out in expressions which went far beyond the original Biblical passages. For example, Eve's suicide suggestion [X, 966ff.] and Adam's counterargument are not even mentioned in Genesis or in Rashi's commentary, and in the very passage where Eve expresses fear of a rival, still another motive is put forth, a desire to "keep the odds of Knowledge in my power" [IX, 820], which is apparently original with Milton. So that the passages where there is no obvious literary parallel, like those where the only parallel is that provided by the rabbis, turn out to be just those where Milton's deep personal feelings would be most likely to spill over repeatedly into the vessel of his fable. Of all topics in the world, John Milton had least need of a rabbi to inform him of these two—why a man contemplates taking a wife and why a wife contemplates gaining advantage over her husband.

These, then, are the major points of evidence linking

Paradise Lost to rabbinical commentary on the Bible; I do not think there is one single item of evidence which is incompatible with the assumption that Milton was a man of strong poetic instincts and social convictions who knew the Bible text well in four languages, who, twenty years before he published *Paradise Lost,* may have read some but not all of the rabbinical commentators, and who had forgotten most of what he read. To presume a closer intimacy is not only to multiply assumptions beyond necessity; it is to send John Milton scurrying through crabbed medieval volumes in search of authority for representing worms crawling on the ground and men wanting women.

The arguments from "angelology" which make up the last half of Mr. Fletcher's book are even more marginal than those which relate to rabbinical commentary. They center upon such points as the fact that by a complex deduction from IV, 782–85, Gabriel can be seen to face the East at this point, and a medieval Jewish tradition says his station is to the east of the heavenly throne. Or a long argument is built up to connect Milton with Bochart's *Hierozoicon* or Spencer's *De legibus Hebraeorum,* books published in 1663 and 1685 respectively, simply because Milton uses the name "Azazel" in I, 534. That Milton could have got "Azazel" from the Book of Enoch through versions as immediate as *Purchas His Pilgrimage* [Whiting, *MLM,* p. 213] is either ignored or forgotten.

The forlorn hope of the argument for rabbinical influence is that though the passages making up the evidence may seem weak individually, cumulatively they are strong. Though none of them is conclusive by itself, as a group—it may be said—they provide evidence of rabbinical borrowings. But the cumulative argument is obviously weakened by the circumstance that Milton frequently and the commentators always wrote with the Biblical text in mind.

They often had a common source; no wonder, then, that they often agree, especially in random trifles and matters of phrasing. The only form in which the cumulative argument would carry real conviction would be a complete listing of all the similarities and differences between Milton and his supposed Hebrew originals. Twenty-five significant similarities out of twenty-six passages would mean one thing; twenty-five trifling similarities out of a thousand passages would be something else again. But it is precisely in those matters where the rabbis depart most strikingly from the original Genesis text or elaborate most remarkably on it that we find Milton differing most notably from them. Rashi has about a dozen very distinctive interpretations of verses in the first two chapters of Genesis; he says, for instance, that the Lord created woman for man so that people should not say Adam was like God in having no partner; he says the serpent offered Eve a chance to build other worlds, like God; he says the tree was a fig tree, and that Adam and Eve took its leaves after the other trees refused theirs; he says that Adam and Eve sinned at about the tenth hour, in the evening; and he says that the serpent originally had four feet, which were cut off for a curse [*Rashi on the Pentateuch,* tr. J. H. Lowe (London, 1929)]. In not one of these details does Milton follow him or reject him or show the least awareness, either favorably or unfavorably colored, of Rabbi Rashi's interpretation.

If Mr. Fletcher could maintain with evidence his assertion that Rabbi Ibn Ezra was responsible for Milton's denial of creation *ex nihilo* and for his corollary doctrine that matter cannot be annihilated, that would be a proof indeed. But Mr. Conklin is abrupt and absolute: "Milton's position . . . is uniquely his, and was independently derived from his exegetical conclusions alone" [*BCHM,* p. 67]. Certainly it seems far more characteristic of the man to take a strong, straightforward, literal position on the interpretation of Genesis 1:1 and stick to it in spite of logical embarrassments than to beat through the thickets of obscure rabbinical commentary to find an authority whom he never so much as mentioned. And it is clear that a useful guide to the whole field of Miltonic readings, though it has been little employed and even less avowed, is the character of John Milton as we know it and as he himself conceived it. Not to labor all the characteristics, he was a protestant individualist, and, above all, in *Paradise Lost,* he was an epic poet. The rabbinical method of exegesis, analysis, and mystical intuition seems downright incompatible with the writing of a long narrative poem, broad and sweeping in its effects and heroic in its dimensions. The grammarians of Alexandria, so far as they succeeded in converting Homer into a perpetrator of muddled moral platitudes expressed as allegories, destroyed him as a narrative poet. The price of Milton the rabbinical scholar seems to be the conversion of England's greatest writer of epic into a seventeenth-century amalgam of Madame Blavatsky and a Byzantine mosaicist. Perhaps Milton had a touch of the mosaicist in him; one is entitled to hope that he had a minimum of Madame Blavatsky. In the light of considerations like these, the rabbis do not seem likely to maintain their claim to more than an obscure corner in one short, crowded period of Milton's life, far removed from his immortal epic.

The image of Milton as a rabbinical scholar represents one high point in the tendency, set under way many years ago by Professor Greenlaw, to create a new Milton capable of rising above Professor Raleigh's oblique but disturbing dictum that *Paradise Lost* is a monument to dead ideas. By liberalizing the poet's theology (liberalizing it sometimes into obscurantist confusion) or by emphasizing his humanism, scholars undertook to rescue Milton from an odious imputation. Perhaps the more cautious course would have been to decline Raleigh's gambit altogether. So long as we assume that Milton's ideas must be "alive" and "contemporary," we shall have to keep changing them to conform to the definition of those highly mutable words. It was strain enough when Professor Patterson invited his students to associate Milton with "modern thinkers, such as Bergson" [*Student's Milton,* "Textual Notes," p. 88]; must the present generation struggle to demonstrate Milton's essential sympathy with Whitehead or Heidegger? After all, Professor Raleigh said nothing worse than that "Paradise Lost is not the less an eternal monument because it is a monument to dead ideas" [*Milton* (New York, 1900), p. 85]. It will be a dark day for criticism when we think that a work of art cannot continue to arouse living and vivid feelings long after its central ideas are dead; "organic unity" will have triumphed then, with a vengeance.

But efforts to warm the frozen labyrinth of Milton's thought have had many aspects more moderate than the rabbinical; and in recent years, perhaps as a revulsion from elaborate and finespun theories, the argument has been widely put forth that Milton's ideas were very largely conventional and traditional in humanist Renaissance circles. Instead of leaping across the slim spans of similarity which bind *Paradise Lost* to various obscure and heretical books, scholars have undertaken to find as much as possible of Milton's materials in the commonplaces of the day—in the summaries, compilations, popular histories, and literary encyclopedias which were available to him and to the average well-educated reader of his time. There is no doubt that this is taking hold of the stick by the right end. Before venturing on esoteric influences, it is the part of mere intellectual economy to make what one can of those books which were immediately available to Milton. What is more, it is always useful to know, irrespective of possible direct influences on Milton's writing, what sort of intellectual milieu he worked with, what sort of information he could count on finding widely dispersed among his readers. But radical oversimplification results when we assume that Milton read only the conventional, widely dispersed books and read them always in a conventional, orthodox spirit. Mr. C. S. Lewis, however valuable his contribution in rescuing Milton from the sentimental Satanists, has gone far toward substituting a figure of whom it is unthinkable that he should ever have departed the Church of England, advocated divorce reforms, defended regicide, or anticipated a proximate Second Coming. How the devil did this "grammarian, swordsman, [and] musician with a predilection for the fugue" [*PPL,* p. 79] come to range himself with an immoderate, inspirational figure like Oliver Cromwell? Why was he not enthralled by the Beauty of Holiness instead? While admitting that some small, ambiguous heresies have crept into the poem, Mr. Lewis argues that *Paradise Lost* is predominantly Augustinian, hierarchical, and Catholic [*PPL,* p. 81]; and he explains Milton's support of the regicides as an assertion of true hierarchy against tyrants. With minor exceptions, he does not even find the poem "specifically Protestant or Puritan" [*PPL,* p. 91]; but if he had pursued the question of tyrants and kings a little further, he might have found both a notable source of heresy and some of Milton's missing Protestantism. Who is to judge when a doctrine is orthodox and when it is heretical, when a king is a proper king and when he is a tyrant? Milton's answer to these questions would have been clear and unhesitating; and it would have been neither Augustinian, hierarchical, nor Catholic. For Milton, the proper judge of what, to be technical, are controversies in faith and religion was the inward conscience of the individual Christian, as enlightened by heavenly grace and guided by right reason. It would not have been a church council, the consensus of the fathers, or any clerical body whatever. If it is true that *Paradise Lost* does not obtrude heterodox conclusions on the reader, it is no less true that the ground of Milton's Protestantism is not far to seek in the poem. Among other places, it is implicit in the image, which recurs over and over again in no very dark or hidden corners of *Paradise Lost,* of truth as abandoned by the many, but defended and triumphantly asserted by one redeeming individual known in his various types as Adam, Abdiel, Noah, Moses, Enoch, or Christ. Against the image of hierarchy which dwells secure and unchallenged in the bosom of Mr. Lewis' Milton or Mr. Rajan's, one may place a much more troubled and troubling image used by the actual Milton. It is found in that passage of the *Areopagitica* where Milton compares the search for truth's mangled particles to Isis' search after the fragments of Osiris. Hierarchy, no doubt, is the pure and radiant image of what ought to be; but for the sad friends of truth, "such as durst appear," the everyday image of life is a piecing together of dusty fragments. *Paradise Lost* must be true to both these images; indeed, it is nothing less than an account of how man's life, which ought to have been the one, came to consist of the other. And no account of Milton or his epic can conceivably be accurate which precludes the possibility that the poet went a lonely journey, looking for truth in strange places, and discovered there some fairly uncouth fragments of the divine corpus. Mr. Lewis, to be fair, does not preclude this possibility; he does minimize it.

The question of Milton's reading does not enter directly into Mr. Lewis' book, though he polemicizes vigorously against Professor Saurat and makes some point of associating *Paradise Lost* only with volumes which already have, or can be given, a respectable and orthodox tinge. The several works which do emphasize Milton's indebtedness to conventional, orthodox Christian thought and the literary traditions in which that thought found expression are perhaps best approached semantically; for the way in which their assertion is framed differentiates them more significantly than the evidence with which they support it.[2] The late Grant McColley, for example, began his learned study in the backgrounds of Milton's epic with the observation that "the hexameral literature stands as the most important single source of *Paradise Lost*" [*BOE,* p. 15]. One would think it might be safer, if less striking, to say that the Book of Genesis was the most important single source of Milton's poem; but, leaving this point aside, one should note that many important questions are begged by stating the question in this form. By treating the hexameral literature as a "single source," McColley was able to dispense very largely with evidence showing that Milton was acquainted with a specific book. Because Milton knew, beyond any question, certain books in the hexameral tradition, the critic assumed his right to discuss all the books in the tradition and their influence on the poet. A major question may be raised as to the sense in which St. Basil and Joseph Beaumont constitute a single source of influence on anybody; an even sharper question may arise as to whether Milton's reading of St. Basil constitutes evidence that he read Joseph Beaumont.

Where it is not explicit and conclusive, the evidence that Milton was acquainted with, or made use of, any particular book is commonly a matter of delicately balanced probabili-

[2] Grant McColley, *Paradise Lost: The Birth of an Epic* (Chicago, 1940); B. Rajan, *Paradise Lost and the 17th Century Reader* (London, 1947); Taylor, *MUDB;* Allen, *THV;* Whiting, *MLM.*

ties. A single random similarity, a casual turn of expression, a thought which might be derived from a widely known source by any man possessed of the powers of reason and the ability to read—these are not evidence sufficient to establish securely the fact that Milton knew a crabbed medieval treatise or a lumbering moral discourse. One of the symptoms of McColley's weakness for attributing a book to Milton's library without making a detailed estimate of the probabilities is his occasional comment that a certain book or author was known to the seventeenth century [*BOE*, pp. 10, 34]. The book was known to somebody in that wildly diversified hundred-year span; therefore it was known to Milton. To be sure, there is sometimes no question at all that Milton did know a particular author or volume; precisely for this reason, it is misleading to huddle all the hexameral authors together under the tacit implication that because Milton was acquainted with Augustine, Philo, and Basil, he was therefore acquainted with Rupertus Tuitiensis, Moses Bar Cepha, Valmarana, and Valvasone.

A degree of immunity accrues to all source hunters of the McColley persuasion from the circumstance that the negative proof in a matter of influence is notoriously hard to establish. But a very rough sort of index to Milton's reading is provided by the authors whom he explicitly mentions. Granted, it is silly to suppose that Milton mentions every author he ever read; conceded, that *Paradise Lost* contains many buried verbal reminiscences of sacred and classical authors which cannot be challenged; still, we do know from biographical and autobiographical comments that major areas of Milton's life were devoted to reading the Bible and the classics. But we do not know that Milton ever devoted any time to reading hexameral literature as such. He does not mention hexameral literature; he does not use the noun "hexameron." And though he is said to mention six thousand authors by name, he does not mention the majority of the writers who are lumped in the hexameral literature. Crude as this procedure is, one may get an image of the problem in its general outlines by checking McColley's index against the index of the *Columbia Milton*. Discounting those proper names, chiefly of Miltonic scholars and editors, where a Miltonic influence is out of the question, one finds McColley referring to about one hundred fifty authors as influences on Milton. He omits, he says, a few of peripheral significance, so that one presumes a more particular significance is intended to attach to the remainder. Now of this significant remainder, more than two-thirds were never mentioned by Milton in his entire career.

The figure of two-thirds is unjust and approximate in various ways. Among the authors not mentioned by Milton it includes a number of names which are introduced only in lists, without any serious argument that Milton knew the writings associated with them; and some of the writers whom he never mentioned Milton surely knew—Du Bartas, for example. On the other hand, among the authors whom Milton did know are included a good many whose influence on Milton has never been questioned and who indicate nothing in particular about the hexameral tradition—for example, Homer, Virgil, Dante, Hesiod, Augustine, and Diodorus Siculus. Also included among authors known to Milton are those whose names he mentions in any context whatever at any point in his collected works, whether or not he evinces knowledge of the particular work which is said to lie within the hexameral tradition. Altogether, one might adjust the statistic in various ways without radically altering the general condition which it suggests, that two out of three authors whom McColley associated with Milton are related to the poet only by conjecture. Their connection with Milton depends on a chain of reasoning, more or less consecutive in nature and more or less probable in its conclusions, but which in fact the reader of *Paradise Lost: The Birth of an Epic* is rarely in a position to estimate for himself. Certainly a temple in which the superstructure of surmise and conjecture is twice as extensive as the foundation of fact does not seem like the most solidly grounded of architectures.

The problem is one of initial presumptions. If we are going to impute to Milton acquaintance with an author whom he does not mention—and sometimes we must and should—let it be at least for a specific and substantial reason, either philosophical or literary. Milton's acquaintance with Du Bartas, a subject of observation and discussion for nearly two hundred years now, provides some striking examples of extravagant and unnecessary guesswork. Even to have a discussion here we must burke the inconvenient fact that Milton never in his entire lifetime mentioned Du Bartas or his poem or the poem's translator by name. But let us suppose that he knew the *Divine Weeks and Works;* what probably was his opinion of this production? Though he would naturally be interested in a long Protestant poem on sacred themes, though in his youth he may well have admired Du Bartas' muscle-bound metaphors and jog-trot meter, though he included in his epic at least one complete line [III, 373] which parallels a line of Du Bartas, the mature Milton is unlikely to have dissented radically from Dryden's judgment that Sylvester's translation was a piece of "antiquated fustian." At least, there is no evidence that the Milton who wrote *Paradise Lost* had any opinion of Sylvester's work more favorable than Dryden's. Milton's own style had emancipated itself from Sylvestrisms; in the nature of things, he is unlikely to have thought highly of an author whose literary tastes and talents were unashamedly pedestrian. (The complete silence of both Milton and Phineas Fletcher regarding Sylvester's existence, in the teeth of the fact that both men pretty surely knew Sylvester's work, suggests that the elder poet enjoyed among England's aggressively Protestant, post-Spenserian versifiers a certain underground, shamefaced popularity, akin to the popularity of Mr. Michael Gold among the proletarian authors of the 1930's and '40's.)

It is clear, then, that the evidence of a borrowing from Du Bartas should be rather more cogent and explicit than that required to establish a borrowing from Spenser, Augustine, or Grotius, authors whom we know that Milton not only read but respected. Yet many of the items which were adduced by Professor McColley as evidence of Milton's debt to Du Bartas consist of the merest commonplaces or the most irrelevant and incidental details. In opening the fourth part of the second day of the second week, Du Bartas asks the Lord, in Sylvester's translation, that his spirit may be "rapt above the pole," and Milton [VII, 23] says he is now to sing,

> Standing on Earth, not rapt above the Pole.

The correspondence of language is presumably evidence that Milton had read Sylvester and was either compulsively moved to imitate him or else wanted in the invocation to Book VII to contrast himself with Du Bartas. The first point is granted for the sake of discussion. The second indicates a distracting psychological peculiarity or a miserable want of verbal invention in the poet; and the final suggestion is artistically disastrous. If Milton is not, as he seems to be, contrasting the first part of his poem with the second, but instead is slyly setting himself up as *less* ambitious than Du Bartas (in the teeth of I, 16), then he simply is an incompetent bungler in verse. His thought is awkward in itself, untrue, and ill formed; and he has given it a slovenly expression. Elsewhere in McColley's volume [*BOE*, p. 64] we find it urged as proof of influence that both Milton and Du Bartas concede that their list of insects is incomplete. Perhaps the very large number and slightly undignified character of the creatures in question may have something to do with this very acute observation. Or, the point is made that Milton's "smelling gourd" [VII, 321] should be explained as a reminiscence of the "fine pepper" which Du Bartas says grew up on the third day; this would avoid Bentley's emendation to "swelling," which otherwise seems attractive enough [see above p. 96]. No doubt pepper smells; but it usually occurs in the form of berries, not gourds, and even if it did occur as gourds, Milton is here describing classes of vegetables, not obscure botanical species; nor, for that matter, is he writing a poem which requires a gloss from Du Bartas before it can be understood. His usual manner of adapting the phrases of others never involves the obscuring of his own lines; an echo from Virgil or Ovid is presented as lagniappe for the learned, but it does not substitute for sense in the English. Milton is not more likely to have used Du Bartas as a crutch for his epic. In the matter of the creation of light, Milton is said [*BOE*, p. 54] to imitate Du Bartas, but with this curious original touch, that he has got the story backwards. In what sense this constitutes proof of influence one does not quite know. Certainly it results in an odd image of the poetic mind, which, while writing an immortal epic forwards, managed to paraphrase a clumsy piece of didactic translation backwards.

It would be unfair to leave the impression that all McColley's argument, still less Taylor's, is on this level. But both critics are alike in treating as grist to their mill almost every random similarity, every conventional epithet, in which Milton and Du Bartas agree; and both fall upon the dilemma that the parallels between Milton's poetic expression and that of Du Bartas rarely involve anything but the crudest sort of raw materials—Milton calls the sun a lamp and so does Du Bartas, Milton says man was to be the masterwork of creation and Du Bartas says the same thing in more words—while the broad structural features of Milton's epic parallel the Bible about as closely as they do Du Bartas. Hence there is no real reason to go beyond the position assumed long ago by Professor E. N. S. Thompson [*Essays on Milton* (New Haven, 1914), pp. 162–64], that Du Bartas is usefully representative of a mass of conventional material to which Milton had access and of which he made not very lavish use as the raw material of *Paradise Lost*. Mr. Taylor is on safe ground when he speaks of Du Bartas as a mine from which Milton quarried some of the material for *Paradise Lost* [*MUDB*, p. xv]. But this is not at all the same thing as saying that Milton imitated Du Bartas or derived from the French poet the diction of his epic, far less its plan. There can be no doubt that Milton read some hexameral authors; perhaps, though he had no real reason to bore himself beyond the third repetition, he read as many as six of the hexamera themselves. But he got from them nothing which he did not radically transform, in such ways as those brilliantly indicated by Mr. Rajan [*SCR*, pp. 39–52] and Mr. Arthur Barker [*PQ*, XXVIII, 17–30]. To suggest that he confused his thought or muddled his expression in order to parallel or reverse a hexameral author is to create an odd image of the epic mind at work; to allow Milton the virtues of a skillful jointer of fragments is to deny him those of an inventive rhetorician; and to clutter the poem with endless analogues, each of which may or may not be significant, but which as a group must inevitably contain a great many irrelevancies, redundancies, and contradictions, is not to advance notably our appreciation of the poet.

One of the great temptations of the influence study as it has been practiced upon Milton seems to be the tendency to reduce all varieties of influence to a one-for-one verbal correspondence, as if one poet must always experience another as a piece of blotting paper experiences wet ink. But Milton would not have been Milton if he had not been a critical reader; and, aside from various stylistic lessons, he could scarcely have failed to learn from a reading of Du Bartas how inadequately extended moralizing substitutes for dramatic interest. A glance at the *Divine Weeks and Works* may suggest a reason for the prominence of Satan in the first four books at least as valid as some of those which have been proposed. Milton had before him a horrible example of what happens to a long poem on sacred themes when it loses narrative force and becomes discursively moralistic. But this is not the sort of influence which can be tabulated, cross-referenced, or entered in a card catalogue.

Mechanical conceptions of literary influence also provide a disturbing aspect of McColley's efforts to relate Milton's catalogue of pagan deities to a popular theogony such as Alexander Ross's *Pansebeia.* It may very well be that Milton's list resembles Ross's more closely than it does anyone else's; but there is a major incongruity in the thought that Milton, who had been studying ancient languages and religions for at least thirty-five years before Ross's book was written, should have adopted, the minute it was published, the terminology and organization of this popular digest. If Milton ever did mention Alexander Ross, it was in a little epigram on *Mel Heliconium* which has been inconclusively attributed to him. But the attribution is less than inconclusive; it is downright unlikely. Probabilities do not suggest that Milton in 1642 would have gone out of his way to inscribe complimentary verses to a man who is referred to, in the title of the verses themselves, as the king's chaplain. It is particularly unlikely that Milton, who ordinarily had a scholar's ferocious contempt for the cheap learning to be picked up from compendia, collections, and indexes, would have broken his rule against commendatory versicles to praise a little bundle of secondhand allegorical commonplaces and to praise them as improving on Ovid, no less. In any event, whether Milton knew Ross or not, one may wonder why the man who at the age of twenty-one could write the poem "On the Morning of Christ's Nativity" without consulting Alexander Ross's *Pansebeia* should have required direct assistance from it when in his fifties he composed *Paradise Lost.* Of all things, learning does not deteriorate at this pace. As with Ross, so too with Natale Conti, the Milanese mythographer. As a matter of fact, Milton had heard of Conti's book [letter from Diodati, *Columbia Milton,* XII, 308–09], which is a handy summary of classic myths and Renaissance allegories. But he no more allowed it to shape his epic than a modern poet depends on the *Encyclopaedia Britannica* for the ordering of his verse. Conti, no less than Ross, is helpful in providing evidence of what interpretations were current and what information about the myths was popularly disseminated; but as a Miltonic "source" he is not significant. Of its own nature, what he says is not distinctive; it has no more shape than any other encyclopedic production; and above all, dependence on such a source is incompatible with Milton's known habits of mind and linguistic accomplishments. The competent general scholar who annotated Pindar and Lycophron and read the Hebrew Bible did not have to depend for elementary information about the ancient deities on Alexander Ross or Natale Conti. Professor Hughes makes ideal use of Conti, holding him up, with classic restraint, to illustrate conventions and highlight Miltonic departures from them, but he constantly adds that the same materials were available to the poet from many other sources.

A recurrent logical oddity of Milton studies is the way in which the argument that certain of Milton's ideas were not esoteric or individual subtly transmutes itself into the argument that Milton knew certain individual books, sometimes fairly esoteric ones. In order to show that Milton was familiar with a story which had been monotonously repeated by seventeen centuries of commentators and exegetes, one must prove that he had read Du Bartas. And so, in order to show that Milton was steeped in the traditional themes of the Renaissance, Mr. Don C. Allen imputes to him acquaintance with a number of books which he may or may not have read but which seem notably irrelevant to the context in which they are invoked. For example, in explaining why Milton wrote "Lycidas" in pastoral form, Mr. Allen refers within four pages [*THV*, pp. 55–58], not only to Polybius' account of Arcadia in Book IV of the *History*, but to Guarini's defense of pastoral poetry, the opinions of Diomedes the Grammarian (who is present under false auspices), Servius, Probus, Sabinus, Donatus, Rapin, Fontenelle, Pierre de Laudun, and William Webbe, with a note on a dissenting opinion of Puttenham, a qualification from J. C. Scaliger, and a license proposed by Minturno. Discounting Fontenelle (born 1657) as largely outside the range of Milton's career, thirteen names are cited here; and of these thirteen names, Milton himself did not see fit to mention, in his entire life, more than three. No doubt Mr. Allen is justified in appealing to the others in order to establish a climate of opinion; but if this is his purpose, it seems odd to omit mention of Theocritus, Sidney, and John Fletcher, with all of whom Milton was definitely familiar and who would have contributed far more to any climate which the author of "Lycidas" could have breathed than Fontenelle, Rapin, or Diomedes Grammaticus. To say Mr. Allen is wrong would be absurd; in the broadest sense, he is right that Milton wrote "Lycidas" as a pastoral because the form was familiar and traditional and offered certain liberties and immunities not elsewhere available. But to list a dozen Renaissance writers, editors, and critics as Milton's authorities is downright misleading; quite aside from the fact that Milton gave no sign of knowing most of them, citation of this sort suggests a formality on Milton's part, a concern for strict categories and literal precedents, which is a critic's virtue, not a poet's, and a most un-Miltonic quality anyway. Without being able to prove the point by any strict canon, I should think Milton got more hints for the free stanza form of "Lycidas" from Tasso, Dante, and Spenser [F. T. Prince, *The Italian Element in Milton's Verse* (Oxford, 1954), and Ants Oras, *MP,* LII, 12–22] than from any dictum of Scaliger's; and if he rummaged through a dozen Renaissance critics for permission to write a pastoral elegy, it was certainly more pains than he took on more important matters.

"Lycidas" itself Mr. Allen describes as "a sensitive re-echoing of ancient elegies, as well as those of Petrarch, Boccaccio, Sannazaro, Castiglione, and Spenser" [*THV,* p. 58]. There is no doubt that "Lycidas" is a pastoral elegy and that the authors cited all wrote pastoral elegies of one sort or another. But in what sense could one describe *Middlemarch* as a re-echoing of *Moll Flanders* and *Emma,* or *Modern Love* as a re-echoing of *Astrophel and Stella?* The echo is there, so far as all works within a genre have similarities; and if an echo exists, it can no doubt be heard by those who are interested in listening for such things. If one approaches "Lycidas" with any other pastoral elegy whatever in mind, echoes will be heard; but the sense in which these echoes are the poem itself is a problem for the metaphysicians. It is customary, I think, to argue that the more richly one reads a poem like "Lycidas," the more fully one is aware of the overtones which arise from its fulfilling certain conventions and defying others, the better one will appreciate it. Perhaps this is so. But there is a point at which this sort of appreciation, however legitimate in itself, stifles the poem as a form of assertion, a point where the echoes drown out the original melody. "Lycidas" is more than the sum of its similarities to and differences from other pastoral elegies; and the sort of virtuosity which reads it in counterpoint with five other pastoral elegies may very well blur and confuse as many harmonies as it creates.

The study of Milton's reading offers, in fact, a major problem in critical tact. The modern investigator suffers, not only from his ignorance of much that the seventeenth century knew, but from his fresh rediscovery of much that the seventeenth century was slowly forgetting. His task is complicated by the enormous range of Renaissance, classical, and Biblically inspired material upon which Milton might have drawn in writing his major poems. It is rendered bewildering by the circumstance that Milton, though he was a man of wide and curious learning and the master of a complex, allusive style, chose to write his great epic about a fable at once primitive and universal, which he undertook to render in its broad and simple outlines. These are complexities enough, inherent in the materials; they are compounded when apologists undertake to help Milton along by modernizing an antiquated creed, humanizing a legalistic deity, or displaying universal knowledge. There is a sense in which Milton has positive meaning for our times, and there is a sense in which he is the product of his own circumstances; but these senses must somehow be held in balance. There is a sense in which the pursuit of his learning is an infinite task and another sense in which that learning is best appreciated as a dim, complex pattern in the background of a tapestry whose main outlines are clear, strong, and simple. Amid these obscurities, it has taken some time for students of Milton's learning to work their way back to Professor Hanford's early practice of starting with the actual list of books which Milton recorded, either deliberately or casually, as his reading, and of holding additions to a minimum. But in recent years a growing number of books and articles have undertaken to explore, instead of this or that particular debt of Milton's, the whole range of information and commonplace within which his thought existed and was communicated. Examples of this new deprecation of the specific influence are Mr. George Whiting's *Milton's Literary Milieu* and Mr. B. Rajan's *Paradise Lost and the 17th Century Reader*. Neither of these books has any particular ax to grind as to Milton's modernity or antiquity; both are concerned to minimize rather than to extend the amount of learning necessary to read *Paradise Lost*. Mr. Whiting in particular has set out to study Milton's literary milieu as Professor Bredvold in a classic volume some years ago studied Dryden's intellectual milieu. Though largely indifferent to the question of literary influence proper, he is careful to distinguish between books which Milton certainly read and those which he left no record of knowing; without forcing casual phrases and conventional epithets into a pattern of correspondence, he yet shows some of the currents of opinion, usage, and information out of which Milton shaped his poetry. Perhaps he does not adequately suggest the shaping quality and controlling interests of Milton's imagination; in studying a milieu, it is always hard to take full account of the growing, changing creatures which complexly adapt themselves to it and it to themselves. Perhaps his performance is not in all instances on the level of his theory; in a field like mythology it is particularly easy to overestimate the one compendious influence, which has an insidious way of seeming a much more economical assumption than a dozen scattered influences. Thus, though Mr. Whiting's general account of mythological backgrounds rightly emphasizes some half-dozen different volumes, all easy of access and copiously informative, his account of Belial is tied, perhaps too narrowly, to the reputation of this unpleasant deity in contemporary Puritan polemic. But questions like this concern relatively minor nuances of emphasis; what is important is that the minute we escape from the concept of limited, specific influence, we breathe a fresh air. The new studies of Milton's learning are most impressive in their perception that Milton read and wrote in depth, that behind Raleigh, Purchas, or for that matter *Pansebeia,* are often found other versions of a fact or fable, versions of which one or several may have served as Milton's "source" even while he counted on his audience catching a reverberation from the more popular volume.

Without limiting themselves to popularizations, the new studies thus make clear something of the difference between books which Milton knew well and used freely and those which were tangential to his central poetic purposes. The histories of Diodorus and Raleigh, the atlases of Mercator and Ortelius, Goodman's popular *Fall of Man,* Burton's *Anatomy,* Augustine's *City of God,* Calvin's *Institutes,* Purchas or Fuller and Plutarch—when we add to these convenient and familiar volumes the Bible itself, Homer, Virgil, Ovid, Hesiod, and Spenser, there remains a surprisingly small area of Milton's poetry for which responsibility must be divided between more or less esoteric reading and the poet's own dramatic and creative instincts. Even at the risk of encouraging lazy readers, one is glad to find Milton a little relieved, by this new emphasis on the commonplace, of that onus which attaches to being the last reward of literary scholarship.

From the reader's point of view, there is of course no degree of learning which is "enough" to read a classic of world literature, particularly Milton's; whatever we know, whatever we do, adds a new dimension to our experience of the poetry. Milton would have been the first to insist that one cannot read his epic rightly without being a "magnanimous" man; and in this one adjective is implied a vast reading of the book of creatures, as well as printed volumes. But if our poet, like other poets, had some concept, however hazy, of an "adequate" reader, upon whom his poem might produce its main blunt effects without meeting major distortions or blank spots, his demands in the matter of reading would not, I think, have greatly exceeded the list given above.

In a word, Milton's own reading, like that which he expected of his readers, was not a set of particular points, not a nudge here from Virgil and a hitch there from the *Zohar;* it was a milieu, a medium. Mr. Whiting's terminology (to put the matter at its very lowest estimate) has the merit of making clear that *Paradise Lost* was not stuck together like a patchwork quilt out of snippets treasured up for the occasion. It is a journey through a landscape, familiar yet enchanted, which recedes on either side through a luxury of rhetorical flowers, through tags and patches and paraphrases, alien grammars and cognate myths, even while it leads us with strong, unhurried energy toward the quiet desolation of its conclusion. Milton triumphs in *Paradise Lost* through the sense of riches glimpsed in passing.

Donne's learning often exists to be dug up and crowed over; in this sense it is intrinsic, that after one has it there is often not much else. But Milton's great poem is, in this respect at least, agreeable to the rational esthetic of the dawning enlightenment; the learning of the poem, like much of its other decoration, is not organically united with its central theme and does not try to be. The esthetic principle behind this division was boldly asserted, in memorable words, by Thomas Hobbes, in his famous "Answer to Sir Will. D'Avenant's Preface Before *Gondibert*": "Judgment begets the strength and structure, and Fancy begets the ornaments of a Poem." By making the "strength and structure" of a poem products of a principle totally different from that which produced the "ornaments," Hobbes authorized and underlined a dichotomy which Milton and Dryden certainly exemplified, even if they did not (as Mr. Eliot once asserted) create it. Esthetically, it is not a very fashionable division in these days, when "organic unity" is an almost unchallenged critical catchword—though this is very far from an ultimate judgment. But historically, the fact is not to be blinked, whether one thinks it deplorable or not. Milton's learning is an ornament to the poem, not a structural part of it; it exists to be caught in passing or not caught at all but merely felt, and there is a genuine sense in which we read the poem best when we do not fully understand it. No doubt we blur the poem's outlines a bit when we do not search out the full impact of every phrase, reference, and image; we do far more radical damage to the basic values which Milton shared with Hobbes when we try to convert the poem's ornaments into its structure.

Almost the only context in which John Milton has ever been associated with the senior citizen from Malmesbury is that suggested by Miss Nicolson, who argued some years ago that *Paradise Lost* was designed as a direct refutation of Hobbist materialism [*SP*, XXIII, 405–33]. Miss Nicolson's prevailing bent in those days was to associate Milton, if not with the Cabala directly at least with the Cambridge Platonists, some of whom were notably aware of Cabalistic and pseudo-Cabalistic thought. Because a thoroughgoing spiritualist like Henry More was much exercised by the materialism of Hobbes, Miss Nicolson supposed, by a natural sort of transition, that Milton must have been too; and though one may feel that her case requires a good deal more proving then anyone has provided in the last thirty years,[3] there can be no doubt that Milton disagreed energetically with the political, religious, social, and mathematical views of Thomas Hobbes; so his widow declared explicitly to John Aubrey [*Brief Lives* (ed. A. Clark), II, 72].

But there are limitations to Milton's philosophical as

[3] Professors Willey [*17th Century Background,* chap. X, sec. 2, subs. 3] and Bush [*Paradise Lost in Our Time* (Ithaca, 1945), chap. II] have both urged that Milton's exaltation of right reason as against doctrinaire Calvinism is a grounds for associating him with the Cambridge Platonists. To be sure, a common interest in reason falls somewhat short of indicating a common interest in the Cabala; it may also be, in itself, a very limited similarity. Within the house of reason there are many apartments. Hobbes believed in reason, actual right reason, as much as Milton or Whichcote [see *Leviathan,* chap. V]; but it is clear that different men meant different particular things, then as now, when they used the same general terms. Whatever Milton's views of reason, as compared with those of Hooker or the Cambridge Platonists, we must not forget that Milton's reason led him to defend regicide, advocate divorce, and run the risk of political execution at the Restoration instead of making a quiet submission, accepting established authority, and occupying a placid college chair. Evidently "right reason" included almost as many distinct meanings during the seventeenth century as modern words like "peace" and "progressive." A very different conception of Milton's relations to the Cambridge Platonists might be obtained by emphasizing the word "conscience" instead of "reason," and by exploring what both parties considered the typical exercise of "conscience."

well as his literary differences with Hobbes, even though they are obscured by the tradition, now three centuries old and probably entrenched beyond correction, that Hobbes was a wicked and subversive cynic, whom a Good Man like Milton never thought of without horror. But Hobbes the ogre of the Restoration divine was a recent creation when *Paradise Lost* was being penned; Milton, though he testified privately to his dislike of Hobbes's principles, was no more likely to center his masterpiece on a refutation of them than a modern poet, writing in a bid for eternal fame, would be likely to concern himself in a central way with dianetics or technocracy. Moreover, Hobbes had been Bacon's favorite secretary, and Milton not only admired Bacon, but testified that Hobbes was "a man of great parts and a learned man" [*Brief Lives,* II, 72]. For both Hobbes and Milton shared a significant aspect of Baconian thought, a belief in the pre-eminence of the rational mind, which, by comparison with the emphasis laid on Bacon's late, modest, and indirect fostering of the experimental method, has been much neglected. Milton and Hobbes, like Bacon himself to some extent, were too profoundly committed to rationalism to feel any great, immediate need for experimental science as such [see Louis I. Bredvold, *The Intellectual Milieu of John Dryden* (Ann Arbor, 1934), chap. III]. I am not arguing that Milton and Hobbes were Baconians and nothing else, nor even that they were in general intellectual agreement with one another. The quality in question is perhaps only a general characteristic of a generation which came to maturity with a kind of sublime and untarnished confidence in the adequacy of its intellectual tools. Milton's confidence in right reason parallels Hobbes's confidence in geometry; and this very Baconian confidence in the empire of the mind was undoubtedly an element tending to render both Hobbes and Milton largely indifferent or hostile to the great scientific events of their day.

To put the matter in perspective, one may recall that the vital questions of the seventeenth century were, to a degree and in a sense unfamiliar to us, problems of politics and religion. The sort of information provided by experimental science was not only impossibly remote from conclusions of a public and social character, but those who built on the foundations of experimental science were often men who had already despaired of more eminent knowledge. *Scepsis scientifica* had not only a passive but an active aspect; men were free to investigate the minutiae of nature because they had left partisan convictions outside the laboratory; they were also impelled to investigate physical things because the war of abstract words had come to seem so inconclusive. But neither Milton nor Hobbes was really distinguished as a doubter; the intellectual patterning of both men was essentially doctrinaire and assertive. Thus both had ample reason to remain unstirred by a movement which, however remarkable in the ultimate consequences which now fill our foreground, must have seemed at the moment to squander every resource of the human intellect in order to set men stirring with dirty hands at little stinks.

Milton, in particular, could scarcely have been less moved by the new science, above all by the experimental spirit of it, which finds such energetic and pervasive expression in a poet like Cowley. It is a commonplace that geography and astronomy were the two sciences to which he was most attracted; they were, by no coincidence, the two least touched by the experimental method, and indeed they were scarcely susceptible to its application. Geography as Milton knew it was largely a science of nomenclature, scarcely at all of measurement or calculation; and the conclusion of

Milton's most radical venture at knowledge of the stars was, "Be lowly wise."

To be sure, Mr. Kester Svendsen has made a series of ventures at proving Milton's familiarity with science and his interest in it [*SP,* XXXIX, 303–27; *PMLA,* LXVII, 435–45; *ELH,* IX, 198–223]; but his case is vitiated throughout by a failure to distinguish even approximately between a more or less "scientific" science and traditional moralizing on the book of creatures. Though Mr. Svendsen does not emphasize the point, his evidence leads to the conclusion that Milton was much more familiar with the sort of lore promulgated by Bartholomaeus Anglicus (fl. 1230–50) than with Gilbert's explorations of the magnet or Harvey's investigations of the heart (neither of which he ever mentioned). And to lump Bartholomaeus Anglicus together with Copernicus and Galileo as "scientific sources" of Milton's thought is to confuse the character of that thought beyond all recognition.

Even in astronomy, the same bias appears. Grant McColley, zealous as ever to tie Milton down to a set of particular sources, argued that the poet had read, and reproduced in Book VIII of *Paradise Lost,* a contemporary scientific quarrel, the debate between John Wilkins and Alexander Ross regarding a multiplicity of worlds [*BOE,* chap. IX]. But while the evidence of specific indebtedness remains inconclusive, simply as a parallel the controversy reveals that in terms of contemporary astronomical issues and opinions, Milton took a conservative, almost an obscurantist position. The point is not simply that Raphael concludes the discussion by telling Adam to think about matters more immediate than the stars; there is a dramatic reason, almost a dramatic necessity, for this conclusion. The dialogue on astronomy, though not unrelated to the central themes of the epic, does not advance the main line of Milton's narrative, and in some way a graceful return must be managed to the human story and the human problems. Raphael speaks not only to Adam, but to the reader of *Paradise Lost,* in urging concentration on personal, moral issues. But the questions originally raised by Adam and the further uncertainties propounded by Raphael are not even framed in astronomical language. What troubles Adam is not a matter of mechanics, but one of dignity; is it right that the large, bright heavens should be obliged to revolve for the benefit of the small, dull earth? Raphael answers him, not in physical terms, but still in terms of God's dignity, which he describes as even more mysterious than Adam had supposed. It is not to be estimated from mere physical appearances such as brightness and magnitude. God's valuation of things, like his arrangement of them, is mysterious and wilful, almost perverse; the most incongruous and unlikely things may be true, and the fact that they mislead us is evidence that they express the will of God. He has made the world an insoluble anagram of his will so that he may be amused by the silly endeavors of men to understand it.

This note of arbitrary malice in the Deity, which is sounded both in his first speech and again in VIII, 237–40, has raised the hackles on a good many readers of *Paradise Lost;* and no doubt it jars on the rationalism to which the poem itself has made such important concessions. Indeed, there is about Milton's Deity in these passages a touch of feeling such as one recognizes in the rabbinical commentators. Rashi, it may be recalled, says that God made Eve in order that no one might say that Adam was like his maker in being unique of his kind. This is not only a jealous Deity; he is jealous in a special, secretive, self-absorbed way—inventing first a parallel, then people to remark it in an invidious way, and finally taking an underhanded action behind an ostensibly generous motive to obviate the imaginary slur. Milton's Deity as represented by Raphael has the same sort of touchy, perverse, and subtle pride. He could just as well have made the universe comprehensible to human sense; he deliberately removed it to a distance and mixed it up so that

> earthly sight,
> If it presume, might erre in things too high,
> And no advantage gaine [VIII, 120–22].

It is interesting that in discussing science Milton should sound like a rabbi, for in discussing rabbis he often sounded like an arch-empiricist. The truth is that, like his contemporary Browne, he stood, not always in complete security, halfway between a world organized around physical, material facts and one organized on spiritual principles. This is not a key to his character, his ideas, or his reading; it is not a conclusion, but a part of a premise. Milton himself never displayed much overt concern with the "conflict between science and religion" which nineteenth- and even twentieth-century commentators find so congenial and comprehensible. The conflicts with which he was consciously concerned were more immediate, more secondary and tangible, if no less difficult. But if we sense Milton as a complex and deeply divided figure living in a complex and deeply divided age, there will perhaps be less temptation to exaggerate a single aspect of the poet's character or thought out of all proportion. The humble craftsman laboring patiently in an ancient tradition with whom Professor McColley concluded his volume represents one aspect of Milton; but this was not the man who made up his own creed out of the naked Scripture and addressed it to all the churches of Christ, this was not the solitary champion who defended regicide against Salmasius while all

Europe rang from side to side. The rabbinical student and delver into medieval Jewish lore whom M. Saurat and Mr. Fletcher emphasized also has a modest claim to existence; but he is not very close kin to the epic poet. And the importance of "right reason" to Milton's thinking is very hard to overestimate; but it was not applied to those matters of science which a modern man is apt to consider its natural province.

Are we then left with a vague and undiscriminating pluralism? Can we say nothing more of Milton's reading than that it took place in a number of areas, which ought not to be minimized, or, in scholarly pidgin, "oversimplified"? That gambit is altogether too easy and tells us too little. Perhaps we may add without rashness, though not without triteness, that the poet's general reading had two magnetic, not wholly compatible centers, the Bible and the classics; and if we give this cliché its full weight, we shall not be liable to mistake Miltonic byways for main-traveled roads by ascribing to editors, exegetes, and imitators what can perfectly well be derived from original sources, the great authors themselves. But this point is obvious enough. More subtle and significant than the letters which Milton read is the spirit in which he read them; and this spirit is scarcely to be summarized in a capsule comment. One approach is to conceive of Milton's mind as profoundly stirred by the two ideals, once more slightly divergent, of heroic individual energy and complete moral responsibility. And to the task of resolving and realizing these ideals we may think of him as devoting all the forces at his command, especially those which he denominated "right reason."

Rationalism in fact offered Milton an arena for energy and a ground for decision more congenial to the heroic egotism which was a basic quality of his mind than almost any other mode of thought available to him. Even his position, halfway between Ramist intuitionism and Aristotelian reliance on the syllogism [see P. A. Duhamel, *PMLA,* LXVII, 1035–53], may be construed as an expression of his need for intellectual elbowroom. A deeply traditional mind like that of Laud or a mind thoroughly impregnated with skepticism like that of Dryden may be a very finely tempered instrument; but it is not likely to give itself the leeway or the footing needed for heroic decision. Milton's theology is cruder and more naïve than that of Laud; by comparison with the controlled equivocations of Dryden, his argumentative tone is that of a bumptious and wilful pedant. Mr. Ernest Sirluck has shown in a brief and brilliantly illuminating article [*MP,* XLVIII, 90–96] how Milton's mistrust of habit and convention, his anxious emphasis on conscious, active, individual decision, caused him to misremember a passage of Spenser. It is but one very striking example of a kind of intellectual independence in Milton which borders very closely on the cranky. Perhaps this is regrettable; it is nonetheless a fact to be accepted if we hope to understand the man, and it may even be susceptible of a kind of defense. No man who raises his own intellectual shelter, building from the foundation and working in the middle of a storm, is to be blamed if he produces a structure less elegant than one which generations of leisured philosophers have worked to perfect. Indeed, the probability must be faced that he will not get all his joints perfectly weather-tight. In this context, Milton's treatment of intellectual authorities illustrates something more than a humorous foible; it lays bare a basic quality of his mind and of the patterns in which that mind worked. The observation is an old one that Milton cites authorities with respect when they support his opinion and discards them with contempt when they do not. When the Bible makes for his view, it speaks prescriptively; when it contradicts him, it is to be taken metaphorically. To gain a point Milton also makes use, on occasion, of the glib, abstract distinction; what his opponents want is "license," what he wants is "liberty." And, as if seeking to bolster a half-sensed weakness, he sometimes attaches an unexceptionable adjective to a debatable principle, for example in that interesting concept to which he often appeals but which it remained for Hobbes to analyze, "right reason." The term as used without definition seems to grow out of a feeling that reason can be applied to both sides of many crucial questions, but that the side favored by Milton may claim a special advantage in its use of reason, an advantage only to be defined in a safe, broad adjective like "right."

Briefly, Milton's intellectual tools were not always adequate to the tasks he imposed on them; and it was more in his character to overload the tools than to cut down on the tasks. His sense of "ought" was more vivid than his sense of "can"; his feeling for a noble architecture went deeper than his feeling for a clean joint. In fulfilling his idea of what was fitting, he was not greatly inhibited by traditions, awed by technical problems, or cowed by the need for popular approval. With the Apostle, he sought to try all things and hold fast to that which was good; he judged all things, including himself, by the lofty standard of his own concept of a complete man. It is a strenuous, an audacious program, which seems sometimes to engender a kind of unsteadiness in the man who makes himself the measure of so many things. But this is the price of heroic assertion; what Milton had to say could not be said within the framework of any strict logical structure, neither could it have been said by a man who was finicky about having precedents for his opinions or who felt major misgivings about the validity of his own temperament. We shall not wholly misrepresent the spirit in which John Milton approached his reading, I think, if we say that for the most part he held up other books, as he held up himself, to the criterion of his own magnanimity; that he approached few authors in the spirit of a man seeking permission to hold an opinion or borrow an expression, but sat over most of his library as a judge, if not as a conqueror. It is, after all, a very Miltonic Christ who tells the Devil, in Book IV of *Paradise Regained,* that the man

> who reads
> Incessantly, and to his reading brings not
> A spirit and judgment equal or superior,
> (And what he brings, what needs he elsewhere seek)
> Uncertain and unsettl'd still remains,
> Deep verst in books and shallow in himself,
> Crude or intoxicate, collecting toys,
> And trifles for choice matters, worth a spunge;
> As Children gathering pibles on the shore [322–30].

The passage is very useful for setting studies of Milton's reading in their proper perspective.

[VI]

Milton's Verse: Efforts at a Judgment

ONE of the most striking anomalies in modern critical opinion is the position occupied by the poetry of Milton. On the one hand it has undergone, for the first time in its history, sustained, widespread attack at the hands of influential and generally respected critics. The climax of this attack, if not the high point, was Mr. Eliot's assertion, made in 1935 and withdrawn in 1947, that "Milton's poetry could *only* be an influence for the worse, upon any poet whatever." Equally impressive in its confidence was Mr. Leavis' challenge, still unwithdrawn, concerning *Samson Agonistes:* "How many cultivated adults could honestly swear that they had ever read it through with enjoyment?" The repudiation of Milton the poet, though generally phrased in terms more tangential and temperate than these, found frequent expression during the 1930's and '40's; a tithing of the comments may stand for a massive harvest of disapproval. Mr. J. Middleton Murry said that Milton has "little intimate meaning for us. . . . He does not, either in his great effects or his little ones, touch our depths"; Sir Herbert Read wrote that "his thought was a system apart from his poetic feeling . . . he did not think poetically but merely expounded thought in verse"; Mr. F. L. Lucas declared that Milton imposed "marmoreal stiffness" on the language, that his organ voice had no *vox humana;* while Mr. Ezra Pound exercised, over the years, a running feud against Milton, now touching casually on his "complete ignorance of the things of the spirit," now gracefully mentioning the "gross and utter stupidity and obtuseness of Milton." [1]

At the same time and on the other hand, critiques exploring and expounding Milton's poetry (critiques which had no visible *raison d'être* if the poetry which they discussed was without literary merit) continued to multiply. These critiques were often strikingly independent of the unfavorable valuations; they did not as a rule involve direct assault on Mr. Eliot or Mr. Leavis or even Mr. Pound. For the most part, these gentlemen were mentioned only in passing and only with embarrassment; Mr. Cleanth Brooks even suggested that the first fathers of his critical school had not read Milton at all, but had merely "hacked away a decadent Miltonism," thus leaving their successors free to appreciate the Real Thing [*PMLA,* LXVI, 1047]. But such explanations were unusual. Generally, the explicators explicated independently, using without explanation or apology every device of modern criticism to display the beauties of an author whom the founders of modern criticism had declared unalterably ugly. While the overt

[1] Eliot in *ESEA,* 1935 (Oxford, 1936), p. 33; Leavis, *Revaluation* (London, 1936), p. 67; Murry, *The Mystery of Keats* (London, 1949), p. 218; Read, *Collected Essays* (London, 1938), p. 84; Lucas, *Studies French and English* (London, 1934), p. 232; Pound, *The Spirit of Romance* (London, 1910), p. 165, *The ABC of Reading* (New Haven, 1934), p. 91.

anti-Miltonists came under heavy fire from such established positions as those occupied by Mr. Logan Pearsall Smith or Professor Douglas Bush, critics who passed as Milton's friends were diligently and effectively at work to change the general conception of Milton's poetic achievements in still a third direction. The situation was strange indeed. While conservative scholars defended Milton against direct assault, they found him brilliantly undermined from within. Siege and countersiege, sortie and countersortie: was the poet suffering more at the hands of his old idolaters, his recent enemies, or his new-found friends? The enemies condemned him for lacking, and the friends praised him for possessing, qualities which the idolaters had never before supposed relevant to a judgment of John Milton. Confirmed partisans like Professor Bush and Mr. Smith, if they were in no doubt about whom to fight, were nonetheless embarrassed to find appropriate weapons and trustworthy allies. I do not think any of the combatants in these critical skirmishes suffered permanent disrepair; but was there not danger that amid such horrid jaculations the battlefield himself might go to rack and ruin?

Superficially, the climate of Miltonic opinion has become milder of recent years. Mr. Eliot has withdrawn, at least partially, some of his strictures; the New Criticism, after beating through the underbrush of the minor poems, has ventured at last to assert that *Paradise Lost* itself has some merit, if read in a perverse and limited way. And a notable slackening has occurred in the sort of gross Milton-baiting which used to proceed on the assumption that *Paradise Lost* might be fairly exploded if only one could prove that Milton was a syphilitic, an albino, or a forger. But I cannot persuade myself that the era of uneasy truce which we are now experiencing is much more than an episode based on mutual misunderstanding. In his second essay on Milton, Mr. Eliot took two notable steps backward, but also three unobtrusive steps forward. The New Critics found themselves able to say kind words about some parts of Milton, but only after radically distorting the character of his poetry. And critics of the older school, a school rooted essentially in Macaulay's heroic rather than Raleigh's anti-heroic nineteenth-century view of the poet, have defended Milton with sulphurous indignation—have showed how unfair and unjust many of Mr. Eliot's and Mr. Leavis' charges are; but they have not opened up any new grounds of esthetic or intellectual sympathy by which a modern reader can approach Milton's poetry and enjoy it. Professor Bush in particular has given many convincing reasons why we ought to respect Milton, urging that his ideas are "very close to what many modern thinkers have been declaring are necessary to our own necessary regeneration" [*PLIOT*, p. 27]. He seems thus to recommend the poetry and the Christian humanism underlying it as a stiff but wholesome dose for the snobs, sentimentalists, and sensationalists [*PLIOT*, pp. 1–5, 43, 93] who determine so much modern taste. But, whatever the modern world needs in order to undergo "regeneration," it seems clear that Milton will not make much more literary headway if recommended as a tonic to our moral fiber than as a way to salvation. Though modern taste may be hopelessly arrogant and perverse (one would not want to defend it against Professor Bush's astringent historical judgment), still, by the very fact of existing and continuing to exist, it gains a certain authority. The Bellman's motto, "What I tell you three times is true," has in this context a perfectly rational and sensible application to literary taste. An audience in actual, physical existence has a good many points of advantage over one which merely ought to exist and almost as many over one which used to exist. In any event, the burden of reforming modern taste in its broad aspects does not rest on Milton or his partisans; and if one does not feel like setting at defiance the first principles of that taste by recommending Milton as a corrective or confining oneself to a purely historical approach, one had better explore ways and means of conciliation.

Preliminary footings for such an effort might well be found in one of Mr. Eliot's double-edged concessions, from his second essay. It is an observation that Milton was a master at displaying his talent, a comment on "his inerrancy, conscious or unconscious, in writing so as to make the best display of his talents, and the best concealment of his weaknesses" ["Milton," *PBA*, XXXIII, 70]. This is not exactly open-handed praise; it smacks, rather, of a baffled antagonist. Considering the total volume of his writing and the variety of genres in which he worked, Milton must indeed have been a remarkable writer if any sizable part of his attention was devoted to concealing inadequacies. A masque, an elegy, a volume of sonnets and shorter poems, a long epic, a short epic, and a tragedy—in a merely quantitative sense, this is a total production of verse which one need not exaggerate to find impressive, especially when one reckons in a slow start, subtracts a decade or two of politics and prose, and takes account of the handicap of blindness. A truly cautious man might, without arousing suspicious comment, have published even less and so concealed his weaknesses even better. Mr. Eliot's observation thus appears curiously uncharitable at first glance.

But for all this, the remark is in fact half correct. Milton's style, like his intellectual talents and verbal habits generally, was ideally suited to the sustained narrative sweep and high dignified style of epic or classical tragedy. It was not a style well suited to the intimate depiction of several individual characters, not, except for occasional contemptuous phrases, a colloquial style. Nothing could mean less than a contrast of Milton's epic style with Donne's lyrical conversational one or Shakespeare's dramatic one which did not take into account the different purposes served by the different styles. Not to labor the point unduly (it has been made more than adequately by Mr. Lewis, *PPL,* throughout), an epic style is narrative, didactic, rhetorical, continuously elevated, and directly exemplary; it cannot go very far in the direction of becoming colloquial or witty or social without ceasing to be epic. It cannot shift tone radically or modulate very far from its major key without seriously throwing things off balance. It simply cannot compete for flexibility and rhythmic variety with the stage or the dramatic lyric. So that Milton, in avoiding the genres exploited by Donne and Shakespeare, did in a sense conceal the weaknesses of his own style—just as Donne and Shakespeare, in avoiding the genres of Virgil and Spenser, concealed the weaknesses of their own styles, and so on.

Most of the onslaughts against Milton's verse bear remarkably wide of this matter of genre. Mr. Leavis has voiced strong protest against the ponderous beat of Milton's verse—"against the routine gesture, the heavy fall of the verse . . . the foreseen thud that comes so inevitably, and, at last, irresistibly." The grand style, he declares, is monotonous; the only people who, "after an honest interrogation of experience," can say they find variety in it are the classically trained [*Revaluation,* p. 44]—men whose ears, presumably, have been dulled by the monotonous rumble of Homer and Ovid, the flat phlegmatic sameness of Pindar and Catullus. The declaration, so pawky and perverse and confused, invites picking apart. But on one point it too is certainly correct. The variety or monotony of Milton's heroic verse is fully apparent only to one who knows the other long unrhymed poems in world literature, i.e., Virgil and Homer. The learned have reached various conclusions on this matter, which the present essay cannot without impudence pretend to resolve in passing.[2] But without any very uncommon learning, one may perceive that heroic poems do have, and are supposed to have, a pronounced, steady rhythm. And without any learning at all one may discover that in point of rhythmic variety there are very few heroic poems in English worthy to stand on the same shelf with *Paradise Lost*.

To say this is, admittedly, to consign Milton's greatest poem to a small, and largely dead, category. The heroic poem is almost extinct; though it flourished mightily as little as a century and a half ago, when Byron thought his own age degenerate because it produced so *many* epics ["English Bards," ll. 189–204], the number of even partially successful epic poems is small. Thus, to have written the very best heroic poem in English might well seem, in purely relative terms, a smaller achievement than to have written the fourth-best drama or the tenth-best love lyric. The standard by which we undertake to measure Milton's position in English literature cannot and should not be that set by *Thalaba, Creation,* and *Gondibert,* or even by *Hyperion* and *The Faery Queen*. Though Milton in the act of composition doubtless had in mind the different styles appropriate to different genres, and the critic in the act of judging should remember it, the distinction is not universal or even general. The influence of Milton's style extended far beyond the province of the heroic poem, and not necessarily, as Mr. Eliot now concedes, to unfortunate

[2] Rather than appeal to the various commentators who have handled the question, one might look at Mr. Richmond Lattimore's rendering of the *Iliad* and Mr. C. Day Lewis's version of the *Aeneid* to gain some idea of the metrical freedom which modern poets find appropriate to a rendering of Homer and Virgil.

effect. So that the significance of genre is strictly defensive; one cannot blame Milton for writing a heroic poem in the heroic manner, but one may perfectly well feel that both *Paradise Lost* and the heroic genre as a whole are obsolete. It is along the lines of this heroic-nonheroic division that the followers of Raleigh diverge most sharply from those whose bent, however worked out, is fundamentally that of Macaulay. If we accept the second horn of this dilemma, most of the problems concerning Milton's subject and style solve themselves almost automatically; we have the heroic subject and the grand style, and if these do not accord with the modern sensibility, so much the worse for the modern sensibility. But if one thinks this strong-minded position likely to produce little more for Milton than the remote respect which is already his as a classic author, perhaps the nonheroic alternative may be investigated. On these terms Milton's style must be shown to have value, either in terms of its own inner relationships or in relation to something larger and possibly vaguer than a genre—the language in general, perhaps, the reader's or the poet's psyche, or the possibilities and requirements of a particular subject, a particular world view. To any one of these entities the style may be shown to be more or less effectively adapted. I am not prepared to argue that any one of these criteria is categorically superior, as a critical criterion, to any other. They all call for judgments which one can scarcely hope to render in more than impressionistic form; a deep-dyed skeptic might say that literary judgments are by definition vague and impressionistic; but they need not be Lord Macaulay's judgments, for all that.

In the first place, it is clear that though an extravagant and unnecessary enthusiasm of the New Criticism for analysis of imagery has sometimes obscured important internal qualities of the style such as plot, character, diction, narrative parallels, scenic balances, and structural analogies, these broadly conceived and boldly executed qualities do contribute in a major way to the poem's effect. Perhaps they are not, strictly speaking, stylistic achievements; yet none of them can be effectively executed without a sweeping, energetic style. And when one adds weight and complexity of reference, one is not far from a skeleton definition of Milton's epic manner.

Thus in the broad, structural aspects of style, those most neglected by the New Criticism, the inner relations of *Paradise Lost* do lead toward a pretty exact definition of its effect; but the attempt to describe or assess Milton's style in terms of its inner contrasts and tensions breaks down in dealing with relatively small units of composition, with individual images and image clusters. For Milton is not everywhere, or consistently, concerned with the creation of tensions and contrasts. He often writes poetry in the form of lists or catalogues, going out of his way, for instance, in the second edition of *Paradise Lost,* to add three lines and six diseases to an original list of eleven diseases displayed by Michael to Adam [XI, 485–87]. As he was chary of major revisions in the text, one naturally looks for an extraordinary occasion requiring so remarkable an addition; and one is disappointed. If Milton wanted seventeen diseases instead of his original eleven, no other reason appears than that he thought a list of seventeen would be poetically more effective than a list of eleven.

But this assumption radically disturbs the approach to Milton's poetry as a tissue of tensions, for the structural connection of the six extra diseases with the narrative of the poem is by no means obvious. There is no evident reason why three or nine would not have done as well; there is no valid esthetic limit, either upper or lower, to the dimensions of Milton's list. The problem, though most obvious here, is not simply local. If we reject the notion of a meddling editor, it appears that Milton himself felt free to riot with the medical dictionary in this passage; and if this is so, can we be confident that he was not merely versifying the atlas a hundred lines before or Galileo's *Sidereus Nuncius* in Book VIII? It is queer enough that he should consider seventeen names of diseases preferable to eleven; most modern taste would, I think, incline to the more stripped statement. But instead of collecting disease names in heaps, whether of eleven or seventeen, modern writers would probably prefer to symbolize morbidity in an image. Milton was perfectly capable of doing so himself; if he preferred the list of names to the image of the thing and the extended list to the short one, it must have been on principle. And the principle that a list may be preferable to an image seems to undermine many accepted esthetic principles, to cut, even, at the very fundamental notion of poetry as compressed and heightened speech.

Hence if we try to assess the Miltonic style in terms of its dramatic tensions, contrasts, and compressions, we shall from the beginning be at something of a loss; since a writer of the most primitive skills who was out to build up inward tensions and contrasts would know better than to use lists for this purpose. The list is extensive, discursive; it has no inherent bound or limit against which its energies can be opposed; it is a bundle of similarities rather than a net of contrasting tensions; and it is irresistibly undramatic.

For all this, it is plain that the list is a part of Milton's poetical equipment and not by any means a minor part. The catalogue of Gods in Book I is a traditional epic device, rather minimized by Milton as compared with Homer and Virgil. But Book VII, the story of creation, is entirely formed on the principle of paraphrasing Scripture and then expanding on the general category with a list of particulars. "God created fowl," says Genesis—"eagles, storks, cranes, swans, and roosters," adds Milton. The catalogues of places [as in IV, 268, or XI, 385] as well as of mythological or romantic persons [I, 576; IX, 385], the descriptive lists of flowers [IV, 690], and the comparative lists of serpents [IX, 503; X, 520] all suggest a general habit of mind. Milton had a distinct interest in naming things, an interest largely unrelated and sometimes opposed to his interest in telling a story, presenting an image, or even writing a poem. He liked to name things, we may presume, for a number of reasons, of which perhaps the least important was that it was a recognized poetical and rhetorical device. Quintilian, Longinus, and Puttenham all discuss and endorse the technique, which Puttenham, with his usual flair for nomenclature, calls *merismus,* or the distributor [*The Arte of English Poesie,* III, 19]. But Milton was not the man to interpret the tepid permission of critics like these as a binding prescription; he would not have used lists if he had not wanted to. Sometimes he may have indulged in lists because he liked the sounds of the words and thought his readers would like them too. The idea is probably painful to critics who think poetic ornament is bound to be "organically" functional, but for all this it seems likely that Milton sometimes indulged in a spate of names for no reason more eminent than that he enjoyed their sound:

from the destind Walls
Of *Cambalu,* seat of *Cathaian Can*
And *Samarchand* by *Oxus, Temirs* Throne,
To *Paquin* of *Sinaean* Kings, and thence
To *Agra* and *Lahore* of great *Mogul*
Down to the golden *Chersonese* [XI, 387–92].

The sound is obviously important here, along with a conscious effort to display large vistas of space and history;

though it seems extravagant to say that the aural imagination has drowned out the visual (Milton's perspective, of a man standing high above the turning globe, is all the more striking for its remote, panoramic inclusiveness), sound is a strong element in the passage, and Milton clearly intended it to be. Other lists may be attributed in part to Milton's plan of relating subordinate myths to his central myth and of including a total body of religious truth (involving some rather curious lore) within the framework of his poem.

But neither of these motives is especially relevant to the disease listing, which cannot even be related very helpfully to the frequent Renaissance conception of the heroic poem as a genre of unusual dignity because unusually informative, unusually copious in matters of practical information. The disease list supplies no information; it is only a list of names. An ingenious strainer of probabilities might argue that the special character of Milton's theme in *Paradise Lost* may have made lists seem specially relevant. On the theological level, a main question of the poem is why God makes use of particular limited agents (like angels and human beings) to achieve a general purpose which could be accomplished directly; the functions of angels and stars are repeatedly discussed in this connection, and the interrelation of general and particular might thus be something which Milton chose to emphasize throughout the poem by means of lists. But this is a pretty esoteric proceeding for Milton; one cannot see it determining his decision to add six more diseases to the list in Book XI.

On another level altogether, Milton's love of names may be ascribed to a peculiar personal delight in exuberant, luxuriant exfoliation—to the sort of feeling that finds expression in Comus' speech to the Lady or the description of Paradise in Book IV. The poet likes words because they are things, it may be said, and the multiplication of them is pleasing to him in itself. This view puts the whole burden of eccentricity on Milton the individual; his style is good because it expresses his temperament, and if our temperament is not Milton's, so much the worse for us. On the other hand, to put the matter less baldly, we may say that because Milton was historically and by temperament a man of the late Renaissance, this fact entitles us to attribute the lists, partly at least, to a baroque esthetic, such as delights in sportive ornamentation, far in excess and even in defiance of function strictly defined. Though critics did not formulate its rules or venture even to assert its basic principle, this esthetic clearly had the impudence to exist; it is the esthetic, say, of Tasso, of Bernini, of St. Peter's Cathedral in Rome. Theorists of "concettismo" like Tesauro, Pellegrini, and Pallavicino were aware of a conflict between wit, the faculty of discovery, and decorum, the faculty of discipline, but none of them seem to have felt that a poetic style could be built on deliberate, difficult violations of decorous expectations [J. A. Mazzeo, *RR,* XLII, 245–55]; yet this "feeling of a difficulty overcome" offered to an observer as casual as Stendhal an immediate explanation of why Southern peoples "like the Marini sort of thing" [*Private Diaries,* Nov. 4, 1813]. Thus, even though a distinctly metaphysical, extravagant esthetic had not been formulated in specific terms, such a concept of authorized excess growing out of difficulties overcome may perfectly well have been one element in planning a structure and a style for *Paradise Lost;* the point has been made, though not in stylistic terms, by Roy Daniells [*UTQ,* XIV, 293–308].

These last notions raise some interesting considerations, which one may approach by way of another observation in Mr. Eliot's second essay.

The peculiar feeling, almost a physical sensation of a breathless leap, communicated by Milton's long periods, and by his alone, is impossible to procure from rhymed verse. Indeed, this mastery is more conclusive evidence of his intellectual power, than is his grasp of any *ideas* that he borrowed or invented. To be able to control so many words at once is the token of a mind of most unusual energy [*PBA,* XXXIII, 73].

So far as they pertain to rhyming, these judgments are dubious; "Lycidas," lines 56–63, will suffice to show that Milton's gift for massive impetus was not dependent on blank verse. But the second part of the judgment is more searching. The words are objects to control, that it is a literary achievement of merit to marshal them into elaborate patterns of assertion (perhaps including lists)—this is an interesting and pertinent criterion for judging Milton's stylistic achievements; and it casts some light on his grammar and his vocabulary as well. Two qualities common to all Milton's mature work are its disregard of normal English grammar through the constant intrusion of Greek, Hebrew, or (predominantly) Latin constructions; and the use of English words in the sense they bear in the language from which they derive. These are, be it noted, qualities independent of, if not opposed to, dramatic propriety; they stand in open defiance of colloquial speech and self-revelation on the part of the poet; they are not traditional ornaments of English rhetoric; and if complexity is involved, the word "ironic" can scarcely be invoked to cover it. But they can usefully be thought of as devices of extension, intensification, and control, and illustrated by reference, not to the Miltonic epic, but to the drama, *Samson.*

The use of Latinate English, a device scornfully described by Carew as "the subtle cheat/ Of slie Exchanges" and shunned by the metaphysical poets, involves a number of different effects. It adds a philological dimension to

English; and with this new dimension, puts at the poet's disposal a number of significant overtones from other cultures. When Samson describes himself as "retiring from the popular noise" [line 16], the adjective carries, and is meant to carry, all sorts of contemptuous feelings from Latin "populus"; the contempt is interestingly augmented by inverting the conventional adjective-noun, attribute-substance relationship, so that the noise seems to outweigh the people who make it. When he speaks of his "capital secret" [line 394], Samson may be seen as making reference to the importance of his secret and the fact that it resided in or on his head, as well as to the fact that like the capitol in Rome it was the center of his power and the residence of a deity. The effect, dear to Ben Jonson as well as to Milton, is that of an overlay; one sees and responds to the English word at the same time that one is aware of a Latin word behind the English, with its own impact and impetus. From the point of view of portraying a psychology in depth, this device is, at least 90 per cent of the time, all wrong; it portrays the word in depth, turning one away from the mind which speaks to the language which is spoken. For mythological figures, superhuman in stature and encrusted with antiquity, it provides a strong, stiff, dignified idiom, on which Milton's occasional contemptuous colloquialisms [as in *Samson,* "blab," line 495, or "draff," line 574] clash very finely. Lastly, in their own nature the "slie Exchanges" give to language a resonant magniloquence which may be impressive and moving precisely because, in Jonson's phrase (Dr. Johnson made the application to Milton), it is, properly speaking, "no language." The style is built on a deliberate contrast between "natural" English and the artificial speech of the poetry; it is a language more rich, complex, extended, and resourceful than English traditionally is. It is so extended, in fact, so muscular and energetic in its contrasted reaching and controlling, as actually to give the sense of compression. There are so many things to be said, so many patterns to be traced and filled out and connected, that even the heroic rhetoric of four languages seems overtaxed. No doubt the poetry is written in defiance of the materials of which it is composed; just so, a statue by Bernini or a fresco by Tiepolo seems to violate the very materials of which it is constructed, the conditions of its material existence. But this is an esthetic condition, not a judgment, and the work of art, just because it distorts its materials, is sometimes seen to conform to more splendid and significant controls—the controls, one might say, of a temperament or a condition with which the audience itself may share a sympathy.

More dramatic in its immediate application is Milton's use of alien grammars as devices for extending or delaying or, sometimes, suspending the flow of an English sentence. Their most frequent controlling use is to render the verse slow and complex; they knot the thread of assertion in loops which, while they delay our untying, are generally capable of satisfying resolution:

> But safest he who stood aloof,
> When insupportably his foot advanc't
> In scorn of thir proud arms and warlike tools
> Spurn'd them to death by Troops [ll. 135–38].

"Advanc't" here may be a participle or an independent verb; the reader must hold the sentence in suspension till the true verb, appearing with a wonderful contemptuous suddenness in "Spurn'd," jolts the whole sentence into resolution. At other times, Milton takes advantage of that free word order which is the crown of an inflected language to delay a crucial modifier strategically or advance it suddenly into prominence. And finally, he derives some fine effects from a mode of writing English as if it enjoyed the grammatical advantages of Latin or Greek, in such a way, sometimes, as to make actual use of those advantages.

> His pardon I implore; but as for life,
> To what end should I seek it? when in strength
> All mortals I excell'd, and great in hopes
> With youthful courage and magnanimous thoughts
> Of birth from Heav'n foretold and high exploits,
> Full of divine instinct, after some proof
> Of acts indeed heroic, far beyond
> The sons of *Anac,* famous now and blaz'd,
> Fearless of danger, like a petty God
> I walk'd about admir'd of all and dreaded
> On hostile ground, none daring my affront [ll. 521–31].

These clauses, strung loosely and episodically together, audacious and blustering in content but aimless and weakly extended far beyond English usage without any major verb at all (unless one supplies a verb for the subordinate clause "when *I was* in strength"), may achieve dramatic propriety in the same way that the last sentence of Dalila's first speech suggests, by the omission of a main verb, the wavering of her approach [lines 743–47]. On other occasions, the extended, audacious piling of clause on clause may serve to express with equal propriety a turbulent, pell-mell rush of motion or an aspiration which reaches beyond rational, and so beyond grammatical, norms. This, I take it, is Mr. Eliot's "almost physical sensation of a breathless leap." The virtues of this extended style, whether aimless or frenetic, whether appropriate to a dramatic situation or not, are not by any means the virtues of the long Latin period, that skillfully braced fabric of complex yet precise interconnections. The style is, rather, glancing and ejaculatory; an epithet or modifier is thrown out, almost at random, without any indication of direction; then, as the sentence rumbles along, it gravitates toward the noun or general idea it is meant to modify; while, from behind the English words, the grammatical connections which would be there in Latin slowly make themselves felt as fixatives, so to speak, of the fluid English grammar. "Our language sunk under him," said Addison; it was precisely this effect of mingled textures, meanings arranged in depth, and subsurface controls slowly rising to our awareness that Milton may well have wanted to produce. Bigness of assertion, complexity of reference, and a deeply ranged sequence of linguistic and grammatical controls—these may serve as criteria for a judgment of Milton's style, though whether anyone will think the standard universally applicable or wholly sufficient may be doubted. At all events, these qualities do seem to play some part in making Milton's manner Miltonic.

One other quality of the style, a quality dramatic but involving the complete absence of tension, may call for comment. The verse of *Samson,* though it is freer, more various, and looser in its rhythms than the verse of *Paradise Lost,* often slides toward the prosaic in the pattern of its assertion, especially near the climaxes of its choruses. Thus, after that wonderfully vivid and searching exclamation which begins, "God of our fathers, what is man!" the chorus falls to describing the sad fate of men once eminent for virtue; and here the alternatives are enumerated in a solemn processional which neither generates nor seems eager to generate any tension built on contrasts:

> Nor only dost degrade them, or remit
> To life obscur'd, which were a fair dismission,
> But throw'st them lower then thou didst exalt them high,
> Unseemly falls in human eie,
> Too grievous for the trespass or omission,
> Or leav'st them to the hostile sword
> Of Heathen and profane, thir carkasses

To dogs and fowl a prey, or else captiv'd:
Or to the unjust tribunals, under change of times,
And condemnation of the ingrateful multitude.
If these they scape, perhaps in poverty
With sickness and disease thou bow'st them down,
Painful diseases and deform'd,
In crude old age;
Though not disordinate, yet causless suffring
The punishment of dissolute days, in fine,
Just or unjust, alike seem miserable,
For oft alike, both come to evil end [ll. 686–704].

Like Michael's list of diseases, this list of calamities is extensive, not intensive; like the temptations of Manoa, Dalila, and Harapha, the misfortunes of the just are anticlimactically arranged, with Milton's gout (a hurt both intimate and bitter, but not after all very dignified) occupying the position of supremacy. Here, rather more cogently than in *Paradise Lost,* one may urge in justification of the style that *Samson* is concerned with the problem of God's special agents; and by contrast with their special calling, the fact that their fate is not special, that they trail off into the common destiny of ordinary humanity, comes with the impact of a discovery. Samson, who has won his greatest victory with the jawbone of an ass, must learn that God's uncontrollable intent may render all special arms a forgery and all special preparations ridiculous. This word "ridiculous," recurring with special frequency throughout *Samson,* is one sort of index to Milton's rather complicated feelings in this drama; it also provides a measure of justification for the rational, prosaic tone of the choruses. The rationality of these choruses has been compared with the rather intricate sophistry of Euripides' choruses; but they do not offer verbal swordplay or rhetorical display: they are not high points but relaxations of the verse. After flashes of exultation, often barbarically rhythmic, sometimes rising to vindictiveness, the choruses of Milton's drama generally return to a stolid, literal level of flat, discursive assertion, almost as a defence against the intensity of expectation.

The old, much-mooted charge that Milton's poem is doctrinally Stoic rather than Christian may have a bearing, indirect and ambiguous enough, on the esthetic point. If it were fully Stoic in feeling, the poem would not emphasize as it does the notion of Samson's special and peculiar destiny, nor would it show Samson as welcoming this notion. Moreover, it would not be lit with those flashes of grim and terrible exultation which are highlights of its poetic expression; its temper would be more moderate, and though its hero might suffer from *hubris,* that interesting condition would not afflict the entire chosen people, would not be a norm in the drama but a departure from another, clearly defined norm. As a matter of fact, the chorus itself has words very much to the point, crying out as Harapha departs:

> Oh how comely it is and how reviving
> To the Spirits of just men long opprest!
> When God into the hands of thir deliverer
> Puts invincible might [ll. 1268–71].

But the exultation, once more, is only momentary; the chorus is soon drawn to reflect that

> patience is more oft the exercise
> Of Saints, the trial of thir fortitude [ll. 1287–88].

The contrast between these two activities of virtue, the first notably Christian (though the words "Heroic magnitude of mind" [line 1279] are applied to it), the second strikingly Stoic (in spite of the Christian nomenclature by which the actors are called "saints"), is nicely resolved in

Samson's final action, which irresistibly combines action and passion; the confusion as to which prevails may be taken as evidence that the two elements are pretty well balanced; and one may usefully think of the style itself as combining in dramatic fashion energy and lassitude, exhausted patience and invincible might. Of course, given other critical premises, one might consider the dramatic propriety of the style less significant than the generic propriety by which the chorus is assigned, not the sentiments of high pathos and active suffering, but those of rational commentary and secondary analysis. And a modest ingenuity might well discover still other proprieties and contrasts by which the quality of these choruses might be explained or even defended.

For Milton's verse contains, and may be related to, many various sorts of contrasts, tensions, and proprieties, including the contrast between a style compact of contrasts and a style without them. There are dramatic proprieties and generic proprieties, ironic contrasts and contrasts between various grammars and vocabularies; and, finally, there is an element of largeness which contrasts with and constantly surpasses both the normal compass of the language and the expectations of the reader. This largeness is not impeached or diminished by the observation that it sometimes involves a fracturing of English idiom; it is not necessarily faulty because it often pours forth in the form of lists and heaps of words, either quite without structural control and limitation or controlled only by the extreme efforts of a radically extended grammar. This is no occasion to argue the abstract question whether poetry can exist without any inner tensions or contrasts at all—though I suppose, privately, that it perfectly well can. One cannot claim that any or all of the proprieties, relaxations, contrasts, and tensions which one can discover in Milton's poetry are responsible, either singly or in combination, for the poet's literary achievement. That achievement is, evidently, a function of all Milton's literary skills in joint operation, his gift for melodic invention and repetition, for alliteration, assonance, and rhyme, no less than for witty contrasts and poetic decorums. But if one concedes to Milton great technical competence in the writing of metrical stuff, some of the peculiar qualities of his verse may be associated with its largeness and boldness of assertion, combined with a complex verbal and linguistic pattern in depth. As to whether these qualities represent virtues or vices, we have evidently to deal with a bewildering number of contexts, whereby the same quality which accords ideally with one set of premises may be seen as irrelevant or objectionable to another. Perhaps it is not too cynical to suggest that anyone who is determined to admire or condemn Milton's verse can find in these varied contexts ample material for either purpose.

When we have exhausted the various inner relations of richness and bigness, decorum and contrast, propriety and tension, without achieving much more in the direction of a poetic value judgment than bemused skepticism, there remain numerous problems of relating the Miltonic style to something outside itself. Our first observations may well concern the language as a whole. Here it would be idle to pretend that Milton's manner represents anything but the final working out of an ornate manner and learned vocabulary which have not taken firm root in English speech. That Milton is not colloquial is no ultimate condemnation, though the observation is doubtless true. One cannot do much more with the grand style than he did, but the grand style is deliberately designed to contrast with everyday English. Perhaps it was necessary in the historical sense to work out a grand style and apply it to heroic matters (as in *Paradise Lost*) before men were able to develop the sort of plain, direct, unadorned style which one recognizes as making use of the essential qualities of English. But this lightning-rod function of Milton's style is no more a legitimate defense of it than the depredations of pseudo-Miltonists are a legitimate grounds for attack. Milton's is simply a very special, very splendid achievement in English verse; like his prose, which is not so splendid and much more special, it represents a particular sort of ultimate. And thus, if one supposes a crowning glory of the English tongue to be its adaptability to many styles and modes of expression (its "negative capability," almost), one may perhaps reach a sort of balance with regard to Milton's style by considering it a creation which goes against the essential grain of English by fulfilling and overfulfilling certain special potentialities of the tongue. This is by no means a negative verdict. What, after all, is the advantage of that much-vaunted adaptability of the English tongue if we are to reject as un-English such extreme variations from the colloquial norm as those of Milton, Crashaw, Hopkins, and Joyce?

Another relationship by which to judge Milton's verse is that touched on above in connection with a baroque esthetic. If one could show that Milton's style was designed to satisfy a more or less organized body of esthetic expectations, the poetic theory might be supposed to justify the practice, as the production of a successful poem would lend authority to the theory by which it was produced. To be sure, there is an element of lifting oneself by one's own bootstraps in this notion. Sir Richard Blackmore invented (substantially) his own poetic, which his poems brilliantly exemplify; but the one creation is as stupid and earth-bound as the other. Still, a sort of authority may be lent to the procedure by increasing its scale. An audience actually in existence and possessed of certain expectations may fairly claim, in this relativistic day and age, the common human privilege of having its wants satisfied. And if we are to pass judgment on those wants and expectations themselves, we must presumably do so in terms of ever-larger culture patterns, all of which are provisional at best. But in coping with Milton's style, we cannot even embark on this cumbersome procedure, supposing that we actually want to do so. For the Miltonic audience is particularly difficult of definition. Mr. Rajan, supposing Milton to have written for a general seventeenth-century reader, has tried to organize an image of this reader. But his conclusion is the discouraging one that such a person scarcely existed after 1660, and he falls back on the paradox that at certain times "a man can only preach effectively by preaching in the wilderness" [*SCR,* p. 58]. This is very likely true, but it does not solve any of the questions about a seventeenth-century audience, except by the indirect device of admitting that none actually existed. Milton had in fact to go through something like the process of inventing one; he created his audience out of his own fantasy; and while there is something rather heroic about this process, whether in Milton or Blackmore, it leads us far and ever farther from a sociological definition of the merits of his verse.

A more promising way of defining Milton's milieu is through the several intellectual creeds, religious movements, and social codes which he accepted. Indeed, the most fruitful Milton scholarship of recent years has been devoted to broadening the conception of Milton's Puritanism by making us aware of humanist and traditional Christian strains within his thought. There are difficulties, of course, about locating any major figure within any major tradition, much more within several; and Milton may seem, on different occasions and in different eyes, to wander up or down the curiously triangular scale which might be constructed with St. Augustine at one corner, Erasmus at another, and Praisegod Barebones at the third. But there were elements of all these personalities in Milton, and however modern scholarship has disagreed over proportions and emphases, we are surely the richer in being able to see light, artistry, and humanity where the nineteenth century saw only gloom and moral earnestness tempered by organ music. For all its occasional one-sided excesses and many internal confusions, the picture of Milton which one might gain by reading three neat little books by Messrs. Rajan, Lewis, and Waldock is immensely wider than any which one could quarry out of Masson's unwieldy volumes, Macaulay's florid recommendations, and Raleigh's witty summary.

But what we gain in breadth and subtlety of understanding, it may well be felt that we have lost in coherence. Though we put it aside for a moment, this question of coherence returns, more insistent than before; and (quite apart from the fact that relating Milton to an intellectual tradition may end in alienating him from the modern reader quite as much as the contrary) Milton cannot be understood coherently in terms of his relation to a single tradition of philosophical or religious thought, such as Christian humanism, simply because he was not wholeheartedly and single-mindedly a traditional man. The best evidence of this fact, a quality which suggests another dimension of Milton's style, derives from a long-standing critical paradox. Milton's language, critics long ago agreed, is not an ideal instrument for revealing psychological nuances; if not exactly opaque, it offers greater resistance to delicacies of feeling and light shadings of character than to the blunter shafts and more deliberate constructs of the rational intellect. Dr. Johnson's opinions on the subject have been echoed by Mr. Eliot's observation about the "Chinese wall" of Milton's blank verse and Mr. Leavis' remark that a process akin to bricklaying produced *Paradise Lost*.[3] Whatever tone one gives to the observation, it contains an element of undeniable truth. But precisely for this reason, it would appear to be a genuine critical curiosity that Milton has so often, over the last hundred and fifty years, been taken as a type of the personal poet. The point is not simply that fervent romantic enthusiasts once tried to read Milton's character into or out of Satan and Samson; eminent and conservative critics of our own time have argued that the true subject of *Paradise Lost* is the state of Milton's mind when he wrote it; and many stirring critical issues have been fought out on these grounds [see C. S. Lewis and E. M. W. Tillyard, *The Personal Heresy*], without much regard for the fact that *Hamlet* or "Adonais" would provide grounds far more obviously relevant.

The reason for this curious obliquity is, I think, a true perception that Milton's poetic style cannot be successfully and consistently related to any single set of values, any distinct audience or philosophy or critical creed or subject matter. Christian humanism itself, the broadest, most distinct and constant criterion so far considered, is taken by the poet of *Paradise Regained* and *Samson Agonistes* at such a special valuation that, without ceasing to be Christian humanism, it becomes a conflict rather than a definition, an emotional warfare against an inner conflict rather than a philosophy in the customary sense. The climactic act of both poems is an act of supreme magnanimity which is directed against the protagonist's own soul, a triumph

[3] Johnson, *Lives of the English Poets* (Everyman), I, 104–08; Eliot, *The Sacred Wood* (London, 1920), p. 87; Leavis, *Revaluation*, p. 60.

over fortune which is achieved by exclusion rather than comprehension. For this reason, critical outcries have been raised about the Stoicism and grim pessimism of the last poems; Milton has even been effectively denied the title of a Christian [J. M. Murry, *The Mystery of Keats,* p. 217; Lord David Cecil, preface to *The Oxford Book of Christian Verse* (Oxford, 1940), p. xxi]. Perhaps these charges are accurate; I am sure only that they bear no more direct relation to the essential poetic value of Milton's later poetry than to that of Yeats's *Last Poems.* In any event, one is fairly driven by considerations of this character toward an expressive view of Milton's poetic activity, as a supplement to the inadequacies of other views if not as an all-inclusive theory in itself.

For the contrasts and tensions which the style builds up do not occur primarily within the minds of dramatic personages (among whom one may feel free to recognize personae of the author himself); the style seeks to establish control over something exterior, either the very words of the poem or an element still more remote, ill defined, and dimly felt within the poet—a subject matter, to some extent, but a temperament more particularly, a set of feelings. Milton the poet, no less than Milton the writer of prose, suffered from a difficulty about his feelings, of which certain ones in particular did not rise easily to fluent, natural expression. His sensuality, especially, lay buried behind, and often beat against, the barrier of his painful ideas and learned style. Not only are those feelings so energetic and vociferous as to give rise to the concept of a "conscious" and "unconscious" poet in conflict with one another [Tillyard, *Milton,* III, 3, 4]; the rebukes which their spokesmen suffer, whether at the hands of the Lady Alice Egerton, the Lord God, or Christ on the mountain, have a uniform character which Milton's best efforts cannot prevent from seeming prudish, parochial, and peevish. Thus we may sense that the Miltonic style is in some measure a weapon against, as well as a voice expounding, certain feelings about the richness and multiplicity and treachery of the world, feelings very striking in connection with the sweet allurements of sex but evident also in Samson's joyful suicide and Christ's stern rejection of humane learning. In a very primitive sense, Milton's style is a device for mastering, controlling, and even rejecting, as well as for describing, the cosmos; it is a sword drawn against its subject, as well as a glass for revealing or magnifying it.

All this may be no more than a repetition of Keats's distinction of Milton as a positive and Shakespeare as a negative capability. Quite aside from the personal interludes in *Paradise Lost* or possible identification of Satan and Samson with Milton the man, the sort of tension on which his poetic style is built is one within the poet's temperament, if not between his temperament and some part of his subject matter; it is one, at any rate, in which his temperament figures as a tangible and consistent element. The style does not fully adapt itself to the subject either in the passive sense of propriety or in the active sense of witty contrast; and sometimes it tries to dominate the subject, not to wrestle discordant feelings into ironic harmony or to exploit the harmonic contrasts between them, not with dramatic metaphysical indirectness, but in the sense of using one set of feelings to conquer another. Mr. Bush speaks perceptively of Milton's turning in *Paradise Regained* and rending some main roots of his being [*The Renaissance and English Humanism* (Toronto, 1939), p. 125]; it is one major expression of a conflict, deep-seated and long lasting, which may be traced back to the poem "On the Morning of Christ's Nativity," and which has, in one form or another, pervaded every major poem in the canon.[4] Still another basis for judging the style may thus be its propriety to a philosophic and emotional conflict which was the author's and may be the reader's, to a sense of psychological malaise and insecurity within established systems and traditions. Feelings of this nature require, and often lay claim to, no more exalted ideological framework, no more elaborate justification, than is provided by the mere fact of their existing.

It is, of course, true, and will always remain true, that the Christian humanist, whether his persuasion be that of Mr. Lewis or Mr. Bush or Lord Macaulay, must necessarily experience Milton's poetry in a specially rich and intimate way. From his point of view, the particular terms of the poetry have a special meaning, which he is right to cherish and which I think (speaking as an outsider) he would be foolish to surrender without the pressure of necessity. That pressure is so strongly exerted by the mere force of daily circumstance as to need no effort on anyone's part to aug-

[4] Elsewhere, Mr. Bush denies [*PLIOT,* p. 101] that there is a central antinomy in *Paradise Lost;* and this is, of course, true so far as it implies that *Paradise Lost* is not formally torn apart or divided. The conflicts of the poem find their meaning in a broad stream of feeling which may be variously defined, but which suffices to produce, for most readers, a broadly unified effect. On the other hand, there was an antinomy in Milton's life (it is impossible to suppose that all the people who have seen and continue to see one are mistaken); and if one looks at *Paradise Lost* with Milton's biography in mind, the stresses and strains half-hidden beneath the surface will come clear. The difficulties of the Mulciber passage are fairly obvious; scarcely less evident are the problems which Abdiel was invented to solve, problems connected with the state of innocence and with the presentation of the Deity himself. The question of an antinomy in the poem is simply a question of context, and we do not really have to choose between the contexts, only to distinguish them clearly for purposes of discussion. The context of my remarks is biographical.

ment it. But there is a natural tendency, helped along by Milton's own desperate, heroic seriousness, for those who cherish Christian humanist values to represent Milton as triumphantly exemplifying them. Such enthusiastic oversights as Mr. Lewis' misplacing of Milton's Protestantism suggest problems of perspective even in the inner shrine.

One way or another, we have had a good deal of Milton as a triumphant figure, Macaulay's harmonious union of the noblest qualities of every party; it may be worth recalling that Macaulay also spoke of Milton kissing the beautiful deceiver (worldly pleasure, one guesses, or something like it) before he destroyed her. There is a suggestion in this rather flamboyant terminology of a higher self triumphing over a lower self; but one need not accept anything more than the perception that Milton was neither harmonious nor triumphant, but a troubled, divided, and deeply ambivalent consciousness. For all the anguish and torment of the tragedies and bitter comedies, there is an inescapable quality of wholeness about Shakespeare, a sense that the ideas he was born with fitted him as well and troubled him as little as his own skeleton. By comparison, Milton was a spoiled soul, one of the spiritually self-conscious and emotionally awkward. There is no need to romanticize him entirely; few literary men lend themselves less happily to a pathetic and passive approach. Yet a measure of distortion, a failure of control, a deficiency in esthetic detachment, is not to be burked from the career. No matter how one manipulates them, there remains something strident and inflexible about many of Milton's ideas, something buried and beyond control about many of his feelings. Many lesser men present a smoother surface, a more unified esthetic performance, a subtler and more intimate texture of thought and feeling, more perfectly controlled and more gracefully exposed for our delectation. From the formal, esthetic point of view, Milton's deficiencies in these respects, though perhaps minor in the full scale of an epic performance, are still deficiencies. But from a more complex and yet possibly a more familiar aspect, these deficiencies may be seen as flaws in a lesser harmony which fulfill a greater. They mar the strictly esthetic performance, but they consummate another, less strictly defined but more intimately experienced; they appeal deeply to our "modern" sympathy for a self morbidly divided against itself, standing free of ready-made systems and yet struggling with heroic human energy for wholeness.

For clearly, Milton was never a man whose sense of life fitted easily into traditional vessels. He had to invent his own version of an epic in *Paradise Lost* as he invented his own version of a tragedy in *Samson;* he had to invent an audience out of his own imagination to enjoy both works. Neither *Paradise Lost* nor *Samson* was really written for the morally uncommitted general reader, at ease with himself and all his surroundings, who sits in his library savoring esthetic experiences as a gourmet savors oysters. For such a reader, Satan is all out of perspective, the ending of *Paradise Lost* is draggy and inconclusive, and the vindictive exultations of *Samson* are barbaric and hysterical [cf. Rajan, *SCR,* pp. 82–85, 105–07]. Milton wrote for the morally committed reader (who is not, alas, the modern reader); but he also wrote from beliefs which constantly surpassed or evaded the formal categories of his art, so that his great literary achievements, like those of Ibsen and Flaubert, Euripides and Swift, end rather in a stalemate than in a fully resolved stasis. The antinomy on which Milton's work centers undergoes a full exploration, not a full resolution; we admire not the formal perfection with which a conclusion is worked out, but the truth and energy with which a conflict is explored down to its last grinding incompatibility. And in certain authors, at least, this characteristic has appealed to many modern readers as almost gruesomely congenial.

In some ways, this position raises more doubts about the validity of literary judgments in general than it resolves; for it removes from us the solid, Periclean figure of the general reader, seeking a genteel combination of pleasure and instruction, and substitutes a tissue of impulses, incompletenesses, and incompatibilities in which one may or may not recognize oneself. But then one may or may not recognize oneself in the easy, uncommitted, gentlemanly connoisseur who is the conventional image of a literary audience. In reshaping Milton after the image of the anxious reader, one may seem to be opening the door to an unrestricted relativism. But in matters of sympathy the door is already open; without destroying the meaning of the word itself, one cannot make sympathy a universal. And a literary situation may be perfectly comprehensible where one sympathizes with a formal defect in a work of art on the grounds that one does not, oneself, stand in a formal, esthetic relation to the subject matter. Thus one might admire the vast achievement of *Paradise Lost* while reserving one's personal sympathy for the more confessional and despairing *Samson;* or distinguish two contradictory aspects (sympathy for necessary failure, admiration for heroic strategies in the teeth of that failure) in one's appreciation of a single poem; or regret that all authors are not like Shakespeare while feeling all the more kinship with them because they are not.

Of course, from another point of view, common enough in contemporary criticism, the trouble with Milton is not that he is a divided figure, but that he is not divided enough. "Divided sensibility" is one of the few critical catchwords which have the happy faculty of serving to convey either praise or blame; it is a bad thing in Milton when we are told that his thoughts were distinct from his feelings so that instead of really writing poetry he merely versified his ideas, but it is a triumph of literary art when Donne or Eliot anatomizes his own divided sensibility. No doubt the important thing is control; if one cannot eliminate the divisions in one's sensibility completely, one had better—so the critics seem to feel—exploit them ruthlessly. The one quality which this convenient dichotomy eliminates is heroic human effort, man's power to erect himself above himself.

It is, of course, futile to quarrel fundamentally with the taste of one's times. For reasons too elaborate and unwieldy to be explored, contemporary taste seems permanently impatient with the heroic mode. Our poetry, when it ventures beyond the mechanical grating of texture on texture, image on image, and tension on tension, tends either to hug the elemental facts of physical existence or to seek an ecstatic unification of experience in mystical contemplation of the godhead. There is nothing to be said against these modes of poetic thought and feeling except that as exclusive alternatives they radically limit the poet's power to deal with human experience. If one accepts these limitations without question, it is futile to pretend that Milton is anything but a peripheral figure; though something may perhaps be learned even from peripheral figures whom one takes the trouble to understand. But if one feels that modern writers of verse, with rare exceptions, exist within narrow bounds of style and convention, bounds which sometimes exclude the whole middle ground of human experience at its most distinctive, one may be impelled to feel not only respect for Milton, and sympathy, but also an emotion no less intimate and genuine than envy.

Among the oddest and most vulnerable of Mr. Eliot's

judgments is his suggestion that Milton's style was capable of coping with only a limited range of subjects. It is true, of course; true of all poets with distinctive and characteristic styles; true of Donne and Laforgue; and true, no doubt, of any poet whose capacities are not, in the Shakespearian sense and to a Shakespearian degree, negative. But Shakespeares are few and far between; and it is probably his scope, range, and variety that most modern poets, whatever their own character, will envy Milton. To make his point, Mr. Eliot exaggerates it and says that *Samson* "was probably the one dramatic story out of which Milton could have made a masterpiece" [*PBA,* XXXIII, 70]. Disregarding Mr. Leavis, who thinks that *Samson* is botched work, one may note a number of recorded sentiments to the effect that the Prometheus story might have undergone effective development at Milton's hands; and surely his perennial fascination with Orpheus suggests tremendous possibilities. Obviously, it is hard to compare offhand the different potentials of the colloquial and the elevated styles; the one is capable of an intimate particularity, the other of heights, depths, and architectural vistas. But in losing the high, heroic tone, perhaps for good, we have lost much more than a single effect—not merely the last octave on the keyboard, but the note of C in all its permutations and combinations and even the broad structures which an undistorted range of harmonies alone makes possible. Though Milton had to struggle to maintain them, and the struggle involved awkwardness, unnaturalness, and ultimately a sort of self-destruction, we are the poorer now that even the possibility of struggling for these harmonies is gone. Even the contrasts which presume a heroism dead and gone are rendered thin and artificial by its remoteness; and structure in the architectural sense sinks into insignificance.

Sustained achievement in verse has not been much celebrated of late; perhaps it is too much to expect that our age should admire what it cannot imitate. But whatever the needs of the age, Milton continues to impose his own quality; and there is perhaps less danger that the modern reader will forget Milton's heroic demands than that he will be alienated by an all-or-nothing character which time and intellectual distance have caused them to assume. Though no modern poet is likely to be seduced into attempting another *Paradise Lost,* the problem at hand is simply to make easier some sympathy for the *Paradise Lost* we already possess—even, one might say, at the risk of taking the poem at something less than its highest valency. It was one of the most generous and accomplished masters of miniature, Andrew Marvell, who made it Milton's special praise that he sang

> with so much gravity and ease;
> And above humane flight dost soar aloft
> With Plume so strong, so equal, and so soft;

and it is in terms like these that we ought to praise Milton, if only we were able. "I too, transported by the mode, offend"; but it will go hard with readers, not to say critics, of Milton, if they must first rival their subject in magnanimity.

Conclusion: Milton and Magnanimity

A PUZZLED shuffling of the fragments: the assiduous reader in Miltonic scholarship and criticism soon finds that articles, books, and even entire careers have risen out of this fragile occupation. An almost infallible index to this activity is the phrase "not enough weight has been given to" or one of its several equivalents. Thus we have seen built and rebuilt, modified, patched, enlarged, and revamped the many different architectures which have passed under the name of John Milton. For the sake of a momentary scheme, these may be classified as variant versions of Milton the Liberal and Milton the Conservative. Milton the Liberal includes the Whig, the rationalist, the tolerationist, the humanist, the sectarian, the Arian, the Hebraist, the Satanist; Milton the Conservative includes, among many versions of Milton the Calvinist and Milton the Puritan, the nineteenth-century organ musician with a cross disposition, also an Augustinian, hierarchical, and Catholic figure of recent origin and an authority on the hexamera. The hero of New Critical studies seems pretty well independent of both these figures because he combines them in such odd proportions. Philosophically he is conservative, if one can judge from his single-minded concentration on one of several well-worn antinomies, such as Good and Evil, Virtue and Grace, Life and Death, or Matter and Spirit. His verbal habits, on the other hand, are liberal, radical, almost fantastic. A coherent, or at least a limited, figure of Milton may thus be built to accord with almost any principle with which one cares to start. And by minor readjustments of critical premise, any one of these images of Milton may be made compatible with extreme critical adulation or deprecation.

Thus the picture of Milton, precisely because so many efforts have been made at unified, exclusive interpretation, is farther than ever from falling into focus. No doubt it will always be true that men, as they approach Milton with different prepossessions, will find in him different aspects and facets of character. What is criticism, after all, but the study of emphasis? But as we retreat down the hallway of history away from John Milton, it becomes increasingly clear that even slight distortions in our social atmosphere may yield major misunderstandings of the poet. From a modern point of view, for example, it is easy to sense that rationality has made such headway in Milton's universe as to leave God, perhaps despite the poet's intention, responsible chiefly for the perverse and incomprehensible acts of the universe, the "acts of God." A modern reader is perfectly familiar with this situation, by which he may be either amused or horrified, but this sort of awareness consorts ill with Milton's announced purpose and results in one more failure of equilibrium for critics to cope with. Professor Waldock has emphasized that modern sophistication in matters of narrative technique leads us to magnify Milton's literary audacity [*PLIC,* pp. 18ff.]; even more fundamental difficulties arise from the anomalous position of organized religious values in a world where belief is essentially a matter of personal election. Of ten people reading *Paradise Lost,* nine will regard Satan as a picturesque superstition who is meaningless if he is not the hero of the poem, and one will be so impressed by his personal discovery of Evil that he will grudge Milton every dramatic liberty, every dramatic effect he grants to the Devil. One dare not underestimate the power of impulses which reduced so Oxonian an Oxonian as C. S. Lewis to slanging Satan as if he were an illiterate sailor at his first melodrama. Thus insight determines outlook. And when one gropes for some third point, other than Milton and one's own sensibility, against which shifting impressions may be checked, still other and more equivocal mists come in sight. Milton cannot easily be related to a single specific audience or a coherently formulated esthetic. When we think of possible influences upon his writing, the names which come to mind are as ill assorted as those of Della Casa, Wollebius, Scaliger, the Fletchers, Castiglione, St. Augustine, and Josephus. When we think of the tradition in which he wrote, we are with St. Basil, Lactantius, and Du Bartas, or else Virgil, Homer, and Ovid; when we think of his actual readers, we are with Denham, Phillips, and Dryden, or else Jonathan Richardson and little Thomas Ellwood. When we remember the millenarianism of the early tracts, we are with the most wild-eyed of the Fifth Monarchy Men; when we think of the dry, austere despair of *Samson,* we are with Seneca the Elder.

The fact is that the problem of Milton's ideas as Professor Raleigh brilliantly posed it, and as most critics have faithfully accepted it, is insoluble. Milton's ideas and some of the feelings which go with them cannot be interpreted into modernity; they are dead, as his art is not. By consigning

Milton's ideas so abruptly to the graveyard, I do not imply anything more than that they are not currently operative; they have to be learned out of textbooks and do not meet with ready acceptance on the current idea market. Here I must simply appeal to personal experience. Though not everyone tells the same tale, I personally have not observed in the common chaffer of intellectual business any brisk trade in holiness, temperance, chastity, heroic individualism, and so forth—nor even an ability to mention these edifying abstractions without embarrassment. As a matter of fact, the most striking evidence that these ideas are dead is that many people who actually practice the designated virtues do not want to use these names to describe them. The demise of Milton's ideas is only one minor incident in the world-wide decay of theistic assumptions about the universe and human behavior; whatever regret we may feel over this change ought not to blind us to its existence. Thus no particular odium attaches to the observation that a writer's ideas are dead. Few ideas have a very long life, and those which do often seem the reverse of exhilarating. On the other hand, the fact that Milton's ideas are no longer current does not reduce us to reading him for his organ music. Some of the feelings which go with his ideas are dead, but by no means all. We may perfectly well read Milton, as we read Lucretius and Dante, for the exercise which such an experience affords to our minds and sympathies, for the pleasure of knowing what it feels like to work out, as richly and fully as possible, a particular set of presuppositions, some of which are generally analagous to some of our own. In this respect, Professor Tillyard's assertion that the real subject of *Paradise Lost* is "the true state of Milton's mind when he wrote it" [*Milton,* p. 237; *The Personal Heresy,* p. 2] seems to offer a wider ground for enlightened sympathy than the narrow position fenced off by the glittering swordplay of his opponent. Whatever Milton's intentions, a modern reader cannot, without a sort of schizophrenia, take *Paradise Lost* as a document which clarifies relations between God and the human race as presently constituted.

Milton's ideas are dead, then, but this fate is so frequent, so close to universal, as not to represent a very significant judgment. More important is the fact that they cannot, like Spenser's, be brought into substantial harmony with a coherent, accepted tradition of thought or even into perfect harmony with the literary works in which they find expression. Spenser's ideas are quite as dead as Milton's—the ladder of love is a Freudian joke and chivalry a long-antiquated antiquity—but they do not interfere to the same degree with the patterns of his poetry; the reason is not altogether that Spenser's art is dead too, but that his ideas and feelings formed a more or less tractable synthesis, to which his style was truly answerable. The sort of analogous unity which I think we must look for in Milton is one of intention, not of achievement. Milton's style as a whole is ultimately answerable, I believe, only to a concept of his self, to an image of a magnanimous man which he formed and tried to embody. This image is larger and more determining than any of the particulars of action, belief, or artistry which comprise it; without the personal image, indeed, these particulars do not coalesce at all. Within the total image are included such particulars as Milton the Christian and Milton the humanist, Milton the lyric poet and Milton the arrogant controversialist, Milton the reader of books, Milton the reader of proof, and even Milton the epic artist. The magnanimous Milton includes a passive Stoic figure and a figure of militant, active virtue; it is an image often confused in details, but never forgetful of a responsibility to the worth and dignity which it represents. Unlike so many of the Milton figures which have been palmed off on us, it is heroically committed to following an inner rule, not tamely submitting to the leadership of an outer guide. The values we expect of such a man are not those appropriate to a perfect synthesis worked out with absolute consistency, but those of a sincere and wide-minded dedication to the realization of man in the wholeness of his powers. Upon a man so dedicated, the heavens may fall without destroying his essential equilibrium; when he walks in steps worn deep by time, he does so by an individual, personal choice; and when he stands alone, he yet finds a continuity with other solitary standers. Without denying the existence of other systems—rather, incorporating them so far as possible in his own structures—he endeavors to make of his soul a self-contained and self-determined system. The failure of such an enterprise, or for that matter its success, is far less important as a criterion of judgment than its scope.

If we take Milton on this level, we are not, I think, committed to finding successful artistic synthesis, logical or emotional consistency, or immediate contemporary relevance in all the logical positions to which circumstances invited him; neither are we required to find literal precedents for all his expressions and ways of thinking nor to fit him by main force into one or another or several previously existing traditions. On the other hand, though he was frequently a tradition to himself, we need not see in him Mr. Eliot's "greatest of all eccentrics" [*PBA,* XXXIII, 69]; for in his very individuality he thought himself, he intended to be, and perhaps actually was, broadly typical. We are not by any means obliged to seek or find a perfect harmony between the ideas actually available to him and the artistic structures in which he clothed that sometimes gaunt and awkward framework. Indeed, we are encouraged to find in the occasional esthetic dissonances which insist on making themselves felt a meaning which is not alien to us, or accidental, but intimate. And as to ultimate judgments, I cannot recognize any reason for considering an author categorically inferior because he finds his fate too complex to fit peacefully into a literary form or religious convention.

Undoubtedly we lose one sort of intimacy by relegating to secondary status some of the specific forms in which Milton's thought was cast. A Christian humanist of the anxious persuasion will always have a particular rapport for Milton which the rest of us may grope at and learn from even while we place our primary emphasis on something more general and remote—an attitude, not a creed, an ideal helplessly flawed and audaciously pursued, not a set of logical propositions and their corollaries.

Surely it is in something like this spirit that educated readers have long since learned to reconcile admiration for disparate authors and philosophies. One does not seek agreement or disagreement with particular beliefs but an awareness of the feelings associated with holding them; one does not cherish specific, literal ideas, which may be true or false, alive or dead, coherent or incoherent, wicked or virtuous, but the fullness of an ideal worked out as thoroughly and largely as may be. I believe that for Milton this ideal is best defined in terms of magnanimity. Professor Hughes has already shown [*SP*, XXXV, 254–77] how an awareness of the tradition of Christian magnanimity enriches and humanizes the picture of Christ in *Paradise Regained;* and Mr. Tillyard, in a brief note, has carried the argument a long step further by demonstrating [*SP*, XXXVI, 247–52] that it may also enrich and humanize the figure of Milton himself. To be sure, the example of magnanimity chosen by Professor Hughes, though striking, even crucial, may also be misleading. Contempt of the world's snares is but one aspect of the virtue of magnanimity as Milton defined it. We are magnanimous, says the *Christian Doctrine* [II, ix] "when in seeking or avoiding, the acceptance or refusal of riches, advantages, or honors, we are actuated by a regard to our own dignity, rightly understood." And the first example he cites is that of Abraham, who accepted the gifts of the king of Egypt, though he rejected those of the king of Sodom. So that we need not think of magnanimity as a high-and-mighty name for the lean and sallow abstinence; it represents, not a type of action, but a motive to action.

Any man who acts as Milton (echoing Aristotle) recommends, out of a sense of his own dignity as he himself understands it, runs the risk of seeming to act arbitrarily. What has been described as "self-conscious ethical selectiveness," sterile to art if not counteracted [M. M. Ross, *Poetry and Dogma* (New Brunswick, 1954), p. 193], comes to dominate many of one's acts, thoughts, and feelings; and then, lacking a social continuum of commonly accepted symbols, a milieu for making one's meaning gracefully visible, one falls back on the bare bones of logical (or, just as often, illogical) abstraction. Perhaps this is a grounds for condemnation; if so, the condemnation falls on many poets besides Milton, for the dilemma of those who find traditional symbolisms inadequate to new purposes has often been thought of as distinctively modern. The various alternative solutions have been much explored and discussed, not always conclusively; even to list them would be a major undertaking, and to decide which is better, which worse, would evidently be a complex and indefinite task, involving an almost infinite number of variables. At least we may easily see that Milton suffered a number of special disadvantages in making his theological ideas concrete and even in making them clear. On the other hand, I doubt if we can usefully consider poets as under a special obligation to invent or accept a sacramental view of life, irrespective of what is implied in the sacrament. Even if we suppose, as Mr. Ross evidently does, that poets of the present day can do no better than return to a sacramental view, it still does not follow that Milton was wrong in departing from it. Communion for the sake of community is a heresy of progressive education, not a tenet of the Old Faith, and it is far from a prescription for the writing of great poetry. Quite properly Mr. Ross sees "the artist himself . . . at the centre of the new firmament of poetry, Milton's firmament" [*P & D,* p. 226]; and this implies that Milton uses dogma and typology (not to mention a great many other traditional disciplines) as peripheral machineries. From Milton's machinery it is, as Mr. Ross brilliantly points out, only a few steps to the "gnostic" machinery of Blake and the almost ventriloqual apparatus of Yeats. Though the content of his faith was in good measure severely traditional, Milton's relation to it was generally that of one who believes for personal if not quite for literary reasons. A distinction between what Mr. Ross calls primary and secondary Christian symbols can undoubtedly be made to resolve a great many confusions about Milton's meaning in *Paradise Lost;* and the importance of this approach can scarcely be overstated. On the other hand, this distinction does not bring us very close to an esthetic judgment of the poetry.

Nobody, I think, wants to establish in literary criticism a Christian–non-Christian antinomy, still less to impale Milton uncomfortably on either horn of this dilemma. Thus there is something a little arbitrary about straining *Samson* at one end and "L'Allegro" and "Il Penseroso" at the other out of Milton's entire career, as shining sacramental poems isolated amid acres of barren machinery. Even if the judgment is accurate (and I think only a little of *Samson*'s total feeling fits into a pattern which could properly be called "sacramental"), its critical significance is open to doubt.

Milton was in fact a poet of individual discriminations throughout his career and in all his poems. He was a poet of discriminations sometimes arbitrary, imprudent, hard to make clear, sometimes colored by egotism either apparent or real; all sorts of criticism could no doubt be brought against them, and without further discussion it seems clear that Milton would not, in a best-adjusted-poet contest, any more than in a humility competition, come out a winner. But his difficulties in this respect were not peculiar or eccentric; they were those of a social situation and a personality type so widespread that they may fairly challenge, against their "sacramental" opposites, the status of a norm. Undoubtedly the adventitious difficulties of pioneering a transitional, a revolutionary age, tend to blur Milton's image. To his own age he seemed a fervent radical; to a modern eye he seems unusually stern, strict, and condemnatory. But this is the price of genuine independence; total freedom always involves something close to total isolation. Any man who accepts a received system and then modifies it in a liberal direction easily acquires a reputation for liberality, however modest his modification and however intolerant the system which he originally embraced. (The True Liberal profits from this ancient principle by protesting vigorously against the cruel treatment of witches; he would have them executed *mercifully*.) By starting from first principles, Milton incurred the special disadvantages and responsibilities, as well as the privileges, of those who reject the ready-made structures of their time. The mode of his thinking is deeply libertarian and individualistic; its content, in many features, is broadly traditional. But it is always his own thought, stamped with the seal of his own responsible choice and interpretation.

Milton thus falls halfway between the soft-minded Whiggish liberals who are horrified that any well-intentioned person should be supposed subject to the wrath of God and the tough-minded pseudo-Byzantines who yearn for the Middle Ages just because the ethical system of those days was so implacably impersonal. A striking token of this confusion appears in the fate of those critics [see, for example, Arnold Williams, *SR,* XLIX, 90–106] who boldly set out some fifteen years ago to defend Milton against his conservative, i.e., Anglo-Catholic enemies. They could not anticipate the brilliant strategy by which Mr. Charles Williams and Mr. Lewis were, at the very moment, taking Milton over for the precise principles in the name of which Mr. Eliot had rejected him. But the whole idea of judging Milton by his conformity or nonconformity with intellectual systems (and this is the latent implication of the sacramental-unsacramental distinction) is clearly beside the point.

The magnanimous man is neither a confused and half-hearted dogmatist (which is the best figure we can salvage from Milton the conservative) nor a frustrated anarchist, ignorant of his premises and terrified of his conclusions (which is the basic character of Milton the liberal). His ideas are intended to be neither abjectly relativist nor rigidly absolutist nor eccentrically individual. His soul projects its own image of itself with the true and glorious ambivalence of a Quixote and builds on this shadow of a shadow, akin to Sidney's "erected wit," an ethical structure which it tries and tests on the rough materials of the world. Some ages are more favorable than others to the realization of any given projection; in some respects, Milton had particularly bad luck, falling as he did between two worlds and involved as he was in a vast emotional commitment at the very moment when the structure which made it possible was being smashed. But Milton never failed, I think, to be equal to himself; and the man of whom this can be said is not to be patronized any more than he is to be sentimentalized into a noble martyr. He is in the simplest sense a law to himself—a man who can do no other than try to make his life a work of art in which is exemplified to the rest of us what the armed soul impelled by its own conscious destiny can endure and accomplish.

One way to understand such a man is to build up from the details of his career a picture which suggests, subject to the distortion of circumstance, the man he intended to be. The process is orthodox and orderly; one would not be understood to say a word against it. But the details so accumulated easily become cloudy and confused, as a natural human impulse leads each investigator to press his conclusions to the limit. Whether he is investigating literary analogues, deep psychological patterns, or those verbal curiosities which Milton was wont to describe as a "toilsome vanity," or, for that matter, whether he is laboring in the gloom and obscurity of textual emendation, does not much matter; when special details and technical trivialities press too closely on one another and on the reader of Milton criticism, it becomes not only possible but necessary to look at the man Milton evidently intended to be and judge from the total picture as to the aptness of this or that particular. There are, naturally, sharp and immediate limits to any scholarly approach which inverts the customary inductive method. But architecture determines bricks as well as bricks architecture; with some of the bricks which have been excavated out of the Miltonic milieu one simply cannot construct, on any terms, the man who wrote *Paradise Lost.*

After all, history and literary criticism are, in a sense, predetermined to their conclusions as the so-called exact sciences usually are not. You cannot write about the *ancien régime* without recognizing that your particular facts must somehow lead to the events of 1789. If they do not add up to 1789, they are wrong facts, and new ones must be found which add up correctly. In history, the result is often what we know best; our real problem lies in determining causes. So with Milton; we are given an esthetic impact, whether measured on our own pulses or on those of readers in other ages. As to its precise size and character, there is room for endless debate; but if we think it essentially large and uniquely independent, we should not hesitate to look for the sort of details and causes which yield this result. It is no triumph to find *disjecta membra;* they are everywhere. The only triumph is an economy; the only test, an ultimate one, is an arrangement, an image—such an image, indeed, that, like Milton's daughter, the knowing reader is drawn to cry, out of all grammar, "I see him! 'tis Him! . . . 'tis the very Man! Here, Here—"

Index